Schriften zur Medienwirtschaft und zum
Medienmanagement

herausgegeben von
Prof. Dr. Mike Friedrichsen
Prof. Dr. Robert G. Picard
Prof. Dr. Elena Vartanova

Band 33

Li Zeng

Beyond the Market Myth

A Research on the Dual Broadcasting System and its Inspirations for China's Ongoing Television System Reform

The philosophical faculty III of Humboldt University Berlin accepted this thesis as a dissertation in the winter term of 2012/2013.

© Coverpicture: fotolia.de

Die Deutsche Nationalbibliothek lists this publication in the Deutsche Nationalbibliografie; detailed bibliographic data is available in the Internet at http://dnb.d-nb.de

a.t.: Berlin, Humboldt University, Phil. Fak. III, Diss., 2012/2013

ISBN: HB   978-3-8487-0371-5
        ePDF   978-3-8452-4680-2

British Library Cataloguing-in-Publication Data
A catalogue record for this book is available from the British Library.

ISBN: HB   978-3-8487-0371-5

Library of Congress Cataloging-in-Publication Data
Zeng, Li
Beyond the Market Myth
A Research on the Dual Broadcasting System and its Inspirations for China's Ongoing Television System Reform
Li Zeng
254 p.
Includes bibliographic references and index.

ISBN   978-3-8487-0371-5

1. Edition 2014
© Nomos Verlagsgesellschaft, Baden-Baden, Germany 2014. Printed and bound in Germany.

This work is subject to copyright. All rights reserved. No part of this publication may be reproduced or transmitted in any form or by any means, electronic or mechanical, including photocopying, re-cording, or any information storage or retrieval system, without prior permission in writing from the publishers. Under § 54 of the German Copyright Law where copies are made for other than private use a fee is payable to "Verwertungsgesellschaft Wort", Munich.

No responsibility for loss caused to any individual or organization acting on or refraining from action as a result of the material in this publication can be accepted by Nomos or the autor(s)/editor(s).

Acknowledgments

This book was accepted by the Faculty of Philosophy III, the Humboldt University of Berlin, as a Ph.D. dissertation. The dissertation was reviewed by Prof. Dr. Wolfgang Mühl-Benninghaus and Prof. Dr. YU Guoming. I alone am responsible for the perspectives, judgements, and any errors in this book.

I would like to thank my supervisors Prof. Dr. Wolfgang Mühl-Benninghaus and Prof. Dr. YU Guoming for their sustained inspiration, attention and encouragement. I am very grateful to Prof. Dr. Mike Friedrichsen for his help in publishing this book. I also extend my appreciation and gratitude to the editors from my publishing house Nomos, notably Sandra Frey, Lucia Pflieger, Doris Hirsch, Dr. Martin Reichinger and Carsten Rehbein. There would have been no book of this title without their professional work and patience.

Finally, this book is dedicated to my family for their unconditional love.

November 15, 2013   Dr. Li ZENG

Contents

List of Abbreviations	9
List of Figures	11
Introduction	13
I. Subject of Research	13
II. Conduct and Methods of Research	16
III. Significance of Research	18
Chapter 1 Some Related Theories to the Transition of Chinese Television System	21
1.1. The model of the gradual transition of Chinese economy from plan to market	21
1.2. Kops' geometric exposition of broadcasting systems	25
1.3. McQuail's media policy change model	28
Part 1 Market as a Myth: the Transition of Chinese Television System	31
Chapter 2 A Historical Review of the Transition of Chinese Television	33
2.1. The Starting Position and the Basic Philosophy	35
2.2. The Experimental Years (1958-1977)	36
2.2.1. The advent of Chinese television	36
2.2.2. The structure of Chinese television system	38
2.2.3. Chinese television under the planned economy	39
2.3. The Proliferation of Television (1978-1991)	41
2.3.1. The "four-level system" policy	41
2.3.2. Advertising and the funding of television	45
2.3.3. The germination and a prolonged setback of the public logic in television	49
2.4. The Rule of the Market Economy (1992-2000)	52
2.4.1. Television "reform" with market mechanism at all levels in the multi-channel era	53
2.4.2. The commercial reality of Chinese television	59
2.4.3. The triumph of the market logic on the eve of China's accession to the WTO	64

Contents

2.4.4. A state-led "supervision by public opinion" and the absent public in television reform	68
2.5. At the Crossroads (since 2001)	72
2.5.1. The restoration of "public service": television institutions redefined as shiye unit?	73
2.5.2. Fair play or closed market?	76
2.5.3. Television and the "public": an emergence of fan democracy, the reflection on vulgarisation of television, and the establishment of "public" channels	83
Chapter 3 Assessing the Transition of Chinese Television	88
3.1. A Working Model of the Transition of Chinese Television	89
3.1.1. Four stages of the extrinsic transition of Chinese television	89
3.1.2. Peculiarities of the transition of Chinese television	92
3.2. Reasons, Consequences and Bottlenecks of the Self-commercialisation of Chinese Television	95
3.2.1. Reasons of the self-commercialisation of Chinese television	95
3.2.2. Consequences of the self-commercialisation of Chinese television	99
3.2.3. Bottlenecks in the ongoing reform process	103
3.3. In Search of an Alternative	107
Part 2 The Dual Broadcasting System and its Inspirations	111
Chapter 4 The Purely Public Service Broadcasting System: the predecessor of the dual broadcasting system	113
4.1. The principles and characteristics of the public service broadcasting	114
4.2. The understandings of broadcasting in the PSB: the BBC as the prototype	117
4.2.1. Broadcasting as a public utility	118
4.2.2. Broadcasting as culture	119
4.2.3. Broadcasting and market	122
4.2.4. Broadcasting and state	124
4.2.5. Broadcasting and audience	128
4.3. The British model of PSB after WWII: domestic criticism, international imitation and European consolidation	131
4.3.1. Domestic criticism and change of the PSB	132
4.3.2. The international imitation of British public service broadcasting and its consolidation in Europe	135

4.4. Theoretical development of public service broadcasting: the case of West Germany	139
4.4.1. Freedom of broadcast	141
4.4.2. Broadcasting as a cultural matter	144
4.4.3. The organisational form of the public service broadcasting	146

Chapter 5 The Dual Broadcasting System in Britain and Germany	155
5.1. Dual broadcasting system: the advent of the market logic and its impact	157
5.1.1. The first encounter with the market logic in Britain: from the 1950s to the 1970s	157
5.1.2. To redefine broadcasting with the market logic: from the 1980s onwards	161
5.1.2.1. Britain: Mrs. Thatcher's reform and the demise of public commercial broadcasting	162
5.1.2.2. British dual broadcasting system in the post-Thatcher eras	168
5.1.2.3. West Germany: the introduction of private broadcasting in 1984	172
5.1.2.4. German broadcasting in the era of the dual broadcasting system	177
5.2. Co-existence, conflicts and coordination in the dual broadcasting system	185
5.3. Beyond the market myth: the criticism of the American purely commercial broadcasting by the dual broadcasting system	193
5.4. Is the dual broadcasting system an anachronism in the era of Internet?	198
5.5. The failure and success of imitating the dual broadcasting system: the cases of post-Communist Europe and Eastern Asia	204

Chapter 6 Theoretical Analyses of the Dual Broadcasting System and the Inspirations for Chinese Broadcasting Reform	213
6.1. Some theoretical analyses of the dual broadcasting system	213
6.2. The theoretical significance of the dual broadcasting system	220
6.3. What can Chinese broadcasting learn from the dual broadcasting system?	227
Bibliography	237
Index	247

List of Abbreviations

ABC	American Broadcasting Company
AC	adult contemporary music
ARD	Arbeitsgemeinschaft der öffentlich-rechtlichen Rundfunkanstalten der Bundesrepublik Deutschland (Consortium of public-law broadcasting institutions of the Federal Republic of Germany)
ATSC	Advanced Television Systems Committee (USA)
BBC	The British Broadcasting Company (before 1927)
	The British Broadcasting Corporation (after 1927)
BR	Bayerischer Rundfunk (Germany)
BverfGE	The rulings made by the German Federal Constitutional Court
CBS	Columbia Broadcasting System (USA)
CCP	Chinese Communist Party
CCTV	China Central Television
CDU	The Christian Democratic Union (Germany)
CEECs	Central and Eastern European countries
CETV	China Education Television
CHR	contemporary hit radio
CPE	Centrally Planned Economy
DCMS	The Department of Culture, Media and Sport (Britain)
DVB-H	Digital Video Broadcasting – Handheld
EBS	Korean Educational Broadcasting System
EBU	The European Broadcasting Union
FCC	The Federal Communications Commission (USA)
FME	Free Market Economy
GATT	The General Agreement on Tariffs and Trade
HDTV	high-definition television
HR	Hessischer Rundfunk (Germany)
IBA	The Independent Broadcasting Authority (Britain)
IPTV	Internet Protocol television
IRA	Irish Republican Army
ITA	The Independent Television Authority (Britain)
ITAP	The Information Technology Advisory Panel (Britain)
ITC	The Independent Television Commission (Britain)
ITN	Independent Television News (Britain)
ITV	The Independent Television (Britain)
KBS	Korean Broadcasting System
KEF	Kommission zur Ermittlung des Finanzbedarfs der Rundfunkanstalten (The Commission of Determining the Financing Requirement of the Broadcasters, Germany)

List of Abbreviations

KtK	Kommission für den Ausbau des technischen Kommunikationssystems (The Commission for the Development of Technical Communication System, Germany)
MBC	Munhwa Broadcasting Corporation (Korea)
MIC	The Ministry of Internal Affairs and Communications (Japan)
NBC	National Broadcasting Company (USA)
NDR	Norddeutscher Rundfunk (Germany)
NHK	Nippon Hoso Kyokai (The Japan Broadcasting Corporation)
NPR	National Public Radio (USA)
NWDR	Nordwestdeutscher Rundfunk (Germany)
Ofcom	The Office of Communications (Britain)
PBS	The Public Broadcasting Service (USA)
PSB	the public service broadcasting (system)
RB	Radio Bremen (Germany)
RIAS	Rundfunk im amerikanischen Sektor (Germany)
RTL	Radio Télévision Luxembourg
SARFT	The State Administration of Radio, Film, and Television (China)
SBS	Seoul Broadcasting Station (Korea)
SCAP	The Supreme Commander Allied Powers (Japan)
SDR	Süddeutscher Rundfunk (Germany)
SFB	Sender Freies Berlin (Germany)
SMEG	Shanghai Media & Entertainment Group (China)
SMS	Short Message Service
SPD	The Social Democratic Party (Germany)
SR	Saarländischer Rundfunk (Germany)
SWF	Südwestfunk (Germany)
VCD	the Video CD
WDR	Westdeutscher Rundfunk (Germany)
WTO	The World Trade Organisation
ZDF	Zweites Deutsches Fernsehen (Second German Television)

List of Figures

Figure 1.1	Four Stages of the Extrinsic Transition from Plan to Market	23
Figure 1.2	Two Types of Transition from Plan to Market	24
Figure 1.3	A Geometric Exposition of the Revenue Structures of Broadcasters, Distinguishing Three Types of Broadcasting Systems (by Kops)	26
Figure 1.4	International Comparison of Public Service Broadcasting Revenue Structures Based on the Categories and Data of McKINSEY 1999 (by Kops)	27
Figure 1.5	Broadcasting Systems in Selected Countries – Internationally Compared (by Kops)	28
Figure 1.6	Sequential model of system change (by McQuail et al.)	30
Figure 2.1	Control and Administration of Media in China (Example: TV)	39
Figure 2.2	Development of Chinese Television (1979 – 1998)	44
Figure 2.3	Advertising Revenue by Type of Medium (1983-1998)	47
Figure 2.4	Comparisons on four main media's advertising revenue and annual growth rate in different Periods	60
Figure 2.5	Sepstrup's definition of "commercial" broadcasting	63
Figure 3.1	Revenue Structure of Shanghai TV in 1979 (in %)	90
Figure 3.2	Revenue Structure of Shanghai TV in 1983 (in %)	90
Figure 3.3	Revenue Structure of Shanghai TV in 1995 (in %)	90
Figure 3.4	Ends and Realities of Chinese Television Reform	105
Figure 4.1	Characteristics of public service broadcasting: two similar models (reproduced by Humphreys)	116
Figure 4.2	Types of European broadcasting systems according to revenue systems	137

List of Figures

Figure 4.3	A classification of some Western European public broadcasting systems according to patterns of politicisation	137
Figure 5.1	Viewing Shares of Individual Channels in Britain 2008	171
Figure 5.2	Market Shares of the German Television Market 2009	180
Figure 5.3	Market Shares of the Gross Television Advertising Revenue in Germany 2009	181
Figure 5.4	Genres of Programmes by ARD, ZDF, RTL, SAT. 1 and ProSieben 2008 (length of transmission in %)	183
Figure 5.5	Media Shares in German Gross Advertising Market (from 1984 - 2010) (in %)	184
Figure 5.6	Two different sets of understandings of broadcasting within the dual broadcasting system	186
Figure 5.7	The scales of dimensions in the arrangements of broadcasting system	187
Figure 5.8	Process of decision-making in the British dual broadcasting system (an example)	188
Figure 5.9	Process of decision-making in the German dual broadcasting system (an example)	188
Figure 6.1	The spectrum and evolution of the PSB character in a few sample countries	215
Figure 6.2	The results of different decision making mechanism in selected dual broadcasting systems	218
Figure 6.3	German dual broadcasting system I: the pyramidal structure	228
Figure 6.4	German dual broadcasting system II: ideas, principles and arrangements	229

Introduction

I. Subject of Research

With China's entry into the World Trade Organization (WTO) in 2001, a new round of reforms on the current television system[1] has been conducted in order to better adjust Chinese television to the changing environment. Their foremost aim was to improve Chinese television's competitiveness to meet the challenges from international media conglomerates.

The participants of reforms, i.e. governmental officials, television practitioners, and media academics, seem to consent that the market mechanism is the most effective, if not the only way, to reform Chinese television. Under the guideline of utilizing the market mechanism to make Chinese television "bigger and stronger"[2], the government started to re-regulate state-owned television institutions and other state-owned media institutions. A series of media conglomerates were merged under the administrative orders since 1999. The wave of fusion reached its climax in December 2001 when the national media conglomerate, Chinese Radio, Film and Television Group, was established. Within the television institutions, market mechanisms have been used in programming management for long. It became even radical when the national broadcaster, China Central Television (CCTV), began to shortlist the programmes on its most influential channel, CCTV1, according to the ratings and advertising value of a programme.[3] Moreover, these reform schemes on television received clear endorsements from the media academics[4], many of whom actively participate in initiat-

---

1 The theme of this dissertation focuses on the television system in China, whilst radio broadcasting has to be excluded as a result of the limited length of the dissertation. However, it is a tradition for most European countries to treat television and radio as an integrated concept of broadcasting in relevant research. Therefore, it will follow the European tradition when the dissertation moves to analyze the television system in Europe, more precisely, a broadcasting system rather than a television system in European context.
2 ZHU Hong (chief secretary of the Chinese Radio, Film and Television Group), *The Status Quo and Development Strategy of the Chinese Radio, Film and Television Group* (in Chinese, 中国广播电影电视集团的现状和发展战略 or *Zhongguo Guangbo Dianying Dianshi Jituan de Xianzhuang he Fazhan Zhanlue*), http://www.people.com.cn/GB/14677/22114/26417/26443/1752509.html, last visited in February. 2012.
3 XIA Yu. *"CCTV shows red and yellow cards: ten programmes are eliminated"* (in Chinese. "央视亮出红黄牌: 10 个节目被罚下" or *Yangshi Liangchu hong huang Pai: shige jiemu bei faxia*). In Southern Weekend (in Chinese, 南方周末 or *Nanfang Zhoumo*), June 27, 2003. http://news.sohu.com/50/96/news210509650.shtml, last visited in February 2012.
4 See authors like YU Guoming, HU Zhengrong, MENG Jian, etc.

ing new reform schemes under the guideline of the market mechanism. At the same time, criticism is either insignificant or too weak to compete with the overwhelming passion towards market economy, which has officially been the centre of the state reform agenda since 1992. All above-mentioned evidences have shown that Chinese television is in the process of self-commercialization, and in a transition from the stated-owned party organ to a more and more market-oriented industry sector, however, the transition happens without cautious reflections on the consequences for the future of Chinese television, especially on the consequences in cultural, social and democratic aspects.

Nevertheless, some foreign academics of Chinese media studies[5] have shown great concerns about the obsession with market mechanism in Chinese television reform. However, these academics outside China, whose majority are Chinese in origin but were educated in the Western, generally follow the research tradition of critical political approaches in the field of Chinese media studies. This means, they focus on criticizing the authoritarian one-party system of the People's Republic of China and the oppression of press freedom by the communist party-state. The recent changes of self-commercialization in China, which is formulated as state-corporatism, have also been included in this critical political research tradition. It seems convenient to attribute the problems confronted by Chinese television to the authoritarian political system in China, which is also true. But not all dimensions of the problems can be summarized through the category of authoritarianism/democracy. For example, the market mechanism is also widely adopted in free democratic countries. Supposing that China is once democratized, will all problems in the television sector automatically disappear? The answer is obviously "No".

Another noteworthy counterweight to the dominance of the market mechanism in reforming Chinese television comes from a number of local Chinese scholars and journalists[6], whose research interests in the public service broadcasting system in Western Europe are becoming more intensive since 2002, in which the State Council proposed the establishment of "public" channels at provincial and/or municipal levels.[7] Through this group of scholars and journal-

---

5 See authors like Chin-Chuan Lee, Daniel C. Lynch and Yuezhi Zhao in the USA, Joseph Man Chan, Yu Huang, Ran Wei and Zhongdang Pan in Hong Kong, and He Chuan, Stephanie Hemelryk Donald in Australia.
6 The group of Chinese scholars and journalists who advocate public service broadcasting include CUI Yongyuan, GUO Zhenzhi, CHEN Jiyin et al., JIN Guanjun et al., CHEN Changfeng, etc. Among them, GUO is a pioneer in the researches on the public service broadcasting in China since the 1990s.
7 However, the aim of establishing these provincial and municipal "public" channels was actually to compensate the municipal and county governments for the abolition of the television stations at these two levels by offering a sharing mouthpiece for them. For details see Section 2.5, pp. 72 ff.

I. Subject of Research

ists, certain public attention to the public service broadcasting system was successful attracted by criticising the ills of commercialised television and the introduction of the public service broadcasting to China was advocated. Their knowledge about the public service broadcasting is mostly no more than just an idea on which lacks comprehensive and detailed study. It goes from bad to worse when Chinese government started to misinterpret the concept of "public service" as part of government functions. After Chinese government declaimed its shift to be a "public service" government in 2005, it began to construct public cultural services (国家公共文化服务体系 or guojia gonggong wenhua fuwu tixi) system, which covers many cultural institutions such as libraries, museums, cultural centres, etc. The result is that the concept of "public" seems to be equated with the "state" in the public perception. This misconception of "public" reached its peak when Chongqing Satellite TV declaimed its reform to be a "public interest channel" in 2011, which is in fact a sheer mouthpiece of the Communist ideologies.[8] Despite an emerging notion of "public service" television with entirely contrary intentions, the market mechanism remains dominant in Chinese television sector.

On the whole, during the process of reforming Chinese television with the market mechanism, no close examination has been made while a number of crucial questions remained unanswered. For those who prefer adopting the market mechanism to reform Chinese television, it should be answered: Where will market mechanism lead Chinese television? Is the market mechanism all in all the best means for reforming Chinese television, when considering the cultural, social and political functions of television beside its economic function? Have all possible means been considered and examined? For those who oppose the present reform scheme, what alternatives can be provided instead? Since the market mechanism or any other mechanism is only a means of reform, not the end of reform, then what kind of television system does China need? Which ends does Chinese television serve? How to reach these ends under the current conditions? Which frameworks should be provided for an "optimal" television system?

It might be too ambitious to answer all these questions in just one dissertation. Nevertheless, my dissertation attempts to achieve at least the following aims. First of all, it should be clarified why the market mechanism has gained such an overwhelming position in reforming Chinese television, how this happens, and which kind of consequences in economic, cultural, social and political aspects it may bring to Chinese television in the short and long term. Secondly, it attempts to discover the functional mechanism(s) to reform Chinese television since Chinese television is not yet under the full control of the market mechanism. It also

---

8 For details, see pp. 86-87.

Introduction

attempts to discover whether there exists a model that can describe the process of transition of Chinese television. Furthermore, it attempts as well to discover the forces that play a decisive role during the transition from the state-owned party organ towards a market-oriented industry sector. Thirdly, more constructive rather than purely analytical, it attempts to evaluate the present reform schemes and to remedy their failures if there are any. The rationales for an alternative scheme have to be provided and argued why the alternative scheme is superior to the present scheme, at least theoretically. At the practical level, it will be discussed what inspirations the alternative scheme can provide for Chinese broadcasting, either in the short run so as to deal with the instant ills of Chinese broadcasting, and in the long term concerning the democratisation of Chinese media.

II. Conduct and Methods of Research

This dissertation answers these questions in length of six chapters, which are divided into two parts after a brief review of the related theories in Chapter 1. Part one (Chapter 2 and Chapter 3) attempts to examine the four periods of the transition of Chinese television in a historical context in the first place. Next, it moves to analyse the reasons and to assess the consequences of the transition, in particular the ills of the self-commercialisation of Chinese television. Subsequently, it puts forwards the necessity to look for an alternative besides the state-owned broadcasting and the commercial broadcasting.

Part two (Chapter 4, Chapter 5 and Chapter 6) focuses on the analysis of the possible alternative, the dual broadcasting system, by which most space of the research has been given to the broadcasting systems in Britain and Germany for a convenient access to the author. As the current dual broadcasting system is actually an extension of the once monopolistic public broadcasting system, my study starts from historical retrospection of its predecessor, the public service broadcasting system, in Chapter 4. The British model as a prototype of the public service broadcasting system and the West German model as a later imitator will be painstakingly analyzed in order to learn how broadcasting was understood in the public service broadcasting: the nature and functions of broadcasting, and its relationship with market, state, and audience. And then, in Chapter 5, it moves to trace back the course of the introduction and consolidation of the dual broadcasting system. The emphasis of the analysis here is to be placed upon how the market logic gains a foothold in the public (in particular political) debates of broadcasting, and finally breaks down the monopoly of the public service broadcasting. Another focus of the research is how British and German decision makers dealt with the conflicts of ideas between the supporters of the public service broadcasting and the commercial broadcasting with different approaches. This has led to very different outcomes in reality, by which the German dual broadcasting system seems a solider model throughout the whole process of development in the past three decades. Some other important issues related to the dual broadcasting system, such as the criticism of the American purely commercial broadcasting by the dual broadcasting system, the future of the dual broadcasting system in the era of Internet, and the experiences and lessons of the imitation by other countries, are also included in this Chapter. Finally, some theoretical analyses and the theoretical significance of the dual broadcasting system will be displayed in Chapter 6. They are the essential source of inspirations for Chinese broadcasting reform both at present as well as in the long term, which will be illustrated at the end of the dissertation.

As a multi-disciplinary research which covers many aspects of the media studies, including media economy, media policy, media history and comparative media studies, various research approaches are to be used in this dissertation.

Political economy approach: Political economy is a broadly adopted perspective in researches on media economy and media policy, which is covered in this research. Chin-Chuan Lee differentiates two approaches of political economy: *radical Marxist economists* and *liberal pluralists*.[9] He summarizes that the radical Marxist economists of communication are more "economist" (focusing on critiques of the capital) and the liberal-pluralist political economists of communication are more "politicalistic" (focusing on critiques of the state). Authors from the "heartland nations" of the US and Britain, like instrumentalists Herbert Schiller, Edward Herman and Noam Chomsky, structuralists Louis Althusser and Nicos Poulantzas, political economists Nicholas Garnham, Peter Golding and Graham Murdoch etc., belong to the radical Marxist group. Lee analyzes that the radical Marxist approach is most powerful in criticizing liberal-capitalist media systems, such as in the US and Britain where market power is strong enough to have the inclination of hurting public interest and the state is not a major threat to media freedom, although he remarks the criticisms of these authors on the established capital order are "intellectually potent but perhaps politically feeble". He implicates that the liberal pluralist approach serves better for authoritarian media systems in many Third World states and the former Eastern Europe because the state here is still an enemy of public interest and media freedom.

In the case of China, where political control is still stern but economic reform is posing a contradiction to it in a gradualist process, Lee suggests that a combination of the two approaches could apply to the analyses of the state and corpo-

---

9 Chin-Chuan Lee (ed.). *Power, Money, and Media – Communication Patterns and Bureaucratic Control in Cultural China.* Evanston, Illinios: Northwestern University Press, 2000. pp. 26-36.

rate power respectively. Following this way of thinking, both radical Marxist and liberal pluralist approaches will be adopted in the doctoral research in proper places. Apart from the analysis of contemporary China, the state of affairs in other countries will also be examined with the two approaches. The contradiction between the state and the market power exists in every country where government and media market co-exist, only to different degrees. Radical Marxists emphasize their criticisms on the impact of corporate reach on commodifying public communication, nevertheless, it is also important to pay attention to the economic dynamics of media besides their political and cultural functions.

Historical approach: Anthony Smith's standard work *British Broadcasting* provides a historical point of view on how to review and assess the development of British broadcasting.[10] He selects documents on broadcasting from Parliamentary Papers, Acts, memoirs and commission reports in order to provide a useful guide and an informed insight to problems in this area. This might be particularly useful for studies on Britain whose legal system is largely based on judicial cases, traditions and conventions. However, one thing remains true that the existing problems and ongoing debates in every country have their origins in the history. Hence, it is meaningful to bear this historical perspective in mind when examining the past and current broadcasting system in a country, for instance, the system transitions in China and in the dual system countries in this doctoral research.

Comparative approach will be applied to discussing the conflicts between the ideas of the American purely commercial system and the dual system, and also to clarifying the similarities and differences between the two models of the dual system in Britain and Germany respectively. As Livingstone points out, cross-national research seems "impossible yet necessary" in an era of globalization.[11] The four models of comparative research suggested by her provide a very useful perspective for applying the comparative approach in media research.[12]

III. Significance of Research

This dissertation attempts to develop a new perspective for the discussions about Chinese television reform. It is novel and timely to incorporate the dual broad-

---

10 Anthony Smith. *British Broadcasting*. UK: David & Charles, 1974.
11 Livingstone, Sonia. "On the challenges of cross-national comparative media research", in *European Journal of Communication*, Vol. 18(4) 477-500. London a. o.: Sage Publications, 2003.
12 Livingstone follows the typology developed by Kohn to categorize comparative research into four models, namely nation as object of study, nation as context of study, nation as unit of analysis, and nation as component of a larger international or transnational system.

III. Significance of Research

casting system into the relevant discussions on Chinese television, which may act as a counterweight to the ideas of the American purely commercial broadcasting prevailing among Chinese decision makers and scholars. It is novel because the current discussions are either lost in the "market myth", or fail to remedy it as previously discussed. As an influential broadcasting system, the dual broadcasting system has not received proper attention to the discussions in China. Indeed, many features of the dual broadcasting system, such as co-existence of public and commercial broadcasting, and partial acceptance of market mechanism, will bring novel perspectives for the future decision making on Chinese television. It is also timely that for now a number of Chinese scholars and journalists have already realised the ills of the commercialisation of television, and there emerges an interest in knowing about the public service broadcasting. However, they do not acquire a good knowledge of the public service broadcasting system. This has largely hindered them from producing convincing argumentations in their advocacy of establishing public service broadcasting in China. On the contrary, public service broadcasting has been misinterpreted by the government as the mouthpiece of the government. These misconceptions about the public service broadcasting need to be corrected.

Besides these efforts to deal with the immediate problems that Chinese television is confronted with, this dissertation also seeks to provide a future prospect of the democratisation of media in China. Democratisation of media means not only the discard of an authoritarian system, but also (or rather) the construction of a new democratic system that can effectively guarantee the freedom and autonomy of media. The dissertation attempts to sort out three main principles of constructing a democratic dual broadcasting system, namely the principle of *distance from the state,* the principle of *distance from the market,* and *the protection of basic rights by organisation*. It further points out which principle will be the emphasis of decision making during the different stages of the development of the dual broadcasting system.

My dissertation also attempts to enrich the researches about the broadcasting systems of Britain and Germany from a comparative perspective. Among numerous literature about the broadcasting systems in leading industrial countries, a large part of that about comparative studies is collective works in which academics from different countries examine their own broadcasting systems individually. In Livingstone's words, "the form of nation-by-chapter reporting [which] leaves the making of comparison up to the reader"[13]. Systematic researches, especially monographs of comparative studies remain surprisingly deficient. My dissertation will attempt to systematically analyse the course of change and de-

---

13 Livingstone.

velopment of the public service broadcasting and the dual broadcasting system, and to compare the frameworks of the broadcasting systems in Britain and Germany during these two historical phases to contribute to a deeper understanding of a world-widely influential broadcasting system – the dual broadcasting system. It is of special significance for those who are interested in the dual broadcasting system yet have scant knowledge about it. The British model has (almost always) been regarded as the very typical model of the dual broadcasting system since Britain is known as the cradleland of the public service broadcasting system as well as the dual broadcasting system. However, the frameworks of broadcasting system between Britain and many other countries are often very different because of the peculiarities of Britain, in particular the role of conventions in British political life and legal system. The German broadcasting system, which has been developed on the basis of consistent judicial rulings instead of vague conventions (for the foreign outsiders), can therefore provide a valuable supplementary model of the dual broadcasting system in broadening the scope of knowledge. Finally, the theoretical analyses of the dual broadcasting in the last chapter are also an attempt of the author to make an original contribution to the theoretical studies on the dual broadcasting system.

Chapter 1
Some Related Theories to the Transition of Chinese Television System

Before closely analyzing the transition of Chinese television system, it seems necessary to build some research frameworks for a comprehensive research. It is essential to make clear: a) under what kind of circumstance the transition of Chinese television system happens; b) how this transition happens; c) from which perspective this transition will be analysed.

Respectively, three related theories are selected to serve these ends: 1) The *model of the gradual transition of Chinese economy from plan to market*[14] offers a practical framework for understanding both the deep changes in Chinese society, foremost changes in the economic sphere, and the far-reaching impact of these changes in other social spheres (in this dissertation specifically in television sector). 2) Kops' *geometric exposition of broadcasting systems*[15] conveniently demonstrates the basic types of broadcasting systems worldwide according to the revenue structure. It also shows the dynamic transition of broadcasting systems within the geometric exposition when the vectors of revenue change. The transition of Chinese television system also happens within the scope of the geometric exposition. 3) McQuail and his colleagues' *media policy change model*[16] offer a specific analytic framework for analysing media system changes.

1.1. The model of the gradual transition of Chinese economy from plan to market

The transition of Chinese economy from plan to market started in 1978 and this became the prelude of the ensuing transition of Chinese society. As the transition of Chinese television system happens subsequently to the transition of Chinese

---

14 CHEN, Pu. *Economic Reform and the Transition from Plan to Market: a model for the gradual approach of transition in China.* Münster: LIT Verlag, 1996.
15 Manfred Kops. *What Is Public Service Broadcasting And How Should It Be Financed? (Summary).* In Working Paper of the Institute for Broadcasting Economics, University of Cologne, No. 145. Germany: Institute for Broadcasting Economics, University of Cologne, 2001.
16 Denis McQuail (et. al). "A framework for analysis for media change in Europe in the 1980s". In Karen Siune and Wolfgang Truetzschler (eds.), *Dynamics of Media Politics: broadcast and electronic media in Western Europe.* London: Sage Publications, 1992. pp. 8-25.

economy and the reform scheme for Chinese television system is currently dominated by market means, it is reasonable to hypothesize that the transition of Chinese television system is in a way associated with the transition of Chinese economy from plan to market. So I choose the model that describes the transition of Chinese economy as a working framework for the analysis of the transition of Chinese television system. A closer examination of this hypothesis is conducted in Chapter 3.

The transition of Chinese economy from plan to market is generally characterized as a transition with a gradual approach[17], which is in contrast to the "big bang" approach or "shock remedy" adopted by some other Eastern European socialist countries for their economy transition from plan to market. CHEN differentiates these two types of transition of economy from plan to market as *extrinsic transition* and *intrinsic transition*.

The extrinsic transition refers to the transition of economy with the gradual approach, which at the beginning "tries to introduce market activities into the economy and promotes them, while keeping the planned economy functioning as before and reforming it step by step."[18] Gradually, a market segment emerges. It functions besides the existing planned segment in the economy and competes with it. In an economy with "freeing up" prices and labour surplus, the market segment has advantages in higher product price, lower wage, and more efficient and flexible production[19]. Hence the market segment grows faster than the planned segment. The share of the market segment continues to increase until it exceeds the share of the planned segment. Consequently, the planned segment either shrinks gradually, or adjusts itself voluntarily or forcedly to be more and more market-like. The transition process ends, when the whole economy is dominated by the free market economy. The process of the extrinsic transition of economy from plan to market is described in a four-stage diagram (see figure 1.1): the transition of economy from plan to market goes through a complementary stage (of the market segment in the whole economy), a development stage (of the market segment), a voluntary adjustment stage (of the planned segment), and a forced adjustment stage (of the planned segment)[20].

---

17 See numerous literature on contemporary Chinese economy, for instance Joseph Stiglitz, LIN Yifu etc.
18 CHEN, p. 1.
19 Ibid, p. 85.
20 Ibid, pp. 97-99.

1.1. The model of the gradual transition of Chinese economy from plan to market

Figure 1.1 Four Stages of the Extrinsic Transition from Plan to Market

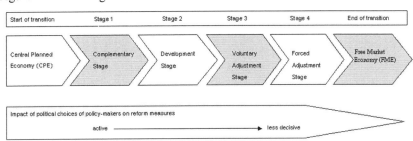

Diagrammatized according to CHEN.

CHEN particularly emphasizes the significance of *timing* of reform and policy making during the process of extrinsic transition. This could be understood from two aspects. On the one hand, some certain policy could promote the transition process only in a certain stage of the transition, whilst it may block the transition process, because the transition is achieved through a series of temporal equilibrium between the market segment and the planned segment. The interaction between the planned segment and the market segment during the transition process makes it a complicated calculation for policy-making and policy implementation. Frequently, a reform policy only designed for the planned segment can also affect the state of temporal equilibrium between the market segment and the planned segment. On the other hand, the influence of the policy makers also differs during the transition process. When the transition is still at the early stages, the policy makers are still able to intervene the process of transition through policies. Once the market segment becomes dominant in the economy, "reform measures are not political choices any longer"[21].

The intrinsic transition, contrary to the extrinsic transition, appeals to an immediate transition of economy from plan to market. Through the establishment of a totally new market based framework and the abrupt abolition of the old planned economic institution, the transition of economy from plan to market is expected to be completed overnight. Policy makers are architects for this sudden transition. The "big bang" approach or "shock therapy", which most Eastern European countries and former Soviet Union adopted at the beginning of 1990s, often results an intrinsic transition.

A comparison between the two types of transition see figure 1.2.

---

21 Ibid, pp. 96-97, p. 125.

Figure 1.2 Two Types of Transition from Plan to Market

	Extrinsic transition	Intrinsic transition
case country(-ies)	– China	– Eastern European countries
the economy at the outset of the transition	– Centrally Planned Economy (CPE)	– Centrally Planned Economy (CPE)
an aimed end of the transition	– no political designed target of a transition towards Free Market Economy (FME), rather a "by-product" of economic reform	– Free Market Economy (FME)
approaches of implementing the transition	– the gradual approach	– the "big bang" approach or "shock therapy"
characters of the transition	– the change starts with establishing a (relatively small) market segment besides the existing plan segment – the transition "growing out of plan" with an quantitative expansion of the share of the market segment and a decreasing share of the plan segment – reforming the CPE "step by step"[22] through introducing and promoting market activities into the CPE, until it becomes increasingly market-like and at the end part of the market segment – accompanied and promoted by a parallel decentralized industrialisation process (highly different from the Eastern European countries)	– the change happens in the plan segment through market-orienting adjustment in the plan segment – radical abolishment of the old CPE and trying to establish a totally new market based framework within short time

---

22 See the four stages of a feasible transition path outlined by CHEN, pp. 97-99.

1.2. Kops' geometric exposition of broadcasting systems

	Extrinsic transition	**Intrinsic transition**
driven force of the transition	– the faster growth of the market segment is the most important driving force of the transition – the built-in mechanism of market had driven the Chinese economy on the way to a market economy	– touched off by reform policies of policy makers
state of society during the transition	– smoother transition	– "shocks" and social disturbance
theoretical framework	– the neo-classic theory of growth – the dual economic model (by Kelly et al.)	– no sound theory owing to the subjective political instrumental character of the intrinsic transition

Summarised according to CHEN, 1996.

This model of extrinsic transition provides a practical framework for the analysis on Chinese television system, whose transition occurs concomitantly with the extrinsic transition from plan to market in China and comes under the impact of it. This also coheres with the consideration that television system transition often involves a very broad range of issues, such as commercial and financial changes, cultural politics and also industrial/economic policy. It complicates matters in an era of globalisation as transnational media also are involved in this process of television system transition.

1.2. Kops' geometric exposition of broadcasting systems

It is widely accepted in broadcasting studies that the world broadcasting systems are categorised according to their revenue structures. Hence the world broadcasting systems can be categorised as three basic types, namely the public service broadcasting, the state broadcasting and the commercial broadcasting, whose revenue sources are public revenue, governmental revenue and commercial revenue respectively. Many countries adopt either one of these three basic broadcasting systems, or a combination of the basic types. However, the broadcasting system in a country is not static and does not stay unchangeable. On the contrary, the broadcasting systems in many countries are experiencing dynamic transitions as the political, economic and social milieus change rapidly in the latest decades.

Chapter 1 Some Related Theories to the Transition of Chinese Television System

In his study on public service broadcasting and its financing, Kops develops a geometric exposition of the revenue structure of broadcasting systems to include the basic types of broadcasting systems as well as to illustrate their dynamic development through the changes of revenue vectors (see figure 1.3).

Figure 1.3 A Geometric Exposition of the Revenue Structures of Broadcasters, Distinguishing Three Types of Broadcasting Systems (by Kops)[23]

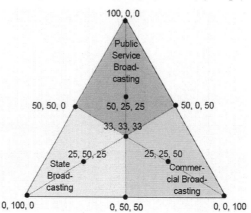

In figure 1.3, public service broadcasting refers to the broadcasting funded by public revenue, such as license fee in Britain or Rundfunkgebühr (broadcasting fee) in Germany. This is described by the vector 100,0,0 and located at the upper edge of the triangle. The governmental broadcasting funded by governmental revenues only is described by the vector 0,100,0 and located at the left edge of the triangle. The commercial broadcasting funded by market revenues only is described by vector 0,0,100 and located at the right edge of the triangle. For a broadcasting system funded by mixed revenue, it can also be described by a vector which reflects the proportion of each sort of revenue and is located in the triangle.[24]

For a country, Kops points out, the revenue structures of all materially existing broadcasters must be aggregated in two steps: first, the revenue structures of the separate existing broadcasters, i.e. public, governmental or commercial, have to be investigated empirically and then positioned into the geographic diagram; second, the revenue structure of the overall broadcasting system has to be deter-

---

23 Kops, p. 10.
24 Ibid, pp. 10-11.

1.2. Kops' geometric exposition of broadcasting systems

mined by aggregating the weighed revenue structure of all separate broadcasters of the country.[25]

Through this way, Kops positions the public service broadcasting of a number of countries into the geographic diagram according to the information available from a McKinsey study in order to make an international comparison of the public service broadcasting systems (see figure 1.4). The sizes of the dots represent the quantities of the broadcasting sectors (per capita) in these countries, and the locations represent their revenue structures, as proportions of public funding, governmental funding and commercial funding.

Furthermore, Kops illustrates the (dynamic) developing tendency of the broadcasting systems in selected countries. Obviously, these countries have a clear tendency towards commercial broadcasting. This brings forward further analyses to the causes for the latest changes in the broadcasting sector. Nevertheless, the triangle also indicates that *theoretically* any broadcasting system may have more than one alternative for its transition. For example, a governmental broadcasting can be transformed into public service broadcasting, or commercial broadcasting, or a mixed form.

Figure 1.4 International Comparison of Public Service Broadcasting Revenue Structures Based on the Categories and Data of McKINSEY 1999 (by Kops)[26]

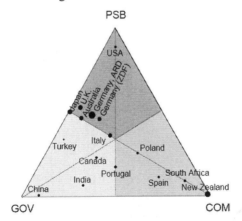

---

25 Ibid, p. 11.
26 Ibid, p. 18.

Figure 1.5 Broadcasting Systems in Selected Countries – Internationally Compared (by Kops)[27]

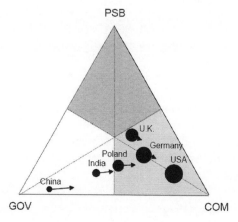

1.3. McQuail's media policy change model

Until the 1980s, the broadcasting systems in most Western European countries remained highly regulated and relatively stable. From then on, substantial changes started to undergo. In order to analyse the unusual changes in the broadcasting sector, McQuail and his colleagues develop a media policy change model.

As the changes in broadcasting sector are prompt and involve a very broad range of issues concerning commercial and financial changes, cultural politics and also industrial/economic policy, MaQuail and his colleagues believe that the medial policy change model is a more proper framework to analyse broadcasting changes in comparison with four existing conceptual frameworks.

The other four conceptual frameworks are: a technological framework; the critical, political economic perspective; the free market, deregulatory perspective; the "information society" framework. McQuail et al. agree that these models offer useful perspectives in handling the facts of change, however, these models have obvious shortcomings in dealing with "something more immediate happening which needs to be captured"[28]. For example, the technological determinist model indicates that the changes are more or less inevitable and logical consequences of the technological innovations in communication, but it appears less analytical, especially in accounting for variations between countries. Both

---

27 Ibid, p. 20.
28 McQuail et al., p. 13.

1.3. McQuail's media policy change model

the critical, political economic perspective and the free market, deregulatory perspectives focus on the logic of capitalist market systems, yet with opposite valuation on it. It seems inevitable that the technology advancements will be exploited by the commercial forces. The question arises as to whether to protect the vulnerable cultural and political communication values primarily (the critical, political economic perspective), or simply to follow a deregulation in a liberal society (the free market, deregulatory perspective). Yet these two perspectives simply deplore or support commercial exploitation of the new communication technologies, whilst it lacks further analysis of the current changes. The "information society" model remains to a large extent a prediction which lacks clear definitions and concrete contents. On the whole, these four frameworks cannot offer a specific analytic framework to capture the essence of the institutional changes.[29]

The media policy change model attempts to explain the media changes with three salient features: 1) the change is being *externally* driven by the powers beyond existing national media and political systems, or by new possibilities of supply rather than increased demand; 2) the change has an element of *conflict* between old and new players in the game, where technological and social-political changes are also incorporated; 3) the change has the sign of *fragmentation*, which means a complex of issues from various sectors and levels are involved, especially in legal and regulatory arrangements. The regulation needs to go beyond the traditional broadcasting sector into telecommunication and computer industry, beyond the national level into the transnational level, whilst the broadcasting itself also becomes more diverse as a result of the proliferating channels, new market opportunities, new audience viewing behaviour, etc.[30]

The model of policy change assumes that media system change takes place as a direct consequence of policy changes (see figure 1.6[31]). McQuail et al. take the example of Western European countries to illustrate the model.

According to the policy change model illustrated in figure 1.6, the system change happens through the following process:

The existing system of broadcasting ("old order") is first destabilised by technological and other changes. This releases commercial opportunities and attracts more players to enter broadcasting sector, and this in turn brings out conflicts and exposes policy vacuum. As a reflection of the conflicts, the policy makers work out a provisional "new order" in order to deal with the conflicts. This provisional "new order" is tested in practice and "some tendencies towards fragmen-

---

29 Ibid, p. 11-13.
30 Ibid, pp. 13-16.
31 Ibid, p. 16.

tation (or diversification) are likely to be experienced"[32]. The "new order" becomes stable after a series of adaptation.

Figure 1.6 Sequential model of system change (by McQuail et al.)

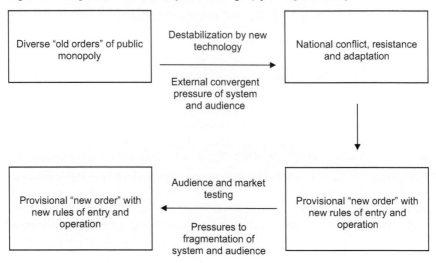

For other countries besides Western European countries, this model of media policy change is also insightful in understanding the prompt changes in broadcasting sector. In the case of Chinese television, this model of media policy change is particularly meaningful when taking the significance of policy making during the process of extrinsic transition from plan to market in China into consideration (see page 22). This policy-specific perspective also helps to narrow the scope of analysis in this dissertation. Through tracing the relevant policies chronologically, we can conveniently capture the trajectory of Chinese television system transition.

---

32 Ibid, p. 17.

Part 1
Market as a Myth: the Transition of Chinese Television System

In this part, the transition of Chinese television system as well as the transition of Chinese television is examined painstakingly in Chapter 2. According to McQuail's media policy change model discussed in Chapter 1, some most salient and crucial policies are chosen as dividing points for the four stages of a historical review of Chinese television, namely the experimental years (1958-1978), the proliferating years (1979-1991), the market economy years (1992 –2000), and at the crossroads (since 2001). The background and the consequences of the policies are also included into the examination. The indicators of the transition are comprised of two aspects: quantitatively, the change of the revenue structure (Kops' geometric exposition of broadcasting systems) indicates the gradual transition of Chinese television from state funded television to market financed television; qualitatively, the transition is manifested through various changes in television sector, ranging from changes of scale and coverage of television, programming, management, personnel in television institutions, to changes of the administration and regulation of television sector. Both quantitatively and qualitatively, it shows that the transition of Chinese television (system) has a clear tendency of self-commercialisation (which is depicted as "market as a myth").

After modelling the transition of Chinese television system by using the model of the transition of Chinese economy from plan to market for reference, it moves to analyse the reasons and consequences of the self-commercialisation in Chapter 3. The stagnation of political reform and the one-sided reliance on economic reform for society development after 1989 are the main reasons for the self-commercialisation of Chinese television. Among others, a serious consequence of the current reform scheme is that the neglect of the potential market failure might bring ill effects to Chinese television, for example, market mechanism has been overused in television system reform at the cost of weakening television's cultural and educational functions. Taking the potential negative consequences of current reform scheme into consideration, it becomes necessary to discuss alternative possibilities for Chinese television system reform.

Chapter 2
A Historical Review of the Transition of Chinese Television

Chinese television is from the very beginning a product of political choice. It follows the fundamental media philosophy of the Chinese Communist Party (CCP), according to which the politically propagandist function is Chinese media's prime function, followed by the educational function, the cultural function[33], while an "industrial"[34] function has been supplemented in the mid-1990s. Therefore, the establishment, development and transition of Chinese television are closely connected with the CCP's propaganda policies, whose task is to serve the significant political decisions of the CCP.

In the 1950s, China imitated the model of "propaganda state" from the Soviet Union, where mass media were used as instruments of thought work[35] to overwhelm the citizens with official information and interpretations of reality. As the result of political decision, television kept in a rudimentary state over its first three decades, was established in 1958 to facilitate the CCP's propagandist thought work and stayed in a primitive state over a long period of time (1958 – 1978) for China's poor economic conditions under the rigid planned economy.

However, since the year of 1978, a bottom-up, decentralised economy reform with the aim at establishing a socialist commodity/market economy enabled the

---

33 XU Guangchun (ed.). *A Brief History of Broadcasting in the People's Republic of China: 1949 – 2000* (in Chinese. 《中华人民共和国广播电视简史: 1949-2000》 or *Zhonghua Renmin Gongheguo Guangbo Dianshi Jianshi: 1949-2000*). Beijing: Chinese Broadcasting Press, 2003. p. 14.

34 Ibid, pp. 474 ff. Cf. GUO Zhenzhi (2004). *WTO, "Chanye Hua" of the Media and Chinese Television (Chinese and English versions)*. Working Papers of the Institute for Broadcasting Economics, die Universität zu Köln, 2004. During the years of planned economy and under the impact of the rigid Marxist-Leninist ideology, media belonged to the ideological domain and were part of the superstructure. The economic property of media was derogated as an exclusive feature of "evil capitalist media", thus the commercial function of television was totally out of question as a result of ideological bias as well as of the de facto primitive state of a consume society in China.

35 As early as in the 1930s, Mao Zedong started to develop Thought Work or sixiang gongzuo (思想工作) as an effective cybernetic technique to correct the deviance of CCP cadre, and to further effect (to "cultivate") their worldviews by undergoing rigorous, public self-examination in small-group study sessions. This was expanded to the mental transformation of the whole society after the establishment of the People's Republic of China in 1949. Mass media, in all forms ranging from the nationwide radio loudspeaker networks to newspapers and the subsequent television at all administrative levels, were treated as conduits of the CCP's propaganda. For a penetrating comment see Daniel C. Lynch, *After the Propaganda State: media, politics, and "thought work" in reformed China*. California (USA): Stanford University Press, 1999.

market means to affect omnidirectionally (notwithstanding following the gradualist approach) nearly all social areas, no need to mention in economic area. For the reason that the paramount task of television has been transferred to serve the CCP's guiding principle of "open and reform", foremost to promote the economic reform, at the same time with the impetus to reach the audience as much as possible and to sell as much advertising as possible, Chinese television has not only remarkably enhanced its scale and coverage with the help of the "four level policy"[36] throughout the 1980s, the content of the television programmes also turned to be audience-oriented and market-oriented, i.e. at the earliest stage of self-commercialisation.

The self-commercialisation of Chinese television was particularly reinforced in the 1990s after the Tian'anmen crackdown of the 1989 student movement, which led to a long-standing stagnation of the political reform and a predominant position of "constructing a socialist market economy with Chinese characteristics"[37] in China's reform agenda. Television, along with other previous *shiye* units[38] such as educational institutions, cultural institutions and other public services like libraries and museums, was redefined and categorised as the "Tertiary Industry[39]" in 1992.[40] Since then the television broadcasters started being managed like business firms, although they were still regarded as cause-oriented in nature and law (*shiye* units).[41]

---

36 The "four level policy" refers to the strategic guideline of developing television proposed in the 11th All-China Broadcasting Work Conference in 1983 – "four levels run television, four levels together cover [the country with television signals]".
37 In 1992, the 14th Convention of the Party Central Committee of Chinese Communist Party definituded that the goal of Chinese economy reform was to construct the socialist market economy. The entire Party was called to seize the opportunity, to accelerate the development, and to concentrate all efforts on economy construction. XU, p. 379. "To construct the socialist market economy" became the paramount (if not the only) theme of Chinese social development.
38 In the planned economy years, public service and enterprise units in China were categorised as either *shiye* or *qiye*. Public service institutions were mostly *shiye* units, while enterprises engaged with producing, manufacturing or commercial activities belonged to *qiye*. The *shiye* units were usually non-profit institutions financed by the state and enjoyed a preferential tax status. For a closer distinction between *shiye* and *qiye* units see Lynch, pp. 75-79.
39 The "Tertiary Industry" is a loose notion covering all industries besides the "Primary Industry" of agriculture and the "Secondary Industry" of of industry (specifically refers to manufacturing, energy, mining) and the building trade. *The Resolution of the Central Committee of the CCP and the State Council on Accelerating the Development of the Tertiary Industry (in Chinese, 《中共中央、国务院关于加快第三产业发展的决定》or Zhonggong Zhongyang, Guowuyuan Guanyu Jiakuai Disanchanye Fazhan de Jueding) on 16 June, 1992.* http://news.xinhuanet.com/ziliao/2005-02/17/content_2586400.htm, last visited in February, 2012.
40 XU, p. 474.
41 Lynch, p. 76.

2.1. The Starting Position and the Basic Philosophy

The degree of the self-commercialisation of Chinese television intensified in recent years after all suspicions and hesitations on market mechanism as a universally applicable means of the reform have been withdrawn through the government's strong conviction along with an up to now unabated boom of Chinese economy over an entire decade, furthermore the alleged externally challenge of the international commercial media conglomerates after China's entry into the World Trade Organisation (WTO) in 2001.[42] Eventually the market logic attained the official endorsement by the CCP leader and the state president JIANG Zemin in 2002 through a euphemism of "the industrialization of culture and broadcasting", which virtually affirmed the transition process of Chinese media as a whole into a business-oriented industry.[43]

2.1. The Starting Position and the Basic Philosophy

Before the start of television, the basic philosophy of broadcasting of the present regime has been shaped through the practice of radio broadcasting, which has acted as a part of the party propaganda during the Anti-Japanese War period (1937 – 1945) and the ensuing Chinese Civil War period (1945 – 1949) since 1940.

Based on the Maoist interpretation of the Marx-Leninist theory, the governmental party, the Chinese Communist Party (CCP), regarded the whole mass media as the mouthpiece of the Party's propaganda and the loyal servants of the Party and the government, whose key tasks were to "propagandize the policies of the Party, educate the masses, organize the masses, and mobilize the masses"[44]. This became the basic philosophy or fundamental ideology and communication model of the whole press (both print and electronic) that can be summarized as *the Party logic* and *the mass logic*.

The Party logic refers that the Party was the sender and the centre of political propaganda, which released policies and instructions through media in uniform means[45], and the masses were (passive) receivers of the thought work. Media's task was to support the current Party and the state policies through propaganda. Media were therefore also part of the ideology and superstructure of China's so-

---

42   Shortly in the process of and after China's accession to the WTO, there were numerous initiatives and papers focusing on the theme of "challenges and opportunities" for a wide range of affected industries once China becomes an official member of the WTO.
43   GUO Zhenzhi (2004).
44   K. LU, cited by Junhao HONG, *The Internationalization of Television in China*. Westport in the USA: Praeger Publishers, 1998. p. 43.
45   LÜ Yu-Nü, *Satellite Era: development and challenge of Continental China's television industry (in Chinese)*. Taipei: Shi-Ying Publishing House, 1999. p. 72.

cialist economy.⁴⁶ While according to *the mass logic*, the mass or the people were stated as the nominal owner and the served target of media. This declamation seemed to never have its true meaning, but de facto a necessary step for the legitimacy of mass media. During the development of Chinese media, it was always under the name of "for the sake of the people" to expand media networks in order to reach the masses as widely and deeply as possible.

In the conference of the State General Press Administration in February 1950, the propagandizing task of the radio broadcasting was regulated in three aspects: releasing news and communicating government order; social education; culture and entertainment.⁴⁷ This has been the ground line of Chinese radio broadcasting. Accordingly, radio programmes were arranged under this ground line, which included three main programme genres of news, knowledge/education, and culture.

Since the beginning of the 1950s, the radio loudspeaker cable networks and radio receiver stations have been established all around the country, so that the propaganda of the Party could reach every corner in a short time, even the remote mountain areas and the minority inhabiting areas. Actually, the development of radio broadcasting in rural areas has been listed as one of the major foci of agriculture development – the core task of the Party in the 1950s and the 1960s.⁴⁸

2.2. *The Experimental Years (1958-1977)*

2.2.1. The advent of Chinese television

Chinese television was established in 1958, which was actually stimulated by the CCP's political adversary. The Kuo-Min-Tang government, which was the former government in mainland China before 1949 and kept its governance in the island Taiwan province (Republic of China) after 1949, announced its plan of television development in the middle of 1950s. In order to show the supremacy of the new regime over the old one, Beijing Television came to life on 1ˢᵗ May 1958 (renamed as China Central Television in 1978) as the first television broadcaster in China. This has made China the fifth country in the Asia-Pacific region

---

46 HONG, p. 44.
47 XU, p. 14.
48 XU, pp. 21-28, pp. 34-38.

2.2. The Experimental Years (1958-1977)

to launch a television network following Japan (1953), Philippines (1953), Thailand (1955) and Australia (1956).[49]

As an expansion of the broadcasting section, television stayed in a primitive state over a long period in comparison to the relatively wide coverage of radio broadcasting. On May 1st 1958, when Beijing Television started to broadcast programmes live, there were only several dozen TV sets in Beijing receiving the programmes. In the following years, more than ten capital cities also established television stations during 1959 – 1960. In 1960, an experiment of colour television was conducted successfully in Beijing, which made China the sixth country in the world with the capacity of testing colour television broadcast.[50]

Since 1959, China got into financial difficulties as a result of both the severe famine and the political crisis of "Great Leap Forward" (1958-60)[51]. In 1961, only five television stations[52] were retained, while the others were cut off in the simplification. This state did not change much in the following two decades. TV sets were rare imported goods and only available in a small number of big cities. Many people watched TV collectively.

The ensuing economic and political turmoil of the Culture Revolution (1966-76) interrupted the normal development of Chinese television. While television has become a popular medium in most industrial countries in the 1960s and the 1970s, there were only 39 television stations located in each of the provincial and autonomous regional capitals in China and about one third of the one billion populations were able to receive television signals.[53] On the whole, Chinese television did not achieve a notable development in the 1960s and the early 1970s.[54] Through the early practices, however, Chinese television practitioners have gathered necessary experiences for the coming proliferation of television in the 1980s.

---

49 Yu HUANG and Andrew Green, "From Mao to the Millennium: 40 years of television in China (1958-98). In David French and Michael Richards (eds.) *Television in Contemporary Asia.* New Delhi: Sage, 2000. pp. 267-91. pp. 269-71.
50 XU, pp. 101-107.
51 Great Leap Forward is a man-made disaster in China's history. In order to establish Communism overnight, MAO Zedong forced the collectivisation of agriculture and kept its continuity with high political pressure. This caused a severe famine that claimed the lives of at least 30 million people. Graham Hutchings. *Modern China.* London: Penguin Books, 2001. p. 164.
52 The five cities which retained television stations were Beijing, Shanghai, Tianjin, Shenyang and Guangzhou. After the Great Leap Forward crisis, more television stations were restored gradually. Before the Culture Revolution (1966), there were ten television stations in the whole country. XU, p. 109, p. 122.
53 XU, p. 172.
54 GUO Zhenzhi. *History of Chinese Television (in Chinese, 中国电视史).* Beijing: Renmin University of China Press, 1991. p. 1.

2.2.2. The structure of Chinese television system

As part of the organs of the CCP and the government, television also followed the basic philosophy of the whole press, i.e. the Party logic and the mass logic. Similar to radio broadcasting, the programme genres of television were also concentrated on news, education and culture. A rudimentary national news network and a further education institution via television, Beijing Television University, were established in the 1960s.[55]

Like other media, the regulatory structure of Chinese television was nevertheless exclusively arranged under the Party logic. More precisely, all culture, arts, and media institutions, including news agency, newspaper, magazine, broadcasting, film, arts and culture, publishing etc., were state-owned and Party-controlled. The Department of Propaganda (中国共产党中央宣传部 or zhongguo-gongchandang zhongyang xuanchuanbu), which was a branch of the Central Party Committee, was the core player in Chinese media system. It was responsible for setting the guideline of propaganda and controlling the political correctness of media content. Other governmental bureaucracies were in charge of the administration affairs on press, broadcasting and culture respectively. In other words, they were executives of the Department of Propaganda's policies. These two columns, the ideological-organisational system of the Party and the administrative system of the government, networked a hierarchy of media structure from central to local level (See Figure 1). As PAN and CHAN pointed out, the Chinese media system was an integral part of the communist political system.[56] This established media system (including television, which extended from two levels to four level hierarchies in 1984) functions until present.[57]

---

55 XU, p. 109.
56 Zhongdang PAN and Joseph Man CHAN, " Building a Market-based Party Organ: television and national integration in China". In David French and Michael Richards. pp. 233-63. p. 236.
57 It is worthwhile to note that Chinese media institutions at all administrative levels enjoy relatively greater autonomy compared with the Soviet-style propaganda states. An "editor responsibility system", by which the editors are appointed by the territorial-level party committees, not by the party propaganda apparatus, applies to both print media and electronic media (including film). Moreover, the broadcasters at the central level has only a "guidance" relationship, not a "leadership" relationship, with the lower level stations and thus can not force them to retransmit the central programmes. See Lynch, p. 147, pp. 160 ff. The autonomy of territorial-level television broadcasters is particularly high for the television stations at the municipal and the county level were invested and built up from null by the territorial-level governments in the middle 1980s.

2.2. The Experimental Years (1958-1977)

Figure 2.1 Control and Administration of Media in China (Example: TV)[58]

Party:	State Council:	Media:
- Dept. of Propaganda, Central Committee of CCP	- Ministry of Culture - State Administration Of Radio, Film and Broadcasting (SARFT) - State Press and Publications Administration	- Culture and Arts Institutions - Radio & TV - Newspaper, Magazine & Publishing

Central	→	Central governments	→	Central (TV since 1958)
Provincial	→	Provincial governments	→	Provincial (TV since 1958)
Municipal	→	Municipal governments	→	Municipal* (TV since 1983)
County	→	County governments	→	County* (TV since 1983)

Notes:
Arrows (top-down) indicate vertical affiliation from central to local level;
Arrows (left-right) indicate horizontal leadership from the party to government and media, and from government to media.

* Chinese government started to transform television stations at the municipal and county levels into relay stations since 2001.

2.2.3. Chinese television under the planned economy

As some scholars observed, the fact that many developing countries established state-owned or governmental television should not be simply attributed to the

---

58 Initiated by LÜ, p. 76. See also PAN and CHAN, p. 238.

government's intention of controlling media. The economic reason, for which these countries did not have a requisite national economy to support a commercial television system or a public service broadcasting system, also plays an unignorable role.[59] Television, unlike print media or radio broadcasting, is a cost-intensive medium and needs a lump sum of investments for its start-up. While in developed countries, where the commercial television broadcasters manage to cover the high expenses of running television through advertising, and the public service broadcasting is funded through license fees from the listeners and viewers, in the developing countries with backward economies, only the government can afford the enormous expenses for television.

But the situation of Chinese television has gone beyond this observation. As a matter of course China was also lack of the necessary economic conditions for a commercial or a public service broadcasting system in the 1950s, for the country was in grinding poverty after years of war and agriculture remained the largest economy sector in China.[60] Chinese people were too poor to afford a public service broadcasting on the one hand, and there were no adequate consumer industries to stimulate a spontaneous development of commercial television on the other hand. Nevertheless, the decisive factor was by all means the Party's guidelines for the country's political and economic system.

China modelled its political and economic institutions after those of the former Soviet Union in the early 1950s with the intention to develop heavy industry, a symbol of the nation's power and economic achievement at that time. Under the Soviet-type planned economy, market discipline was abolished and most private initiatives in economic activities were prohibited. Private enterprises were nationalized in the beginning of the 1950s. Production, distribution and allocation were controlled by the State.[61] Moreover, market was ideologically defamed as "evil" of capitalism and fiercely criticized by the official rhetoric. Private ownership and market mechanism were out of the question over two and a half decades.

Under this distorted model of the Soviet-type planned economy system, all media institutions were "shiye danwei" (事业单位) and state owned. Shiye danwei is a contrary category to "enterprise". Its literary connotation and func-

---

59 Charles Curran. A Seamless Robe. London: William Collins Sons & Co Ltd, 1979. pp. 28-32. And Sydney W. Head, *World Broadcasting Systems: a comparative analysis*. USA: Wadsworth Publishing Company. 1985. pp. 59-60.
60 According to LIN, 89.4 per cent of the population resided in rural area and industry consisted of 12.6 of the national income in 1949. LIN Yifu, "Lessons of China's Transition from a Planned Economy to a Market Economy". *Working Paper Series of China Centre for Economic Research (2004-2), Peking University*. http://ccer.pku.edu.cn/download/296 3-1.pdf, last visited in March 2005. p. 5.
61 LIN, pp. 4-10.

tion are similar to a public service. As shiye danwei, major media organizations were fully financed by the government, while most media institutions were financially subsidized. No private media ownership was allowed, nor was foreign media ownership permitted.[62]

From 1958-1978, all Chinese television stations and their outlets were financed by the state allocation, both for their start-up and later operation. The state allocated around US$ 250,000 as start-up capital and around US$ 400,000-500,000 annually for each major provincial station and its outlets. This was a huge sum of spending. However, with this means television could only maintain a tiny scale in China. Television set ownership was estimated at three million in 1978, which was insignificant compared to the one billion population of the country.[63]

2.3. The Proliferation of Television (1978-1991)

In 1978, the "reform and open" policy was confirmed in the Third Plenary Session of the Eleventh Party Central Committee of Chinese Communist Party, which marked the start of transition in China. "Reform and open" became the new guideline in every field of the country. In television area, a "four-level system" policy, put forward on the 11th National Meeting on Radio and Television in 1983, facilitated the proliferation of television in China. The contemporary economic and political reforms in China in the 1980s also had a tremendous impact on television. In economic aspect, advertising has become an important financing source besides the state allocation with the introduction of commercial movies on television. The market logic started to emerge during this period. In political aspect, the public logic, a democratized version of the mass logic, was strangled in its infancy (also in the television area) along with the ups and downs of the political reform in the 1980s.

2.3.1. The "four-level system" policy

Chinese government started the economic reform and political reform from 1978 onwards. Actually, reforms were conducted in every sector in order to construct "the socialist material civilization and spiritual civilization". In media sector, the Party regarded television and radio as the "most powerful modern tools to educate and inspire the Party, the army and all the nationalities within the country

---

62 HONG, p. 45.
63 HUANG and Green, pp. 272-73.

toward building a socialist material civilization and spiritual civilization".[64] Therefore, it required a rapid development and sweeping reforms in the television sector to maximize the medium's propaganda potential as a means for political and cultural propaganda[65].

The 11th All-China Radio and Television Work Conference was held in Beijing in 1983. It was for the first time that television was listed next to radio as an independent sector of the broadcasting area. In this meeting, a series of significant guidelines and policies of developing broadcasting in the long term and in the short term were ratified and subsequently forwarded as the No. 37 Document (1983) by the Central Committee of the CCP. Among others, the "four-level system" policy was the paramount one that moulded the present landscape of Chinese television.

The "four-level system" policy is the short form of "four levels run television, four levels together cover [the country with television signals]". Besides the existing television stations at the central level and the provincial level, the municipal and the county level were also permitted to establish television stations. The major share of investment in infrastructure and maintenance of local television stations and relay stations, including personnel, should come from territorial-level government budget, while the central government would only play a supplementary role in investing in nationwide significant projects such as the launch of broadcasting satellites and other important technical projects.[66]

The original intention of the "four level policy" was to use local funds to expand the nationwide television coverage with minimum financial burden of the central state budget because the central government itself suffered from serious budge deficits during the early years of the reform[67]. The capacity of the lower level television stations was carefully limited to retransmit central and provincial programmes instead of originating local programmes. However, the ensuing development of lower level television stations proves to have gone far beyond the original intention of the central government, foremost from the incentive of the local governments to recover their investments and furthermore to gain profits

---

64 This was stressed in a document from the Central Secretariat of the CCP in 1981 to state the fundamental character and task of broadcasting. Later this was complemented in the No. 37 document of the central committee of the CCP with a further point that "broadcasting is also the most effective means for the Party and the government to connect with the masses". XU, p. 217.
65 Jinlu YU. "The Structure and Function of Chinese Television, 1978-1989". In Chin-Chuan LEE (ed.) *Voices of China: The Interplay of Politics and Journalism*. New York: The Guilford Press, 1990. pp. 69-87. p. 69.
66 XU, p. 325. In addition, the central and the territorial-level finances have been separated since the beginning of the 1980s as part of the fiscal reform, which resulted higher autonomy of finance for territorial-level governments. See XU, p. 324, and LÜ, p. 106.
67 Lynch, pp. 31 ff.

2.3. The Proliferation of Television (1978-1991)

through advertising revenue, Many lower level television stations also produced their own programmes to attract local audience and to sell their own advertising time although officially they were not allowed to do it.[68]

The consequence of the "four level policy" is twofold. On the one hand, the scale and television coverage rate of Chinese television were enormously enhanced since 1983. As Figure 2.2 presents, the quantity of television stations multiplied strikingly ten times from 1983 to 1993, most of which lay in the municipal and county levels. The coverage rate on total population also rose from 59.9% in 1983 to 82.3% in 1993, which means that most populace of the country was being able to receive television signals either terrestrially or via cable or satellite[69]. Television became the most influential medium of the day. Programme making began to flourish and many genres of programmes, such as news, culture and arts, sports, social education, science and technology, TV plays, were developed in the first decade of the reform. The entertainment function of TV surpassed the informative (propagandist) function to be the first reason that most of the audience watched Television.[70] However, the local-level originated programmes were frequently in poor quality, not to mention a glut of illegally transmitted pirated videotapes of "vulgar" teleplays from Hong Kong or Taiwan.

Another consequence of the "four-level system" policy was the aggravation of the decentralization[71] of the television system. It was cleared by the State Council in 1980 that television stations at the territorial levels (by then the provincial

---

68 According to Lynch, there were 880 (licensed) stations which originated 66 per cent of the television hours broadcast in 1996, while in 1982 there were only 32 stations broadcast regularly. Furthermore, some 2,000 county-level retransmission stations illegally converted into semi-autonomous broadcasting stations originating their own programming. In extreme cases, these county-level stations broadcast their own programmes instead of retransmitting the programmes of the central broadcaster China Central Television (CCTV). This has increased tension between the central television station and the lower level stations. See Lynch, pp. 141-44.
69 There always exists an enormous imbalance of the television coverage between the urban areas and the rural areas, between the eastern costal areas and the western mountainous and desert areas. To facilitate the access to television for populace in the rural areas and the western mountainous and desert areas has always been an official target of Chinese television authorities. In 1998, a policy of "facilitating access to television in every village" by the end of the 21st century and a "Tibet and Xinjiang" project in 2000 were proposed to reduce the imbalance of television coverage rate in the lagging areas. XU, pp. 505-511. Satellite broadcasting, which has started broadcasting service since the mid 1980s, is of special importance for the enhancement of television coverage in mountainous and desert areas. XU, p. 328.
70 Audience survey conducted by CCTV in 1987–1988. In Dai Yuanguang, *Chinese Journalism and Communications in the Twentieth Century: Band of Communications (in Chinese,* 《二十世纪中国新闻学与传播学：传播学卷》*or Ershi Shiji Zhongguo Xinwenxue yu Chuanboxue: Chuanboxue Juan)*. Shanghai: Fudan University Press, 2001. pp. 136-40.
71 HONG, pp. 91-94.

Chapter 2 A Historical Review of the Transition of Chinese Television

television stations) were administrated by both the local governments and the central television authority, while the local governments had the chief administrative authority, and the television authority's task was to "guide the propagandist work" and to "lead the construction of television". This principle was reinforced along with the establishment of the "four level system". When the territorial-level governments (this time primarily the municipal and the county govern-

Figure 2.2 Development of Chinese Television (1979 – 1998)

Year	Number of terrestrial TV station	Coverage rate on total population* (%)	Number of Channels	Hours of self-produced programme	Number of satellite TV relay stations
1979	38	-	-	-	-
1980	38	-	40	-	-
1981	42	49.5	48	-	-
1982	47	57.3	54	-	-
1983	52	59.9	60	-	-
1984	93	64.7	104	-	-
1985	202	68.4	219	-	-
1986	292	71.4	325	-	1,598
1987	366	73	405	-	4,609
1988	422	75.4	465	-	8,233
1989	469	77.9	512	-	12,658
1990	509	79.4	554	-	19,505
1991	543	80.5	596	108,492	28,271
1992	586	81.3	644	148,143	39,627
1993	684	82.3	755	218,260	54,084
1994	766	83.4	848	280,841	73,337
1994	837	84.5	932	383,513	96,528
1996	880	86.2	983	550,738	133,000
1997	923	87.68	1032	616,437	149,962
1998	347**	89.01	1065	-	188,798

* The coverage rate of television is calculated with a mixed means of coverage, namely a co-existence of transmission by microwave and satellite, and receiving with terrestrial or cable TV.

** In 1998 all radio, television and cable stations were re-registered and fused by the Ministry of Radio, Film and Television, the former authority of broadcasting and film.

Source: *CCTV Yearbook 1998, 1999 (in Chinese). Beijing: Chinese Radio & TV Press, 1998, 1999; Yearbook of Chinese Radio & TV 1997, 1999 (in Chinese). Beijing: Yearbook Press of Chinese Radio & TV, 1997, 1999;* LÜ, pp. 109-110

ments) were stimulated to invest to construct the infrastructure of television, they were also authorised to have the chief administrative discretion of television, while the role of the television authority at the respective levels was merely supportive.[72] At the same time, the territorial-level governments were delegated the discretion for personnel appointment and recruitment by the Central Organisation Work Conference in 1983, according to which the higher level television authorities were only responsible for managing the chief leading cadres of the next level down.[73]

Under the "four-level policy", Chinese television not only largely enhanced its scale and influence among the populace, but also reinforced its autonomy in institutional operation, personnel management, programme production etc. In the 1990s, Chinese television further gained its economic autonomy, when all television institutions were asked to be "responsible for profits and losses" (自负盈亏 zifuyingkui) in the process of constructing a socialist market economy.

2.3.2. Advertising and the funding of television

As discussed in 2.2.3, Chinese television was funded exclusively by the state funds during the time of planned economy. This situation has been changed since the economic reform was implemented in 1978.

The 11th All-China Radio and Television Work Conference in 1983, at which the "four-level system" policy was ratified, also adopted an economic policy to encourage television stations to "enhance economic benefits, to widen financial sources for the sake of supplementing the insufficient part of state funds"[74] for the reason that television was extremely cost-intensive and the funds from local governments would be far from affluent. This economic policy authorised television stations to use market means to create income. As ZHAO points out, media outlets "created income" with all means they could explore, including economic activities like running hotels, restaurants, or establishing grain process service or transportation service, etc.[75] Nevertheless, the lion's share of the "created income" in television sector came from advertising revenue in the 1980s.

In January 1979, Shanghai Television first started to air television commercials. Some television stations soon followed broadcasting advertising. As the "four level policy" has conveyed the responsibility for constructing television

---

72 XU, pp. 349-53.
73 XU, p. 372, and Lynch, p. 32. .
74 XU, p. 513.
75 Yuezhi ZHAO. *Media, Market and Democracy in China: between the party line and the bottom line.* Urbana and Chicago: University of Illinois Press, 1998. pp. 206-07.

stations and expanding the nationwide television coverage from the central state to local governments, the local governments had strong incentives to recover their investments and furthermore to gain profits through advertising revenue. Advertising, which was once condemned as the tool of capitalism and even forbidden during the Culture Revolution[76], was rehabilitated and promoted by the Party and the government as a "potential tool for economic reform, the four modernisation, and social change".[77] The fast developing economy also demanded effective channels of advertising to promote products, especially mass consumer goods.

With favourable government policies, a rapidly expanding market economy, and the incentives of the local government to gain profits, the advertising revenue of Chinese television grew rapidly during the 1980s at an annual growth rate of 60.4 per cent from 1983 to 1991 (calculated according to Figure 2.3) alongside the rapid and strong growth of advertising in media sector as a whole (see Figure 2.3). Television was also the medium profiting mostly from advertising compared with other type of mass media like newspaper, magazine and radio, because on average per television station shared more advertising revenue than other any other type of medium outlets.[78]

As television advertising revenue grew at such a phenomenal speed, the funding structure of television also began to change. Advertising revenue gradually substituted state funds as the main source of financing. For example, in 1979, advertising revenue only accounted for 11.7 per cent of the total revenue of Shanghai Television Station, while the state funds still had the largest share of 88.3 per cent of the total revenue. And the rest of the total revenue came from the revenue of economic activities and other sources.[79] In 1983, the state funds have decreased to about 67.8 per cent of the total revenue.[80] Another research on the whole broadcasting sector – radio and television together – shows similar results: the entire broadcasting sector obtained 11.5 per cent of its income from advertis-

---

76 HUANG Shengmin. *Analysis to Chinese Advertising Behaviour with Positivist Approach (in Chinese,* 《中国广告活动实证分析》 *or Zhongguo Guanggao Huodong Shizheng Fenxi)*. Beijing: Beijing Broadcasting Institute Press, 1992. pp. 17-27.
77 ZHAO (1998), pp. 55-56.
78 Lynch, p. 58. Again, there existed great imbalance of television advertising revenue between the television stations in the richer areas and those in the less prosperous areas. For example, the advertising revenue of the monopolist national broadcaster CCTV was nearly 500 million yuan which accounted 25 per cent of the total national television advertising revenue in 1992. ZHAO (1998), P 57.
79 LÜ, p. 204. But LÜ does not give details on which kind of economic activities she refers to. It is therefore unknown whether these commercial activities were correlative to media sector or not.
80 Ibid. In 1995, the revenue from advertising and economic activities has accounted 97 per cent of the total expenditure of Shanghai Television Station. The three per cent state funds appeared little more than a symbolic subjection of the television station to the Party's rule.

2.3. The Proliferation of Television (1978-1991)

ing and "related activities" in 1982, while this figure rose to 20.2 per cent in 1986. The research further reported that in 1993 television received only one-tenth of its expenditure from state funds.[81] The revenue structure of Chinese television experienced a fundamental change.

Figure 2.3 Advertising Revenue by Type of Medium (1983-1998)

(10,000 yuan)*

Year	Television	Newspapers	Radio	Magazine	Total
1983	1,624.37	7,330.34	1,806.93	1,081.12	11,842.76
1984	3,397.00	11,864.72	2,322.99	1,297.54	18,882.25
1985	6,869.58	22,011.35	2,670.71	2,809.28	34,360.92
1986	11,514.37	25,602.77	3,563.95	3,565.23	44,246.32
1987	16,297.26	35,549.21	4,721.22	4,542.91	61,110.60
1988	27,178.90	53,411.58	7,028.62	7,164.87	94,783.97
1989	36,190.20	62,940.10	7,459.90	8,506.40	115,096.60
1990	56,136.80	67,710.50	8,641.60	8,683.00	141,171.90
1991	100,052.10	96,187.60	14,049.20	9,989.30	220,278.20
1992	205,471.00	161,832.40	19,920.00	17,267.00	404,490.40
1993	294,390.70	371,109.90	34,944.30	18,447.00	718,891.90
1994	447,600.00	505,442.00	49,569.00	39,506.00	1,042,117.00
1995	649,800.00	646,768.00	73,769.00	38,229.00	1,408,566.00
1996	907,894.00	776,891.00	87,267.00	56,096.00	1,828,148.00
1997	1,144,105.00	968,265.00	105,776.00	52,709.00	2,270,855.00
1998	1,356,380.00	1,043,546.00	133,036.00	71,328.00	2,604,290.00

* excludes advertising agency and "other" recipients of advertising revenue

Source: Ma (cited by Lynch, p. 59); Modern Advertising Magazin. Chinese Advertising Industry over the Past Two Decades: a compilation of statistic data (in Chinese, 《中国广告业二十年：统计资料汇编》or Zhongguo Guanggao Ershinian: tongji ziliao huibian). Beijing: China Statistic Press, 2000.

The impact of advertising on Chinese television is far-reaching. First, besides the stated funds, advertising revenue provided the urgently needed financing for the fast expansion of Chinese television under the guideline of the "four-level system" policy in the 1980s, by which television experienced a ten-fold growth with regard to the number of television stations and channels. The nationwide cover-

---

81 Lynch, p. 72. It is noteworthy that according to XU the revenue from advertising and economic activities only accounted 43.46 per cent of the total expenditure in broadcasting sector in 1991, which was less than state funds. p. 514.

age rate also went up substantially to cover most territory of the country through this decade. Second, advertising "liberated" television (and other mass media as well) from mouthpiece of sheer Party propaganda and rendered television programming more audience- and society-oriented during its partaking in shaping a consumer society. This has promoted, along with the relatively liberal political reform, the germination of a "public logic" of media sector in a civil society in the mid 1980s. (See further discussions in the subsequent section)

However, owing to the sluggish and insufficient regulation of advertising activities by the state, and overly rapacity of the television institutions seeking advertising revenue, various negative impacts of advertising on television medium also emerged. Among others, the most disturbing phenomenon was that advertising and other market mechanisms started to get involved in television programming and even the operation of television institutions. Individual journalists were involved in "paid news" (or "envelopmental journalism") to seek for extra income from business enterprises by disguising information on products or enterprises as neutral, regular programme contents.[82] Later this has evolved into organised, collective activities of television institution with a euphemism of "soft advertising" (similar to PR news).[83] This led to an extensive ruin of the journalistic ethic and professionalism, which were still appreciated as basic moral principles among journalists despite their poor development under the authoritarian political system.

On the whole, it has to be emphasised again that during the 1980s the increasing dependence of television on advertising revenue has altered the revenue structure of Chinese television from state funded to commercial financed, and therefore fundamentally changed the property of Chinese television from state television to (state-owned) commercial television. In the 1990s, the dependence of television on commercial finance continued to aggravate. As some authors point out, the introduction and dependence on advertising was only the lower stage of the commercialisation of Chinese television. The further development of Chinese television in the 1990s shows that a higher stage of commercialization – the "industrialization" of television – finally attempted to restructure television from "non-profit" semi-public services financed with commercial means to "for-profit" sector of purely commercial enterprises.[84]

---

82 Lynch, pp. 61-64, "Paid News". See also LÜ, p. 208.
83 Ibid. pp. 64-72, "Soft Advertising".
84 GUO (2004), p. 21. XU, p. 514.

2.3. The Proliferation of Television (1978-1991)

2.3.3. The germination and a prolonged setback of the public logic in television

As Kitley and his colleagues observe, state-owned, public television was developed as "a central element in the political and cultural processes of nation-building" in many Asian countries. This is at odds with the public service broadcasting in Western countries which functions as an essential component of public sphere discourse in a civil society.[85]

The primary reason that there lacked a public television in China at all lies in the understanding of television of the CCP. Chinese television was established with clearly cultural and political motivations, and television has been regarded as an effective and modernised means to access and govern national populations in a paternalist manner. In short, Chinese television was established and operated under *the Party logic* as discussed at the beginning of this chapter, which emphasised that media's tasks were to support the current Party and the state policies through propaganda. This was re-strengthened at the beginning of the reform years. According to a resolution of the Tenth All-China Broadcasting Work Conference in 1980, the central task of radio and television was fixed on "serving the economic construction, serving the realization of the Four Modernisations", since the focal point of the Party work has shifted (from class struggle during the Culture Revolution) towards the construction of the socialist modernization.[86] An ensuing higher rank document from the Secretariat of the CCP in 1981, which functioned as part of the television policy or even de facto enjoyed the highest authority in the context of contemporary Chinese politics, reinforced the function of radio and television as:

> "radio and television are the most powerful modernized instruments to inculcate and invigorate the whole Party, the whole military, and people of all nationalities in construction of socialist materialistic and spiritual civilisations. This is indeed the fundamental property and task of broadcasting work".

Later this resolution was revised by supplementing an extra sentence of "(radio and television are) also the most efficient instruments for the Party and the government to get connected with the masses".[87]

Besides the political and ideological reasons, another argument emphasizes the fact that there simply lacked a civil society in China renders the absence of a public television both economically and socially. The definition of civil society in Western tradition embraces a normative separation between state and society,

---

85 Philip Kitley. "Introduction: First principles – television, regulation and transversal civil society in Asia". In Philip Kitley (ed.) *Television, Regulation and Civil Society in Asia.* London and New York: RoutledgeCurzon, 2003. pp. 3-34. p. 3.
86 XU, p. 190.
87 Resolution of the Secretariat of the CCP on November 16, 1981. XU, p. 211 and p. 217.

where a civil society, in forms of civic associations or other civic activities like civic debates, acts to take on social responsibilities in areas where government is increasingly abdicating.[88] However, the separation between state and society was removed under the governance of the CCP by "making everything public"[89]. State paced beyond the political domain and exercised as the agent and administrator of the public in economic and social domains, no matter whether it concerns healthcare, housing or employment, consumer goods. When everything the state-owned has been regarded as "public ownership"[90], a monopolistic state-funded television could therefore conveniently be interpreted as a "public" television, especially under the ostensible claim of the state television of "serving the masses", namely a nominal *"mass logic"* (briefly discussed on p. 36), which also strengthened the false impression of Chinese television being "public".

Despite the non-existence of a genuine public television in China, Chinese television did bear some characteristics of the *"public logic"*[91], especially when civil society is understood in a broad sense as "specific practices and normative codes through which people are made accountable and responsible to other members of society"[92] that exists at any phase of the human history. Beyond the ambiguous connection with the ostensible *"mass logic"* of serving the people, the *"public logic"* of television started to germinate in the mid 1980s in a relatively liberal political circumstance. As political reform, involving topics like the separation of government administration from Party ideological leadership, more openness in government, democratic decision-making, and public participation, was pushed onto the Party's agenda after the economic reform in the mid 1980s, journalism reform was also put on the national agenda. When reformers and aca-

---

88 Michael Keane. "Civil society, regulatory space and cultural authority in China's television industry". In Kitley. pp. 169-87. p. 169.
89 Ibid, p. 176.
90 There has been always a confusion about the likeness of the public service broadcasting and Chinese state-owned television in China. This confusion probably arises from the insufficient knowledge on the public service broadcasting among Chinese media scholars, and also from the blur terminology of the "public ownership" (公有制 or gongyouzhi, "namely, ownership by the whole people and collective ownership by the working people), which is identical to the state ownership and comprises "the basis of the socialist economic system of the People's Republic of China". See Article 6 of *The Constitution of the People's Republic of China*. English version. http://english.people.com.cn/constitution/constitution.html, Last visited in February 2012.
91 The principles of the public service broadcasting (in an old order) are summarised by Colin Seymour-Ure. See Colin Seymour-Ure. *The British Press and Broadcasting since 1945* (2nd edition). UK: Blackwell Publishers Ltd. 1996. pp. 60-63. Brandts and Siune also define the public service elements of public service broadcasting in Europe of the 1990s. See Karen Siune and Olof Hultén, "Dose Public Broadcasting Have a Future?".In Denis McQuail and Karen Siune (eds.) *Media Policy: convergence, concentration and commerce*. London: Sage Publications, 1998. pp. 23-37. pp. 24-25.
92 Kitley, p. 15.

2.3. The Proliferation of Television (1978-1991)

demics were dedicating themselves to discussing concepts like press freedom and the "people principle" instead of the "Party principle"[93], or to drafting a press law to protect journalists from the Party's arbitrary power[94], media self also actively participated in reporting the political reform and other civic-related topics where the state-society relations were being reshaped as a result of the economic reforms[95]. Moreover, it is also noteworthy that television institutions gained certain autonomy through a decentralised "four level policy" and partially financial independence from state funds with the help of advertising revenue.

The *public logic* in Chinese television during the 1980s was shown from the following aspects:

– it aimed to provide universal access within the territory and offered free-to-air television service to all members of the country who could afford a television set. The programmes were comprised of mixed and pluralistic schedules with emphasis to information (dissemination of news and the policies of the Party), social education, culture and entertainment, and with considerations to minority interests, such as ethnic minority, children, peasants and other special interest groups.

– besides the "public" finance of state funds, advertising revenues were principally gained for programming or programme-related purposes, not made for profit of its own sake.

– television institutions enjoyed increasing autonomy in finance, routine operation, personnel management and programming as a result of the implementation of the "four level policy". In fact, as it lacked efficacy of regulation in China for historical, legal and cultural reasons, self-regulation (also self-censorship) has become the dominant model of activities[96] in many areas, and in television sector as well.

– genres of television programmes blossomed omnidirectionally, as it was in entertainment like teleplays or gala shows, and in political news reporting and civic related topics as well. Television critics pertaining the misuse of power by some cadres and various social problems[97] absorbed audience's attention quickly. The public found a new channel to register complaints, though in a limited scale, in that there were still obvious political taboos for

---

93 What are dangxing and renminxing?
94 ZHAO (1998), pp. 35-45.
95 PEI argues that "as the state continues to withdraw its influence in economic and social activities, Chinese society has gradually gained more space previously claimed and controlled by the state under the pre-reform regime". He anticipates the growth of civil society with the evidence of the rise and growth of civic organisations. See Minxin PEI. The Growth of Civil Society in China. In James A. Dorn (ed.) *China in the New Millennium.* Washington D.C.: Cato Institute, 1998. pp. 245-66.
96 Keane, p. 179.
97 Jinglu YU. pp. 78-79.

television critics – no critics were allowed to make on the fundamental problems of the system, nor on the high rank leaders.[98]

The crackdown of the pro-democracy movement in June 1989 not only suspended the practice and theoretical discussions on media reform, but also brought the process of democratisation and political reform into a severe setback thereafter. In the sequent two years, the Party focused on cleaning up the pollution of "Western bourgeois liberalisation" in media sector by dismissing the active journalists and theorists during the pro-democracy movement and the editors-in-chief who failed to stick to the "Party logic" in the struggle against bourgeois liberalisation. The work on drafting a press law was also suspended.[99]

As political reform pertaining democratisation as a whole was removed from the Party's reform agenda after 1989, it turned to be a taboo for discussions on press freedom or the "people logic" in media sector. From the latter half of 1989 till the end of 1991, media were forced to reflect on their performance during the pro-democracy movement by "unifying the thought" that "the Party logic principle is the cornerstone of Chinese press reform".[100] Media were again the tame mouthpiece of the Party's guidelines and policies. However, television underwent a profound transformation in the ensuing years of constructing a "socialist market economy" from 1992 onwards.

2.4. The Rule of the Market Economy (1992-2000)

A series of talks of the former Party leader DENG Xiaoping at the beginning of 1992 marked a new era of the Chinese economic reform. Under his advocation for more economic openness and reiteration of the importance of economic construction, the Fourteenth National Party Congress in October 1992 formally declared that the target of Chinese economic reform was to "construct a socialist market economy with Chinese characteristics". However, the market mechanism soon went beyond the economic sphere and spread to other social spheres (such as educational institutions, cultural institutions and other public services like libraries and museums, as well as media), where the market mechanism was officially encouraged to be adopted as an effective means of reform. At this stage, television intensified its self-commercialisation at all levels, from micro-level of programme teams inside the television institutions, to the meso-level of the tele-

---

98 Ibid.
99 ZHAO (1998), pp. 45-47.
100 LI Liangrong. "Retrospections and Expectations of the Press Reform in the Past 15 Years". (in Chinese, "十五年来新闻改革的回顾与展望"or "shiwunian lai Xinwen Gaige de Huigu yu Zhanwang"). In *Journalistic University (in Chinese, 新闻大学 or Xinwen Daxue)*, 1995 Spring: 3-8.

2.4. The Rule of the Market Economy (1992-2000)

vision institution towards a profit-oriented enterprise, to the macro-level of television "industry" as a whole. This, consequently, caused far-reaching changes to Chinese television landscape, whose scope and scale have been largely extended with the remarkable development of cable television and satellite television throughout the 1990s. In short, Chinese television transformed from state-owned public service to state-owned commercial enterprise under the cover of *"shiye"* unit (Chinese version of non-profit public service). The commercial reality of Chinese television actually was embedded in the deeper societal ethos throughout the 1990s, an enthusiasm for market mechanism promoted by the majorities of the governmental officials, academia, and television practitioners as an efficient means of reform. This zeal for market economy, which is here depicted as a market myth, reached its climax on the eve of China's entry into the WTO which symbolised China's integration into the global market. In contrast to the dynamic development of television economy, television as a medium of monitor over social problems still made some progress under the Party's prudent control and restricted tolerance. The public, namely the audience of television, appeared to be absent in direct participation in television reform, because they were deemed either as public who needed "correct guidance" from the Party, or consumers of advertisement by the commercialised television institutions.

2.4.1. Television "reform" with market mechanism at all levels in the multi-channel era

Without presetting a blueprint for the television system reform, Chinese television intensified its commercialisation from 1992 onwards as a result of the radical cut in government's budget on social welfare and public services, and also as a result of gradually deregulating frameworks for commercial operation in television sector. Nevertheless, when the government and the whole society were enthused by the ethos of "reforming with market mechanism" and there lacked an efficient counterbalance of rational public debates at the same time, it seems no coincidence that Chinese television transformed from a semi-public service into a profit-oriented industry.

In June 1992, the Central Committee of the CCP and the State Council jointly adopted a resolution to call for accelerating the development of the tertiary industry[101]. Media, which used to be regarded as *"shiye"* units, were for the first time categorized into the tertiary sector and endowed with a new property of "in-

---

101 *The Resolution of the Central Committee of the CCP and the State Council on Accelerating the Development of the Ternary Industry (16 June, 1992)*. http://www.people.com.cn/GB/33831/33836/34146/34190/2543468.html (last visited in May, 2005).

dustry". The resolution also pointed out that the self-development mechanism of the tertiary industry should be oriented towards "industrialization" (产业化 or chanyehua). Most institutions in the tertiary sector should be established as economic entity or operated enterprise-like to be able to "operate independently and be responsible for profits and losses". Most of the existing institutions in the tertiary sector in social welfare model, public service model and "shiye" model were demanded to "transform into business model and be managed enterprise-like".[102]

This resolution, together with the cornerstone resolution of the ensuing economic reform, namely the salient resolution of the Fourteenth National Party Congress in October 1992 which set the target of Chinese economic reform as "constructing a socialist market economy with Chinese characteristics", legitimated the market mechanism as a means of reform in economic sectors as well as in social sectors under the new categorisation of the tertiary sector. As it proved in many social sectors such as education, healthcare or housing (which used to be part of social welfare until then), market means has been utilised for further "reform" forthrightly as if it was the most efficient way for problem-solving.

In television sector, the market mechanism as a means of reform was adopted spontaneously first in some pilot projects by television institutions following the commercially successful attempts of some radio stations[103]. In January 1993, Shanghai Bureau of Broadcasting established the second television station of Shanghai, Shanghai Oriental Television, beside the monopolistic Shanghai Television with an intention to introduce competition in local television sector. Since then, "reforming" television with market mechanism, as a spontaneous, bottom-up attempt of television practitioners rather than being stimulated by policy-makers, was carried out successively at micro-, meso- and macro-levels.

---

102 Ibid. Article III / Subarticle 11.
103 A sub-channel of Guangdong People's Radio, Pearl River Economic Radio (PRER), which located and broadcast in Guangdong Province – a region with a premature market economy for its geographic and economic proximity to Hong Kong, was the first "economic" (a euphemism of "commercial") station in China since 1986. It imitated the programming and format from Hong Kong commercial radio and became extremely successful soon after its broadcast. However, it was eight years later in 1992 that the first similar commercial radio station in the inner area (in contrast to Guangdong), Shanghai Orient Radio, was established. Compared with PRER which is a daughter channel of Guangdong People's Radio, the specificity of Shanghai Orient Radio lies in the fact that it is an independent (both financially and organisationally) radio station parallel to the Party organ Shanghai People's Radio. See ZHAO (1998), pp. 95-111.

2.4. The Rule of the Market Economy (1992-2000)

reforms at *micro-level* since the beginning of the 1990s

Two conferences of the television sector in the early 1990s cleared the way for reforms at micro-level. On the "All-China Provincial Broadcasters Conference for Exchanging Experiences on Administrative Work" in November 1992 right after the Fourteenth National Party Congress, the representatives conformed that the focus of reforming television administration was to reform personnel system, allocation system and financial system. The internal reform had to be oriented to the principle of "*shiye* unit, operated enterprise-like".[104] The guidelines for reforming financial system were reinforced on the "All-China Radio and Television Financial Administration Work Conference" in 1993, according to which *shiye* units should gradually be responsible for its revenue and expenses and be not dependent on state funds.[105] Consequently, the national broadcaster China Central Television (CCTV) started a pilot project of the "producer mechanism" since 1993 in the newly established News Commentary Department. The producers of programme were endowed with the responsibility and autonomy for content and format of programming, personnel recruiting (open to applicants outside CCTV for the first time), fund raising through a fixed proportion of the advertising revenue of the programme. This new mechanism stimulated the innovation and the consciousness of competition among television journalists. Two pilot programmes under the new mechanism, *Oriental Horizon (《东方时空》 or Dongfang Shikong)*, and *Focus (《焦点访谈》 or Jiaodian Fangtan)*, soon became not only the most successful news magazines but also the most lucrative advertising media of the country.[106] In 1996 this model was institutionalized for other CCTV programme teams with 10 per cent of the programme time being allocated to advertising, while 50 per cent of the advertising revenue were allocated for production funds.[107] Beijing Television (BTV) also introduced a similar mechanism in 1995 by dividing its 800 production personnel into 103 "programme groups" (jiemuzu), each of which was responsible for generating the funds necessary to pay for the operating expenses of the single, regularly broadcast programme[108]. In short, the programme teams inside the television stations were either encouraged or forced to be responsible for generating its daily operating expenses and even giving some certain percent of advertising revenues to the television institution, as an exchange the programme producers obtained production autonomy.

---

104 XU, p. 534.
105 Ibid, p. 535.
106 XU, pp. 390-92.
107 Ibid, p. 517. The other 50 per cent of the advertising revenue would be turned over to the finance department of CCTV.
108 Lynch, p. 65.

reforms at *meso-level* since the mid of the 1990s

Although the establishment of Shanghai Oriental Television in 1993 marked the reform of television at meso-level, i.e. television broadcaster as an institution to be reformed with market mechanism, it was until 1996 that the broadcasters started to be operated enterprise-like, after the then General Secretary of CCP JIANG Zemin gave the media sector a clear signal in his talk during his inspection to the People's Daily in 1996, whereby he advocated that "the Newspaper Office of the People's Daily should make endeavour to improve its business management while running the newspaper well".[109] Again, CCTV promptly grasped the messages of JIANG's talk, and explicitly put forward that CCTV would "endeavour to develop the tertiary industry". Although it is vague enough to fully understand how to develop the "tertiary industry" in this context, what CCTV has done afterwards shows that it started to be diversified into television-related business in an enterprise-like manner. For example, CCTV established a number of subsidiaries in the fields of programme production, programme dealing, studio management etc.; it even established a VCD production line for its own programmes. Another salient development of television institutions at the meso-level is that some subsidiaries of television broadcasters practiced "the operation of capital" (资本运作 or *ziben yunzuo*) by turning joint-stock companies and raising funds from stock exchange. These joint-stock companies included Oriental Pearl Joint-Stock Company (the subsidiary of Shanghai Broadcasting Bureau) in 1992, Chinese International Television Communication Joint-Stock Company (the subsidiary of CCTV) in 1997, and Television & Radio Communication Joint-Stock Company (the subsidiary of Hunan Provincial Television) in 1999, etc.[110] The above-mentioned two developments indicate that the property of Chinese television institutions has to some extent metamorphosed from public service or *shiye* to commercial enterprise.

reforms at *macro-level* since the later 1990s

Although lagging far behind the reforms conducted by the television institutions at micro- and meso-levels for the reason that "industrialisation" (产业化 or

---

109 XU, p. 525.
110 Ibid, pp. 528-31.

2.4. The Rule of the Market Economy (1992-2000)

Chanye Hua[111]) of television remained controversial among policy-makers, some further reforms with market mechanism conducted by the central government and the national authority of radio and television, SARFT, show that the transformation of television sector still happened at macro-level, especially in the restructuring of the television sector at national level. In 1999, a "No. 82 Document" of the Office of State Council demanded "a separation of cable network and cable television station". According to this high-ranking document, the existing cable television stations at four levels would be integrated into the respective terrestrial television stations, while the cable network would be "industrialised" as an independent entity at provincial level and national level. Instead of its original function of transmitting television signals and generating television programmes as well, now the cable network would be operated as a sheer transmission network with value added services such as video-on-demand, long distance education etc.[112] If the intention of restructuring the cable network was to rationalise the reduplicative and very often excessive constructions of both terrestrial television and cable television, another fusion of media institutions conducted by the SARFT since 2000 seems to be a direct response to the ostensibly inevitable challenges of the international conglomerates while China was in the process of entering the WTO[113]. After analysing the strengths of the international conglomerates as "mega media", the officials from the SARFT concluded that Chinese media had to be "bigger and stronger" in order to meet the competition from international conglomerates. This consequently led to a wave of "conglomeration" (literally "grouping", 集团化 or *Jituan Hua*) of television institutions and other

---

111 GUO (2004) conducted an exhaustive research on the Chinese concept of Chanye Hua (literally "industrialisation"), which has to be understood within the Chinese context of mediascape. GUO concludes that Chanye Hua is indeed "a rhetorical device to push for the marketisation of the Chinese media". The conception of Chanye Hua gradually gained its currency among media managers and some scholars in the late 1990s, which expressed the desires of media managers to use the media to make profits. However, the concept of Chanye Hua remained controversial among policy makers in television sector until the state president JIANG Zemin finally gave an official endorsement of the industrialisation (Chanye Hua) of television in a talk in 2002. Since then, Chanye Hua became a buzzword among policy makers in television sector. See GUO: *WTO, "Chanye Hua" of the Media and Chinese Television (Chinese versions).* pp. 9-11.
112 XU, pp. 526-28.
113 Actually there exists an "audio-video exemption" in GATS and the later WTO agreements, which means China does not have to open its television market after its entry into the WTO. If the officials from the SARFT were well informed about this matter of principle as they ought to be, it could be speculated that it was just an excuse for the advocators of conglomeration to claim that there exists an urgent challenge from the multinational media conglomerates after China's entry into the WTO. The real intention lies probably in two aspects: first, the practitioners' ambition of economic expansion; second, the SARFT utilised this opportunity to tighten its control on broadcasting by creating an umbrella organisation of media conglomerates of economically powerful institutions.

media institutions. After the conglomeration of some provincial media institutions in 2000 and 2001, the biggest media conglomerate of China with the involvement of almost all radio, film and television institutions of the national level, Chinese Radio, Film and Television Group[114] (中国广播影视集团 or Zhongguo Guangbo Yingshi Jituan), was established in December 2001, fitly following China's accession to the WTO in the same month.[115]

It has to be stressed that these reforms with market mechanism on television sector throughout the 1990s took place at a time when cable television and satellite television flourished in China. Since the mid 1990s, a plan of "merging satellite and cable television into one network" based on the scattered development of satellite and cable television since the 1980s was carried out by the state authority, with the aim to improve the quality of transmission and to further enhance the nationwide coverage rate of television, which proved to be particularly difficult, if not impossible, in the remote mountain areas alone with terrestrial relay stations.[116] This has tremendously impacted on the landscape of Chinese television in terms of scope and scale. Owing to the large capacity of cable television, the number of channels doubled from 554 in 1990 to 1065 in 1999; this figure doubled again to 2058 in the year of 2002 (See Figure 2.2. on page 44). CCTV alone had 9 channels in 1999, including a full programme channel CCTV 1 and a clutch of "professional" channels, which were theme-oriented niche channels ranging from economic affairs and life-style, sports, movie, to military affairs, agriculture and children programmes, even including an English-speaking channel.[117] Other major television stations at the provincial level had a similar structure of channels like CCTV. Moreover, satellite television enabled nationwide access to provincial channels, which used to be accessible only to the audience of the respective province. By the end of 2000, all central and provincial television broadcasters had at least one satellite channel that can be received nationwide. It was fairly common for a family among the 84 million households with cable television access[118], mostly in the urban area, to receive about 50 channels in 2000.

To sum up, the development of satellite and cable television in the 1990s has brought Chinese television into a multi-channel era, when the channel resources all at once became abundant and the attention of audience became a scarce resource. This in turn formed the infrastructure of commercial competition for au-

---

114 The fusion involved a cluster of central radio, film and television institutions covering areas of infrastructure, delivery, content production and other auxiliary business like publishing, advertising etc.
115 ZHU Hong.
116 XU, p. 495.
117 www.cctv.com/English (visited in August 2003).
118 XU, p. 498.

2.4. The Rule of the Market Economy (1992-2000)

dience share and advertising revenue among television institutions. The reforms of Chinese television with market mechanism at the micro-, meso- and macro-levels which were proceeding at the same time, have finally brought the commercialisation of Chinese television into reality.

2.4.2. The commercial reality of Chinese television

After a decade of reforms with market mechanism at the micro-, meso- and macro-levels, Chinese television has transformed from stated-owned public service into state-owned commercial enterprise under the rhetoric of "(television institutions are in their nature) '*shiye*' units (Chinese version of non-profit public service) but operated enterprise-like". The commercial properties of Chinese television were evident in many aspects.

First, Chinese television was not only heavily dependent on advertising revenue as source of finance, but started profit-seeking by selling advertisement throughout the 1990s. As discussed in 2.3.2., Chinese television received only about one-tenth of its expenditure from state funds in 1993. In 1998, the state funds received by most provincial television stations were less than ten per cent of their expenditure, while the state funds to a large extent showed a symbolic significance of the state-ownership and state control over television stations; on the contrary, these television stations handed over more than tenfold of the received state funds to the respective authority.[119] Television advertising became a highly, if not the most, profitable advertising medium, when Chinese advertising industry kept an average growth rate of 51.7 per cent annually from 1983 to 2001 (see Figure 2.4.).[120] Of course there existed a tremendous imbalance in advertising revenue among television stations as a result of size or the geographic locations in economically advanced areas or economically backward areas. For example, the advertising revenue of the monopolistic national broadcaster CCTV was more than 4 billion yuan in 1997, which alone accounted for 36.6 per cent of the total national television advertising revenue of 11.4 billion yuan; the advertising revenue of the 32 provincial television stations accounted for another 38.8 per cent of the national television advertising revenue; the rest 24.6 per cent of the total television advertising revenue was shared by 60 municipal television

---

119 LU Di. *A Research on the Development Strategy of Chinese Television Industry* (in Chinese, 《中国电视产业发展战略研究》 or *Zhongguo Dianshi Chanye Fazhan Zhanlue Yanjiu*). Beijing: Xinhua Press, 1999. p. 97.
120 YU Guoming, *"Six key Points of the Development of Chinese Media Industry"* (in Chinese, "中国传媒业发展的六个关键词", or *"Zhongguo Chuanmeiye Fazhan de liuge Guanjianci"*), a speech given on 30. May 2003. http://media.sohu.com/14/34/news209663 414.shtml. Last visited in February 2012.

Chapter 2 A Historical Review of the Transition of Chinese Television

stations and more than 3000 other types of television stations, which unavoidably needed a subsidy from the respective level of government. Moreover, the disparity of the average television advertising revenue between television stations in more prosperous eastern coastal areas and those in impoverished western mountain areas could be very big.[121] Nevertheless, television was no more a mouthpiece needing a huge sum of investment from the state, but "an industry that adds value"[122].

Figure 2.4 Comparisons on four main media's advertising revenue and annual growth rate in different Periods

	1983-2001 average annual growth rate in the past 18 years	1997-2001 average annual growth rate in the latest 5 years
Newspaper	37.8%	15.6%
Magazine	33.7%	17.2%
Television	51.7%	14.8%
Radio	30.5%	16.6%

Source: YU Guoming, 2003.

Second, the commercial patterns of management and operation, such as the ratings, bidding, were adopted inside television stations as means to enhance competitiveness or to maximise advertising revenue. In 1995, CCTV established CVSC[123], a professional audience research company, which conducts audience surveys and provides television ratings data. The ratings system has since then become a decisive indicator for advertisers to decide in which programme they wished to launch advertisement. Those top rated programmes, such as the main news programme of CCTV at the prime time, *Newscaster* (《新闻联播》 or *Xinwen Lianbo*) at 19:00 on CCTV 1, and the succedent news commentary programme *Focus* at 19:40 on CCTV 1, became extremely lucrative.[124] The five-

---

121 LU (1999), p. 97.
122 Ibid, p. 88.
123 Later CSM, a joint-venture of CVSC and TNS Group, the leading French market research group.
124 For example, in 1999 *Newscaster* still had 30 per cent ratings on average with an enormous viewship of about 400 million audience nationwide; the ratings of *Focus* were 25% on average with a viewship of about 300 million audience nationwide. These two programmes were the most viewed programmes in China. See ZHANG Ning, *A Ratings Analysis to the Bidding of Advertising Spots on CCTV (in Chinese,* 中央电视台广告招标段位收视分析 or *Zhongyangdianshitai Guanggao Zhaobiao Duanwei Shoushi Fenxi).*

2.4. The Rule of the Market Economy (1992-2000)

second-advertising-spots between the two most often viewed programmes in China, *Newscaster* and *Focus*, were so in demand that the Advertising Department of CCTV finally initiated a bidding system since 1995 to ease the tension between the limited supply of advertising-spots time after *Newscaster* and the excessive demands from the advertisers. The starting price was 7 million yuan for a five-second-advertising-spot and it increased to 12 million yuan in 1996.[125] The starting price keeps rising annually at a rate of 10% and the highest bidding price was often rocketing. This activity of bidding hosted by CCTV and the highest bidder of the year, the so-called Bidding King (标王 or biaowang) which often bid at a record-breaking price of thousand million yuan[126], have since then been a phenomenon of Chinese television advertising. The revenue generated from the bidding alone accounts for about a half of the advertising revenue of CCTV. Under the circumstances, programme teams had to struggle to be ahead in the ratings, which indicated the value and competitiveness of a certain programme in the television advertising market on which programmes depended for survival, and for profit as well.

Third, the content and format of television programmes became overwhelmingly market-oriented. As more channels and airtime were available owing to the development of satellite and cable television in the mid 1990s, television programmes in all genres flourished and thematised channels were becoming a dominant trend. For instance, the trendsetter of Chinese television CCTV was expanding from two terrestrial channels (the full programme channel CCTV 1 and the economic channel CCTV 2) to nine channels until the end of 2000, while the latest established channels (only accessible via satellite and cable television) were all thematised channels of music and Chinese opera (CCTV 3), international reports (CCTV 4), sports (CCTV 5), movies (CCTV 6), military affairs, agriculture and children programmes (CCTV 7), TV plays (CCTV 8) and English-speaking programmes (CCTV 9).[127] However, many lately broadcast programmes were congested with two types of content: informercial and entertainment, while the former is either paid news or an expanded version of conventional advertisement, and the latter one covers those entertaining contents attracting more audience and is therefore more attractive to ratings-concerned advertisers.

---

http://www.a.com.cn/cn/mtyj/mtalfx/2001/hyzl-ssfx.htm. Last visited in February 2012. However, in recent years the ratings of *Newscaster* drop to less than 11 per cent as a result of the explosion of channels, but it remains the most viewed single regular programme of the country (with the exception of the occasional high ratings of some popular TV plays). See www.xhby.net/xhby/content/2004-07/16/content_484641.htm. Last visited May, 2005.

125 ZHAO (1998), p. 58.
126 Several Bidding Kings even ran into difficulties and went bankrupt after their blind bidding.
127 www.cctv.com/English, visited in August 2003.

Chapter 2 A Historical Review of the Transition of Chinese Television

Following the success model of PRER in the mid 1980s, the first economic radio (a commercial radio in reality) in China, many economic radios and television channels were established at the beginning of 1990s.[128] CCTV 2, the thematised channel of CCTV for economy and information, emerged to be a typical informercial channel and was later widely imitated by other regional economic television stations. Apart from the regular economic news, CCTV 2 had three other regular programmes broadcasting "the second type of advertising" (二类广告 or erlei guanggao), whose contents were comprised of detailed promotion of industrial and consumer products or a boast of corporate image.[129] Other programmes of CCTV 2 with special interest, such as cars, high technology, finance and economics, lifestyle, were also filled with PR news or sponsored contents. If informercials were directly selling broadcasting contents to the market, the entertainment programmes were attempting to sell audience share to the market. Not only did Chinese television transform many of the lately established channels to entertainment in the broad sense such as movies, sports or music, entertainment programmes in a narrow sense, especially new formats of entertainment programmes such as game shows, dating shows and quiz shows, also became phenomenally popular. Provincial satellite channels, which were by then receivable nationwide, were extraordinary vigorous in exploring new formats of entertainment programmes in order to compete with CCTV for nationwide audience share and to attract advertisers. Hunan Satellite TV was the first provincial channel that succeeded in gaining high nationwide audience share with its entertainment programmes. In 1996, the first successful game show in China, Base Camp of Happyniess (快乐大本营 or kuaile dabenying) from Hunan Satellite TV reached a high rate of 33% on average in the ratings. Consequently, the advertising price of the programme overtook the average advertising price of CCTV for the first time.[130] Nevertheless, many of these entertainment programmes were simply plain "clones" of overseas entertainment programmes, mostly from Taiwan, Hong Kong, Europe and USA. The domestically successful formats of entertainment programmes would again have to live with inferior clones from other regional channels, therefore generally Chinese television presented a tendency of convergence in terms of content and format.

Preben Sepstrup once summed up the two key elements for defining commercialisation (of broadcasting). The first element is the presence or absence of a profit motive, and the second element is the presence or absence of advertising

---

128 ZHAO (1998), p. 124.
129 ZHAO Bin. Mouth Piece or Money Spinner? – the double life of Chinese television in the late 1990s. *International Journal of Cultural Studies*, 1999 Vol. 2(3): 291-305.
130 XIE Yungeng and WANG Caiping. *A Report on Chinese Television Entertainment Programmes (in Chinese. 中国电视娱乐节目报告 or Zhongguo Dianshi Yule Jiemu Baogao)*. www.cddc.net. Visited in August 2005.

2.4. The Rule of the Market Economy (1992-2000)

revenue.[131] In this explicit and practical definition, broadcasting with one of the two elements or both will be categorised as commercial. (See Figure 2.5) Broadcasters can be further differentiated from others, given which element(s) it possesses.

Figure 2.5 Sepstrup's definition of "commercial" broadcasting

	Advertising income	**No advertising income**
Profit goal	Private commercial broadcasters	Private commercial pay-TV broadcasters
No profit goal	Commercial public service broadcasters	Non-commercial public service broadcasters

Source: Sepstrup, p. 32.

Accordingly, Chinese television not only heavily depended on advertising revenue as financial source by the end of the 1990s, but also turned profit-oriented in practice. Therefore, it is fair to conclude that Chinese television has been commercialised during the 1990s; moreover, the process of commercialisation was occurring in a bottom-up, built-in way, which means that it was the Chinese television institutions themselves who led the process of commercialisation, instead of a top-down, administrative intervention by government or a direct involvement by market force. In addition, Chinese television institutions went far beyond generating advertising revenue, but expanded their practices in an enterprise-like way in terms of the management and operation of television institutions and the production of contents and formats. The reality of Chinese television in the late 1990s was de facto a commercialised state-owned television by nature.

Corresponding to this commercial reality, the quasi-public remit of Chinese television was by and large declining and marginalised: the cultural and the educational functions of television were shrinking when the entertaining role of television kept expanding. At the same time, television also lost its interest in "speaking for the people" as it did in the 1980s[132] and turned to pander to the advertising-relevant, lucrative upper middle class, which only accounted for a small minority (less than 20%[133]) of the whole population.

---

131 Preben Sepstrup. Implications of Current Developments in West European Broadcasting. *Media, Culture & Society*, 1989 Vol. 11: 29-54.
132 Yuezhi ZHAO. Media and Elusive Democracy in China. *Javnost*, 2001 Vol. 2: 21-44.
133 Ibid. According to HE Qinglian's research on contemporary Chinese social structure. p. 34.

2.4.3. The triumph of the market logic on the eve of China's accession to the WTO

Behind the television reform with market mechanism and its later reality of being commercial, there are some deeper, external determinants that precipitate the transformation of Chinese television. In 1992, Deng's talk on furthering the reform and constructing a socialist market economy endorsed the legitimacy of market reform agenda. At the same time the state kept suppressing liberal and democratic forces in public debates throughout the 1990s since the consideration of maintaining political and social stability has been the prime task of the Chinese society and regime. The ensuing booming economy during the 1990s and the tub-thumping official campaign for China's entry into the WTO in the late 1990s glorified the gloss of global capitalism. It is no surprise that there emerged a market myth – a blind faith in market economy – among governmental officials, media academia and television practitioners in the late 1990s as a result of the one-sided stress on market reform agenda and political repression. In fact, these three groups all "benefit" from and collude in the commercialisation of Chinese television.

There was once an attempt inside the Party to restore ideological campaigns against the Western "peaceful transformation" after the crackdown of Tian'anmen movement, even at the cost of ceasing economic reforms. The former Party leader DENG Xiaoping, who was then already in his retirement, elaborated the importance of furthering economic reform in a series of talks during his private visit to several Southern Chinese cities in 1992. His salient prestige inside the Party marked his talks as a turning point of the path-choosing for Chinese society. The ensuing Fourteenth National Party Congress in October 1992 formally declared that the target of Chinese economic reform was to "construct a socialist market economy with Chinese characteristics". Market mechanism was soon accepted as a general means of reform not only in economic sphere but also in many social spheres, including public institutions like educational institutions, cultural institutions and other public services like libraries and museums.

Television, which was categorized into the tertiary industry by the central government in 1992 yet still kept its *shiye* property, was no exception. Not only must television institutions earn their own livings from the market instead of expecting state funds, they must hand over a certain proportion of profits to their governmental administrators – SARFT at the central level and the broadcasting bureaus at all levels. A model of "social market"[134] of Chinese television, never-

---

134 Some scholar described it as "entrepreneurial State". See Duckett, cited by Chien-San FENG. "Is it Legitimate to Imagine China's Media as Socialist? The state, the media and 'market socialism' in China". In *Javnost* (2003), Vol X (4), pp. 37-52. p. 40.

2.4. The Rule of the Market Economy (1992-2000)

theless in the form of "rent-seeking", emerged. In this "social market" model, television institutions with strength to generate advertising revenue would have to give a (quite large) proportion of their revenues to the respective broadcasting bureau. The broadcasting bureau would then use this money to subsidise money loosing television institutions in poorer area, to invest in cost-intensive infrastructure, or to invest in minority interest but "politically correct" projects and programmes. At the same time, a chunk of the money secretly and illegally went to some officials' pockets (corruption), or was used to improve welfare of employees in the broadcasting bureau (semi-overt rent-seeking). What television institutions could get was autonomy and favourable policies for their economic expansion. Various scholars have observed this "social market" model in China. For example, Lynch observed that in economically backward Yunnan province, Yunnan Provincial Television handed over most of its profits to the provincial broadcasting bureau between 1993 and 1999, and then this money was used to construct cable infrastructure in rural areas which benefited over two million households. Feng also observed the operation of the "social market" model in CCTV. As the most lucrative television institution in China, CCTV, whose advertising avenue totals more than 1/3 of all China television advertising revenue, handed over 12.6 percent till nearly 30% of its income to the SARFT between 1994 and 1997. Although further data from 1998 onwards was no longer publicised, it was certain that over one billion RMB was spent in 1998 and 1999 in constructing TV infrastructure in 100,000 remote villages. This investment was largely generated from the contributions from television institutions all around the country, including CCTV. At the same time, the channels of CCTV increased to 12 channels, among which some were non-profit and served for political ends. For example, the West Channel was launched to propagate the central government's policy of "developing the West".[135] Heavy investment in equipment and new technologies, which facilitated the fast development of Chinese television throughout the 1990s, largely depended on broadcasting revenues, foremost advertising revenues. Therefore, through adopting favourable policies to encourage television institutions to be engaged in market- and profit-oriented activities, broadcasting bureaus employed the market mechanism intensively as a means to enhance their administrative power and to improve governance, while the economic development has become the major index for assessing cadres' performance.

Owing to the monopolistic position of Chinese government organisations in policy making and a lack of effective checking mechanism for the potential mis-

---

135 Ibid, pp. 40-43.

plays[136], the government's (here SARFT and broadcasting bureaus at all levels) standpoint on the role of market mechanism in television reform therefore emerged as an overwhelming guideline in television sector. Media academia and television practitioners, who act as a critical check force of policy initiation and policy implementation in Western democracy, had ultimately played a coadjutant role in Chinese government's one-sided stress on market mechanism for expedient reasons.

Media academia, which was once very active in enlightening public involvement in the pro-democratic movements as well as in the attempt to erect press legislation in the 1980s, was ruthlessly suppressed in discussing media reform publicly after the Tian'anmen crackdown in 1989. After a stifling interval, however, some media scholars tuned to be engaged in a burgeoning branch of media studies – media economics, which incorporates the modish Western theories on market mechanism into media studies. These scholars[137] gradually gained currency from the government soon after the government envisaged its need for academic aid in policy initiation and policy formulation.[138] The motives for the unduly zeal[139] of media academia in media economics probably remains various. Some scholars[140], who were pro-democratic reformists during the 1980s and now moved closer to the liberal position, once presumed that the development of economy would help China to be a more open and justice society, whereby some forms of evolving public spheres would empower the media to play a watch-dog function.[141] This optimistic presumption was later proved largely in vain as the party-stated still kept good control over Chinese society. Some other media economists, criticised by GUO as the school of administrative research[142], applied themselves to pragmatic and business-oriented researches by serving the establishment – foremost government and media enterprises – as their consultants. Despite their various starting points, both groups of media economists found their common interest in American-style commercial television system,

---

136 PENG Bo. The Policy Process in Contemporary China: mechanism of politics and government. In: Catherine Jones Finer (ed.) *Social Policy Reform in China*. England: Ashgate, 2003. pp. 37-50.
137 They are comprised of a group of the most active media scholars in media studies in China. Among others, the representatives in television studies are HUANG Shengmin, DING Junjie, YU Guoming, etc.
138 See GUO (2004).
139 Feng ironically refers to one communications scholar's protest that media studies was becoming synonymous with the studies of media economics in late 1990s. See Feng (2003), p. 43.
140 For example, SUN Xupei and YU Guoming.
141 Feng (2003), p. 46.
142 GUO Zhenzhi. *"My View on Political Economics of Communications"* (in Chinese, "传播政治经济学之我见" or *"Chuanbo Zhengzhi Jingjixue zhi Wojian"*). http://academic.mediachina.net/article.php?id=2963. Last visited in February 2012.

2.4. The Rule of the Market Economy (1992-2000)

which symbolises the highest level of commercialisation of television. This USA-mania in turn became trendy among governmental officials and television practitioners.[143]

Television practitioners have always been the most active initiators for reform schemes with market mechanism at the grassroots micro-level. However, their bold attempts like "producer mechanism" at CCTV or "programme groups" at Beijing TV were conducted under the tolerance or even with encouragement of the respective broadcasting bureaucracy to "reform". This means, so long they did not challenge the political ideology and governance of the CCP, any attempt or innovation within the economic domain would be tolerated. After sensibly grasping the hint of the Party line as the bottom line[144], television institutions expediently left the news sector a demesne of the Party while promptly starting to extend their economic expansion in other genres of television programmes. The broadcasting bureaucracy's heavy reliance on television institutions as dairy cows for the rush of investment in the construction of politically relevant infrastructure enlarged the elbow room for television institutions to expand throughout the 1990s.

Nevertheless, the economic expansion of television institutions, starting with advertising revenue generation, reached a new stage by the end of the 1990s. Owing to the market logic, the self-commercialised Chinese television institutions now expected the benefit of scale economy and an abolition of the existing administrative boundaries in pursuit of a larger market.[145] Western media conglomerates, which were widely admired by many Chinese television practitioners as the most advanced models of commercial media, opened another dimension of economic expansion – cross-media ownership – with a wave of megafusions and acquisitions (such Time-Warner AOL fusion) on the eve of the new millennium. It seemed imperative for Chinese media to get "bigger and stronger" by any means, since China was awaiting its entry into the WTO and Chinese media were compelled to face the potential challenge of the multinational media conglomerates. Moreover, after years of practices with market mechanism, television practitioners now were skilled businesspeople. They began to set foot in more complex economic activities such as capital performance, building a closer cooperative relationship with foreign media conglomerates. It seemed that television practitioners are shaping up nicely with the help of market mechanism.

---

143 There were numerous articles illustrating the American television system in governmental official's reports, essays from media academics and television practitioners.
144 ZHAO Yuezhi (1998).
145 Joseph Man Chan. Administrative Boundaries and Media Administration: a comparative analysis of the newspaper, TV and Internet markets in China. In Chin-Chuan Lee (ed.) *Chinese Media, Global Contexts*. London and New York: RoutledgeCurzon, 2003. pp. 159-76.

2.4.4. A state-led "supervision by public opinion" and the absent public in television reform

In the post-1989 China, the democratic reform was stagnated at least in official agenda; nevertheless, as Frolic observed, a kind of state-led civil society kept developing drastically and predominated the emerging Chinese civil society, while the conventional civil society of the West also developed parallel in China but only at a very incipient stage.[146]

A state-led civil society refers to the organisations and groups established, organised and directed by the state and serve the state where it is confronted with difficulties in managing a complex and rapidly expanding economy and changing society. Frolic comments the state-led civil society in China as a unification of two strands of authoritarian politics: those of the socialist authoritarian state in transition, and those of the ascendant East Asian communitarian state whose examples include other East Asian states like Japan, Korea and Taiwan. The organisations and groups in a state-led civil society, although with limited autonomy, still serve as training grounds for the development of civic consciousness and function as intermediaries between the state and society, which may lead to a social transformation to form a (democratic) civil society in the long term.[147]

This form of state-led civil society also found its examples in Chinese television sector. Despite creating social organisations or groups, a state-led civil society in television sector[148] was strengthened first and foremost through a series of "news reform" since 1993. Taking CCTV as an example, it first increased the daily frequencies of broadcasting news programmes. Based on the existing four main news programmes of Morning News (8:00-8:30), Noontime News (12:00-12:30), Newscast (19:00-19:30), and Evening News (22:00-22:30) on CCTV1, daily news programmes were extended to 13 with extra brief news every hour on the hour to update the latest news and therefore enhanced the immediacy of television news reporting. The way of broadcasting news programmes also changed into live broadcasting from pre-recorded broadcasting. With the extension of news hour and the improvement in a more attractive layout of news programming, the content of news was diversified from boring "conference news" and "cadre's talks" into more facts-based, informative and also human interest news. Secondly, besides conventional news, CCTV opened more programmes in forms of news magazine, news talk, news commentary, and live coverage of significant events and breaking news. Many of these newly founded

---

146 B. Michael Frolic. State-Led Civil Society. In Timothy Brook and B. Michael Frolic (eds.) *Civil Society in China*. New York and London: M. E. Sharpe, 1997. pp. 46-67.
147 Ibid.
148 See also FENG's (2003) analysis on a party-state led public sphere, pp. 46-48.

2.4. The Rule of the Market Economy (1992-2000)

programmes like *Oriental Horizon (1993), Focus (1994), Tell It Like It Is (《实话实说》 or Shihua Shishuo, 1996), News Probe (《新闻调查》 or Xinwen Diaocha, 1996)* became immensely popular among audience. Thirdly and most importantly, the function of television news as a way of "supervision by public opinion" (舆论监督 or yulun jiandu) has been reinforced during the "news reform" in television news sector. Programmes like *Focus and News Investigation* were featured with their critical perspective of news commentary and excellent professionalism of television journalism. Soon after its birth, *Focus* began to position its peculiarity as a programme of "supervision by public opinion" by setting 1/3 of its programmes as criticism on social problems, 1/3 as objective reporting, and 1/3 other type of reporting (for example, international news reporting with depth of background knowledge). *News Probe*, a programme combining investigative journalism and news commentary, sought to explore news events in depth and at length. It focused on social problems which bore universal significance in an era of social transition. Two other programmes, *Oriental Horizon* (news magazine) and *Tell It Like It is* (news talk), on the other hand, were known for the human angle of ordinary people in content and format. One section in *Oriental Horizon*, "Living Space" ("生活空间" or "shenghuo kongjian") was well-known for the reportage on ordinary people and daily life in a form of short documentary, while *Tell It Like It is* invited ordinary people as studio audience to take part in discussing and commenting on social problems.[149] In official rhetoric, these news programmes provided an ideological function of "correct guidance to public opinion" and "maintaining political stability".[150]

However, the critical function of these news programmes remains largely circumscribed. For example, these programmes criticised a wide variety of social problems ranging from fake products and products in inferior quality, ecological crises, economic and social policy, to the inefficiency of bureaucracy, corruption of officials, and cases of unjust judicature etc., but they would not criticise corruption of high rank officials and further explore the root of the institutionalised corruption in Chinese society – which is profoundly embedded in the lack of transparent supervision by elected representatives, a free press, and an independent judicial system. Besides, the topics of the programmes like *Focus* would be pre-selected by programme team leaders in the weekly editorial meeting to filter out some most sensitive ones; then the finished programmes would be previewed at the station president level with some 10 per cent being rejected before broadcast[151]; after broadcast, the programmes would be double-checked by the officials from the Department of Propaganda if the "bottom line" of the Party was

---

149   XU, pp. 380-406.
150   ZHAO (1998), p. 117.
151   Ibid. p. 121.

touched. When some significant or sudden event happened, the journalists would follow the uniformed official announcement of the governmental news agency – Xinhua News Agency. This means, there existed a cautious self-censorship from the journalists themselves and an unaccountable (sometimes loose sometimes tight) censorship from the top. The journalists were by no means independent and their critical function worked in an associated way in areas where the state tolerated certain "supervision by public opinion".

Furthermore, it should not be overlooked that to some extent it was the lucrative advertising revenue that motivated CCTV to open more news programmes besides the circumscribed state-led "supervision by public opinion" and a sense of social responsibility among journalists. Among others, news programmes are always one of the most popular genres of television programmes among Chinese audience. *Newscast* still owned a regular viewship of 400 million audience nationwide in 1999 and also the highest national audience rating (about 30 per cent) of all CCTV programmes despite the fierce competition from other news programmes and other types of popular programmes; *Focus*, the programme right after *Newscast* and national weather forecast on CCTV1, had a second highest national audience rating of 25 per cent;[152] 62% of the audience of morning programmes during 7:20-8:00 were watching *Tell It Like It is*; *News Probe* also had a relatively high share of audience. Therefore, it is no surprise that these news programmes became the most lucrative programmes of CCTV. As discussed previously, the advertising-spots time after Newscaster even "enlightened" the Advertising Department of CCTV to initiate a bidding system because of the excessive demands from the advertisers. The advertising revenue from news programmes accounted for a tremendous part of the total advertising revenue of CCTV. This fact also suggests that the "supervision by public opinion" might be affected by market forces once the public interest conflicts with market interests, although direct pressure from advertisers was not yet a problem owing to the monopolistic status of CCTV and the popularity of the programmes, according to ZHAO[153].

Nevertheless, the success of these news programmes first initiated by CCTV soon led to a wave of imitation by numerous local television stations. News programmes of various types flourished throughout the country and were widely welcomed by the audience. Senior officials of the party-state like Premier ZHU Rongji, Chairman of the National People's Congress LI Peng, and Vice President HU Jingtao also conveyed their encouragement to news journalists on the issue

---

152 ZHANG Ning.
153 ZHAO (1998), p. 122.

2.4. The Rule of the Market Economy (1992-2000)

of "supervision by public opinion" on several occasions.[154] This verifies that this circumscribed independent critical television journalism was endorsed by the party-state to encourage certain "supervision by the public opinion" in media sector that functioned to a certain extent as monitor on social problems. If we understand the emergence of a democratic civil society as a process of long-term development and transition, and leave it open to different interpretations on civil society aside from the conventional democratic ones[155], this type of state-led "supervision by public opinion" could be seen as a further development in the public sphere of Chinese society. This means, although the spontaneous development of democratic civil society during the 1980s was constantly repressed in the 1990s, Chinese civil society in general still kept growing, only under more cautious controls from the party-state and in a more or less fluctuant way.

Another fact has to be pointed out that the audience as the public or civil citizens were almost absent during the development of the state-led civil society in television sector. Besides being treated as public who needed "correct guidance" from the Party, the audience would at best be paid ample attention when they were seen as consumers of advertisement most of the time, which were represented by figures of ratings or market share of a programme. Therefore, the flourish of news programmes was also a reflection of the "advertising value" of these programmes. The public logic function of television kept weakening during the self-commercialisation of television. One evident example is that the majority of Chinese population, namely peasants who constitute 70 to 80 per cent of the whole population in China, were categorised as "minority" in programming.[156] Most television programmes targeted on the well-off, better-educated young urban "consumers" because this small group was attractive for advertisers. Educational and cultural programmes also plunged into difficult situations under the consistent pressure of ratings war whereby entertainment programmes were almost always at evident advantage. The government still retained some public functions with political significance, such as financing politically significant projects like "television access in every village" ("村村通" or "cun cun tong") or "Project of (full television coverage in) Tibet and Xinjiang" (西新工程 or xi xin

---

154 XU, p. 396-401. See also LI Xiaoping, "Focus" (Jiaodian Fangtan) and the Changes in the Chinese Television Industry. In *Journal of Contemporary China* (2002) Vol. 11, No. 30, pp. 17-34.
155 Joseph Camilleri. State, Markets and Civil Society. *Asia Pacific: the political economy of the Asia-Pacific region*, Volume I. USA: Edward Elgar, 2000. pp. 357-60.
156 In CCTV, programmes for peasants were queerly packaged on the channel of CCTV7 with other "minority programmes" of military programmes and children programmes.

gongcheng)[157]. Many newly emerging opportunities in television sector like developing new technologies and services of digital television or IPTV were by large left to market forces, which possessed abundant financial resources. The state and the market pushed the fast development of Chinese television, with little direct participation from the public.

2.5. At the Crossroads (since 2001)

In November 2002, the CCP completed a peaceful power shift for the first time after 1949. The so-called fourth generation of Chinese leadership, the HU-WEN[158] regime presented a new style of governance compared with their predecessor JIANG. Different from JIANG's tendency of elitism and focusing on the success of economic development, HU-WEN regime paid more attention to the problems remaining while keeping "perfecting the socialist market economy". A series of policies addressing the benefits and needs of ordinary people helped the new regime to win a public image of "close to the people" (亲民 or qinmin) and "pragmatic work style" (务实 or wushi) and to further consolidate its power[159]. The impact of the new regime on media sector was, nevertheless, rather suppressing. By emphasising the "Party's firm initiative", the Party-state tightened the control over media. While the new regime kept following the existing policy of the industrialisation of television, it also reappraised the reform schemes, especially those regarding ideological work. As Chinese television kept developing under the new political, economic (post-WTO) and social conditions, uncertainties were manifested not only in a zigzag in television (and media in general) policies, but also in the further development of Chinese television market for

---

157 To improve the coverage rate of television and radio throughout the country has been always a core task of the broadcasting bureaucrats, for broadcasting is deemed efficient in conveying policies and ideological propaganda of the Party and the state. This is of special importance for rural areas and border regions of ethnic minorities because these places are the weakest link of the Party control and "the frontline against the penetration of foreign hostile powers". Therefore, the project of "cun cun tong" which aimed to further improve the coverage rate of television in rural areas, and the "Project of Tibet and Xinjiang" in remote border areas like Tibet and Xinjiang, were listed as top task of broadcasting administration in the 1990s and heavily subsidised with governmental funds from all levels under the fiat of central government. XU, p. 486-512. Here these projects are counted as signs of governmental public function for they do facilitate the development of technical infrastructure in the poorer hinterland, which would be otherwise an enormous difficulty without governmental support.
158 President HU Jintao and Premier WEN Jiabao.
159 See Joseph Fewsmith, China's New Leadership: a one-year assessment. *Orbis: a Journal of World Affairs*, 2004, 48, 2, Spring, 205-15; Young Nam Cho, Political Reform without Substantial Change. *Asian Perspective,* Vol. 28, No. 3, 2004, pp. 61-86.

2.5. At the Crossroads (since 2001)

both domestic and international players, and in a dividing yet ambiguous understanding of audience as consumers and the public.

2.5.1. The restoration of "public service": television institutions redefined as shiye unit?

As some scholars observed, the policies of the new HU-WEN regime did not merely inherit those from its predecessors. On the contrary, it tried to "hollow-out" the old policies by revising the ideas and adding new interpretations as part of the project of consolidating its powers.[160]

In television sector, reform schemes were also revised since the new regime came into power. In 2001, a "No. 17 Document" on "deepening the reform in press, publishing, radio, film, and television industries", which was co-promulgated by the Office of the Central Committee of CCP and the Office of State Council, marked a watershed in Chinese television policy making. On the one hand, it still reiterated the policies on conglomeration of television and radio institutions by clarifying the property of television and radio institutions as "public servie yet being operated enterprise-like" (事业单位企业化经营 or shiye danwei qiyehua jingying). On the other hand, the No. 17 Document proposed the establishment of "public" channels at provincial and/or municipal levels. Though the actual aim of establishing these provincial and municipal "public" channels was to compensate the municipal and county governments for the abolition of the television stations at these two levels by offering a sharing mouthpiece for them, it stimulated discussions among academia on public broadcasting which have been ignored over a long period of time in China. Since then, the decision makers of Chinese broadcasting policy have been always wavering between conglomeration of television institutions or firmly persisting in the ideological function of television throughout the following years.

One governmental document on the industrialisation of cultural industry, the No. 105 Document of the Office of State Council in 2003 which focused on "the development of cultural industry and the switch of the property of cultural institutions from shiye (public service) to qiye (business enterprise) in the pilot projects of cultural institution reform", also followed the existing guiding princi-

---

160 Cho, p. 72-74.

Chapter 2 A Historical Review of the Transition of Chinese Television

ple of industrialisation, indicating to "retain a shiye segment and leave the rest to market".[161]

However, at the end of 2004 the vice head of the SARFT declared that no more requisition of establishing radio and television groups with shiye property would be ratified. The further development of television policy indicated that there was a revision on the idea of industrialisation of television institutions. On the one hand, television as an industry kept the process of industrialisation, however, it was confined in programme production – and in fact in producing programmes excluding the genre of news. The existing "radio and television communication" groups switched their property to business enterprise to replace the ambiguous old principle of "shiye unit, opereated enterprise-like". Television and radio institutions, on the other hand, were extracted from the existing groups, retaining their property as shiye unit (public service institution) whose functions remained as "serving as the mouthpiece of the Party-state and the people under the leadership of the Party".[162] A clearer separation of shiye (public service) and qiye (business enterprise) in television sector was the tendency for the further development of Chinese television system.

These changes in television policy might be understood as a reflection on the precipitate policy-making of conglomeration as immature and unreasonable for Chinese television[163], which is true at this point. However, the revision of the conglomeration of television institutions was also one of the many steps whereby the new regime started to tighten its control over media. In fact, HU-WEN adopted a series of measures to overall restore the Party's control over mass media which seemed to have gained "too much" autonomy from their market practices.

The HU-WEN regime first started with a conventional "thought work" campaign. The new regime advocated the "three closes" (三贴近 or san tiejin) for the media soon after it rose to power in March 2003, whereby the media should be "close to reality, close to the masses, and close to life" instead of providing extensive coverage of leasers and conferences.[164] The rhetoric was nothing new as these principles are always regarded as part of good traditions and fundamental dogmas of the Party, while it seemed also to be in harmony with the new regime's "close to the people" policy and "pragmatic work style" at the same time. However, the "three closes" were reiterated by the new regime at a time

---

161 CUI Baoguo (ed.). *A Report on the Development of Chinese Media Industry (2004-2005) (in Chinese,《中国传媒产业发展报告（2004-2005）》 or Zhongguo Chuanmei Chanye Fazhan Baogao (2004-2005))*. 2005. http://www.china.com.cn/chinese/zhuanti/chuanmei/903305.htm. Last visited in February 2012.
162 CUI.
163 LU Di. "2004 Report on Chinese Television Industry" ("2004 年中国电视产业报告" or "2004nian zhongguo dianshi chanye baogao"). In Cui (ed.)
164 Cho, p. 16.

2.5. At the Crossroads (since 2001)

when the media sector and the majority of people in Chinese society were still indulged in the "market myth" of the JIANG's era. Later it was proved that this was only the prelude to the tightening of control on media sector.

The next major step was rather a measure aimed at press market. Again, being in harmony with the idea of "close to the people" and "pragmatic work style", the majority of newspapers and magazines published by state agencies and Party organisations at various administrative levels were cancelled since July 2003 in order to lessen economic burden on the people caused by administrative forced-subscription[165]. It required that only one newspaper and one magazine published by Party organ would be allowed to retain at the central and provincial level, only one Party organ newspaper at municipal level, while one governmental gazette would be gratis distributed. Other newspapers and magazines published by state agencies and Party organisations would have to cease publishing, fuse with other newspapers or magazines, or to be separated from the Party-state system and exclusively depend on the press market.[166] This measure helped to clarify the fact that the press was now an industry rather than shiye, and its further development would be guided by market mechanism. Despite a clear market-oriented press policy, the new regime also strongly advocated that the mass media, as mouthpiece of the Party and state, should contribute to the realisation of Party policies. Not only should mass media make more efforts to report the success and achievements of the Party, newspaper and magazines editors were asked to send reports for a preview by the Party in case of significant or sensitive issues.[167]

Moreover, the new regime kept tightening control on "muckraking" media and outspoken journalists. Since 2003, some senior journalists, editors-in-chief and managers with critical views on social problems and Party policies have been either forced to leave their positions, or heavily punished on irrelevant

---

165 See the No. 19 Document co-promulgated by the Office of the Central Committee of CCP and the Office of State Council on 15th July, 2003, "The circular on further straightening out newspapers and magazines published by state agencies and Party organisations and the misuse of authority in subscription, and to lessen the burden on primary levels and peasants" (in Chinese,《关于进一步治理党政报刊散滥和利用职权发行，减轻基层和农民负担的通知》or guanyu jinyibu zhili dangzheng baokan sanlan he liyong zhiquan faxing, jianqing jiceng he nongmin fudan de tongzhi). http://testcnci.cnci.gov.cn/2008/12/7/law-0102160000-3125.shtml. Last visited in February 2012. Up to January 2004, there were altogether 1452 titles of newspapers and magazines being included into the action of "straightening out"; the ceasing publishing resulted a decrease of 1,2 billion copies of newspapers and 340 copies of magazines. See CUI.
166 www.xinhuanet.com/newmedia, accessed on October 2005.
167 Cho, pp. 77-78.

criminal charges.[168] Press criticism on social problems and political reforms was overtly suppressed at an unprecedented degree since 1992.

All these indicate that Chinese media, including television sector, was experiencing a period of zigzag in policy, whereby the Party attempted to restore its control and influence over the mass media which seemed to go far enough into the market. However, it is also clear that the restoration of the Party power would not risk sacrificing economic development as the cost, for economic growth and the improvement of living standards rather than ideology have been the main source of the Party's political legitimacy in the reform era. However, the attempt of the Party to restore its control over mass media also indicates that the hope of the emergence of liberal, democratic media along with the economic development, as it once happened in some other Asian countries and regions like South Korea and Taiwan during the 1980s, would be even far from realisation in contemporary China.

2.5.2. Fair play or closed market?

The zigzag in television policy inevitably brought uncertainty for the development of television market, but at the same time Chinese television industry itself was also experiencing some acute changes. Among others, that competition was gradually replacing monopoly turned to be a growing tendency in television market, especially the competition between the existing market players of television institutions, and the competition between the existing players and new participants including independent production companies, multinational media conglomerates, and new patterns of television service like Internet Protocol televi-

---

168 For example, the manager YU Huafeng and editor-in-chief CHENG Yizhong of the popular mass newspaper Southern Metropolis Daily (《南方都市报》 or nanfang dushi bao), which first reported the outbreak of the epidemic SARS and the death of SUN Zhiqiang owing to the arbitrary regulation on vagrancy, were arrested and heavily sentenced on charges of bribery and embezzlement. See Cho, p. 78; the chief editor LI Datong of another influential investigative weekly supplement on social problems and intellectual discourses, Freezing Point (《冰点》 or bingdian) of China Youth Daily (《中国青年报》 or zhongguo qingnian bao), was forced to leave his position. Freezing Point was closed for some time for "internal reorganisation". See "Leading Publication Shut Down In China" in Washington Post, http://www.washingtonpost.com (accessed in January 2006) and many other reports.

2.5. At the Crossroads (since 2001)

sion (IPTV), Digital Video Broadcasting – Handheld (DVB-H), mobile television[169], etc.

competition between existing players in television sector

The existing players in television market, namely the state-owned television institutions at all levels[170], intensified their competition first and foremost for the market share of their satellite channels. Originally the satellite channels at provincial level were first launched in 1989 to improve the bad reception of television signals in geographically remote areas and mountain areas like Tibet, Xinjiang, Sichuan, Guizhou and Yunnan provinces. Later other provinces also began to request their own satellite channel from the SARFT, since they found out that this enabled a nationwide reach of their programmes. This became reality with the launch of more communications satellites by Chinese government during the 1990s.[171] By the year of 1999, all 31 provinces had their own satellite channel which could be received nationwide, while CCTV alone had 13 satellite channels up to 2004, China Education Television (CETV) had two satellite channels.

These provincial satellite channels were at first regarded as a window of each province, and were therefore full programme channels with similar schedules but various provincial contents. Since 2002, some provincial satellite channels, especially those in Middle and Western provinces, started to adopt marketing strategies of individual "positioning". For example, Hunan satellite channel became quite successful as an "entertainment channel", Sichuan satellite channel was positioned as a channel of consumer brands, Anhui satellite channel as a channel of TV serials, and so on. These marketing strategies of individualised positioning indicate the efforts of provincial satellite channels to shape a unique image in the convergent domestic satellite programmes market. The impetus behind was the desire to reach more audience nationwide and to increase advertising revenue cross-regionally. These new strategies proved quite effective. According to ratings data on satellite channels in 2004, among the top ten channels nationwide, 6 of them were provincial satellite channels, while the rest 4 channels were

---

169 So far there lacks a widely accepted definition for mobile television since the related technology and market are still taking shape. When discussing mobile television in Europe, it usually refers to DVB-H among researchers and practitioners; nonetheless, in China, mobile television refers to digital video broadcasting with mobile antenna and receivers on bus, ship or train, whilst DVB-H is regarded as a parallel category.
170 Since 1999, the television stations at county level were abolished and became sheer transmission stations instead of programme generating units. Therefore, there are currently three levels of state-owned television institutions, i.e. national, provincial and municipal.
171 For details see LÜ, pp. 55-67.

from CCTV.[172] This has not only challenged the traditional monopoly of CCTV in national satellite programme market[173], but also attempted to change the traditional advantage of affluent Eastern provincial channels over economically backward Western provincial channels, in that 5 of these 6 provincial channels were those of Western provinces[174].

Nevertheless, the monopoly of CCTV and the advantage of Eastern provincial television stations would not change so easily in the short term. CCTV remains as the only national television broadcaster and monopolises various resources both politically and economically. For example, CCTV has the priority in reporting domestic and international significant events, which guarantees a high market share in news sector. Its abundant advertising revenue also enables it to keep its dominant advantages in the programmes of all genres except television serials.[175] The imbalance of economy between Eastern and Western provinces would also affect the development of television industry in the respective regions. As some data indicate, the programmes of local television stations still own evident advantage in local television ratings,[176] and this would in turn be reflected in the local television advertising revenue. Provincial satellite channels might offer those television stations in economically backward provinces a chance to break through the limitation of local economy with national viewship. However, this

---

172 LU (2005).
173 According to a survey of CSM in 2003, CCTV enjoyed an obvious advantage in national television market as its 12 channels had 65.9% of national television market share, while the 31 provincial satellite channels shared the rest 33.7% of the national market. CETV had a tiny 0.5% of national market share. See WU Dong and CAO Heng, *2003: Analysis of the Viewer Behaviour of Chinese Television Audience and the Competition of Viewer Market (in Chinese, 2003 年中国电视观众收视行为与收视市场竞争分析 or 2003nian zhongguo dianshi guanzhong shoushi xingwei yu shoushi shichang jingzheng fenxi)*. http://wenku.baidu.com/view/b81f41b765ce050876321363.html. Last visited in February 2012. The monopoly of CCTV in national television market was also manifested in its advertising revenue which accounted for nearly 1/3 of total television advertising revenue; 31 provincial television stations and hundreds of municipal television stations each received 1/3 of total advertising revenue respectively. See WANG Xuewen, *An Analysis of the Structure and Market Share of Chinese Media (in Chinese, 中国传媒结构与市场份额分析 or zhongguo chuanmei jiegou yu shichang fen'e fenxi)*, 2004. http://www.china.com.cn/chinese/zhuanti/2004whbg/504166.htm. Last visited in February 2012.
174 The total television advertising revenue of 12 western provinces in 2000 only accounted for 8% of the national television advertising revenue, even less than the advertising revenue of one single television station in eastern China like Shanghai TV or Beijing TV. See WU Xinxun, *The Imbalance of Media Economy between eastern and western China and Countermeasures (in Chinese, 中国东西部传媒经济的失衡与对策 or zhongguo dongxibu chuanmei jingji de shiheng yu duice)*, 2005. http://media.people.com.cn/GB/22100/51194/51195/3572501.html. Last visited in February 2012.
175 WU and CAO.
176 *The Rankings of All-China TV Programmes (in Chinese, 全国电视栏目收视率排名 or quanguo dianshi lanmu shoushilü paiming)*, 2004. http://data.icxo.com/htmlnews/2004/11/26/480455.htm. Last visited in February 2012.

2.5. At the Crossroads (since 2001)

would only indicate that the competition between provincial satellite channels would be intensified once the satellite channels in affluent Eastern provinces also timely adjust their marketing strategies. Moreover, as a result of the unregulated "seller's market" of local cable network and the rise of local protectionism, the provincial satellite channels were confronted with a difficult situation in keeping national viewship since 2004. Many local cable network operators, particularly those from the affluent areas, started to raise the price of receiving and transmitting satellite channels of other provinces. The costs have reportedly reached more than 20% of the total advertising revenue of a satellite channel.[177] This has become a heavy financial burden for most provincial satellite channels and seriously limited their further development. So far there still lacked governmental regulations to tackle this problem. The existing administrative and policy obstacles further hindered provincial satellite channels from free capital performance and free cooperation in terms of cross-region and cross-industry.

competition between the existing players and new participants

Parallel to the competition between the existing players of state-owned television institutions, more participants joined the competition along with the further development of Chinese television market, China's integration with global economy after its entry into the WTO, and the latest technological advancements. Among others, three groups of new participants deserve a mention here.

The first group is literally generalised as "civilian-run television" (民营电视 or minying dianshi) by Chinese media sector. Actually this inaccurate parlance refers to all Chinese domestic television institutions excluding state-owned television broadcasters. The majority of them are independent production companies, which are in question here. Although generalised as "civilian-run television", these companies have various properties – state-owned, private, or mixed-ownership – however, they share one common feature: they have no broadcasting channels of their own.[178]

---

177 *The regions "close the door", and the landing of satellite channels confronts a conundrum of "non-market"*(地方"闭门"卫视落地遭遇"非市场"难题 *or difang "bimen" weishi luodi zaoyu "fei shichang" nanti)*. http://news.xinhuanet.com/newmedia/2006-03/29/content_4360287.htm, last visited in February 2012.

178 WANG Jifang and LI Xing. *An Interview to the President of Guangxian Television WANG Changtian: To develop film and television should not merely depend on television stations. (*光线电视总裁王长田：发展影视不能只管电视台 *or guangxian dianshi zongcai wang changtian: fazhan yingshi buneng zhiguan dianshitai)*. http://news.xinhuanet.com/newmedia/2004-10/10/content_2071640.htm, last visited in February 2012.

The so-called "civilian-run television" emerged in the 1990s, at the time when the state-owned televisions stations were the sole television broadcasters and programme producers. The advent of a multi-channel era in the early 1990s led to an enormous hunger for television programmes in large quantities and wide varieties. As the operation system inside television institutions became comparatively flexible with the reform under market mechanism since 1992, some programme teams inside television stations started to outsource (often in a loose way) some of their programme hours for outside institutions like newly established independent production companies. These independent production companies developed under very tough conditions since they were actually not yet authorised to produce programme for television stations – this has been regulated as an exclusive task of state-owned television stations.[179] Therefore, independent production companies had to accept unfair deals from the programme teams of television stations. Nevertheless, the independent production companies first proved their strength with a large number of popular products in TV serial production, and later to many other genres like entertainment, life-style, science and education.

In the late 1990s, there were once discussions on a separation between "broadcasters" and "producers", which purported that the existing television stations would mainly act as broadcasters of programmes, and (a certain part of) the programmes would be commissioned from professional production companies. This idea cheered numerous Chinese independent production companies but hardly became a reality owing to the resistance from television stations and the hesitation of government about opening "ideological sector". It was until 2003 that a first group of 8 independent production companies was licensed by the government for TV serial production. Another 16 independent production companies were licensed in 2004. With the increasing demand for programmes with high quality and loosening restriction on the entry of "civilian" capital into television market, Chinese "civilian-ran television" institutions will hopefully become vigorous competitors against the existing television stations, for these independent production companies are highly market-oriented and audience oriented, and are particularly expert in specific genres, especially in the lucrative TV serials and entertainment programmes. Nevertheless, the state-owned television institutions still remained the main players during the process of separation between "broadcasters" and "producers". CCTV declared its pilot project of "separation between

---

179 It was made clear in 1988 at the All-China Broadcasting Office & Bureau Heads' Conference that television was exclusively run by broadcasting sector. Neither orginisations of other sector, nor private persons and foreign capital were permitted to run television. See XU, p. 330.

2.5. At the Crossroads (since 2001)

broadcasters and producers" in 2003, first with 10 programmes.[180] In 2009, Shanghai Media & Entertainment Group (SMEG) declared its reform of separation between "broadcasters" and "producers" with the establishment of Radio and Television Shanghai as public service (shiye), and Shanghai Media Group as enterprise (qiye), which has been the first successful case of the seperation between "broadcasters" and "producers" among provincial broadcasting groups.

The second group is multinational media conglomerates. This group is small in number but powerful in terms of media economy due to their advantages of resources ranging from contents, capital, personnel, to management and knowhow. As early as in the early 1990s, some of these powerful multinational media conglomerates like AOL Time-Warner, News Corporation, Disney, Viacom, Bertelsmann, attempted to enter the huge but tightly protected Chinese media market, although these efforts were mostly fruitless as Chinese media market was then completely insulated from external investors, no matter if they are domestic or international ones. However, along with the self-commercialisation of Chinese television over the 1990s, particularly when Chinese government's official agenda of entering into the WTO reached a crucial phase in the late 1990s, Chinese television sector gradually altered their attitudes towards multinational media conglomerates. On the one hand, Chinese television still firmly protected themselves from prompt competition with multinational media conglomerates through policy protection; on the other hand, Chinese television started to model itself on multinational media conglomerates, including professional and managerial aspects as well as the ideas of commercial television. Probably the most noticeable impact of multinational media conglomerates on the policy making of Chinese television was the conglomeration of Chinese television institutions under administrative fiat on the eve of China's entry into the WTO. The alleged rationale behind was to improve the competitiveness of Chinese television (and media in general) against the powerful multinational media conglomerates in the post-WTO era.

In fact, the multinational media conglomerates were not welcomed with an open Chinese television market in the post-WTO era owing to the existence of an "audio-video exemption" in the WTO agreements. Chinese television market remained well protected against foreign capital. As discussed in an earlier section, the real intention of the conglomeration lies probably in two aspects: first, the practitioners' ambition of economic expansion; second, the SARFT utilised this opportunity to tighten its control on broadcasting by creating a superintendent in-

---

180 WU Jin. *An analysis of the developing opportunities of civilian-run television (in Chinese.* 解析民营电视的发展机遇 *or jiexi minying dianshi de fazhan jiyu).* http://qnjz.dzww.com/gdst/t20060224_1365785.htm. Last visited in February 2012.

stitution of media conglomerates over economically powerful television institutions.[181]

Nevertheless, multinational media conglomerates still obtained more elbow room in Chinese television market in the processes of the internationalisation of Chinese television and the globalisation of Chinese economy. For instance, the commonest business activities of multinational media conglomerates in China were to establish joint-venture production companies. Star TV, the Hong Kong based subsidiary of News Corporation, has been the most active foreign player in the field of co-production with an annual production of more than 700 hours.[182] Besides, foreign investors were permitted to establish subsidiaries of television advertising agencies since 2004. Star TV has established its own advertising agency in 2004, which is the first advertising agency exclusively invested with foreign capital in China. Multinational media conglomerates can now cooperate more closely with Chinese television institutions in event organising and management. CCTV-MTV Music Awards, an annually held event cooperated by CCTV and MTV, has been a successful case with a history of 7 years. Foreign investors can invest through capital performance such as portfolio investment in Chinese media companies which are quoted on overseas (mostly Hong Kong or US) stock exchanges, or venture capital investment in new markets of digital television, IPTV, mobile television, animated cartoon production etc.[183] Although still in a fairly limited extent, the multinational media conglomerates have shown strong competitiveness compared to their Chinese counterparts.

The third group is composed of hybrid members of television service providers in new patterns, such as IPTV, DVB-H, mobile television, etc. All these new patterns of television service are the outgrowth of the latest technological advancements like digital technology, information technology and telecommunications technology. In addition to the conventional TV set, audience can now view television via personal computer, mobile phone, or while being aboard a bus, train or ship. These new patterns of television service are still at a nascent

---

181 HU Zhengrong. "The Post-WTO Restructuring of the Chinese Media Industries and the Consequences of Capitalisation". *Javnost*, 2003 Vol. X 4: pp. 19-36. pp. 22-24.

182 At the end of 2004, SARFT and the Ministry of Commerce co-promulgated the "Provisional Regulations on the Administration of Joint-venture and Sino-foreign Cooperative Radio and Television Programmes Production Companies", which specifically regulated foreign investment in the field of broadcasting programmes production. This regulation severely lagged behind the reality like many other regulations in China; nevertheless, it officially confirmed that foreign investors were permitted to invest in the field of broadcasting programmes production in China.

183 LI Zhijian. *A Forecast on Foreign Investment in Chinese Television in 2005 (in Chinese. 2005 外商投资中国电视业展望 or 2005 waishang touzi zhongguo dianshiye zhanwang)* http://media.people.com.cn/GB/40724/40727/3121990.html. Last visited in February 2012.

2.5. At the Crossroads (since 2001)

stage and pose no immediate threats to the conventional television in the short term. As the development of these new patterns of television service is not strictly confined to the monopoly of broadcasting sector, their emerging markets are open to external capital (outside television industry) of investors from various industries, which means private capital, foreign capital from many sectors are relatively free to invest in new patterns of television service. Among others, telecommunications are particularly aggressive in the fields of IPTV and DVB-H. In 2004, SARFT has licensed more than 80 companies to provide the service of IPTV, many of which were cooperation between programme production companies and broadband network operators; in the same year, telecommunications companies in provinces of Guangdong, Shanghai, Beijing, Sichuan, Jiangsu, Hebei began to provide DVB-H service to their users.[184] Therefore, these new patterns of television service not only break through the monopoly of television institutions as broadcaster, but also join the fierce competition for television advertising revenue. This would inevitably be a challenge for the existing television institutions.

2.5.3. Television and the "public": an emergence of fan democracy, the reflection on vulgarisation of television, and the establishment of "public" channels

In recent years, there are increasing discussions about the audience as the public in Chinese society, notwithstanding in quite limited scope. On the one hand, the changing role of the audience brought new perspective for the relevant discussions, for example, the audience as fandom of the successful contest show Super Girl, which is a Chinese imitation of American Idol whilst being hailed as a rise of entertainment democracy in China by some thrilled domestic and international observers; on the other hand, some scholars and journalists paid closer attention to the public functions of television as a reflection on the (over-) commercialisation of television in the past decade. Moreover, "public", as an undefined term, was to some extent misused by the government: dozens of "public" channels were established as an expedient compensation for the removal of television stations at county level since 1999. This misleading usage of the word "public" makes it somehow difficult to clarify what "public" television means in China.

As a result of the increasing intensification of the competition between television stations at all levels and a slowdown of the growth of advertising industry since 2000, many television stations, especially the provincial satellite channels

---

184 LU (2005).

under tremendous pressure from the market, fought arduously for a larger audience share. Entertainment programmes have been counted as a favourable genre to enhance ratings and market share by television practitioners.[185] In the latest wave of entertainment on Chinese television screen, Super Girl[186], a Chinese imitation of the contest show American Idol produced by the provincial television broadcaster Hunan Satellite TV, has been a phenomenal success of entertainment programmes in 2005 – both in terms of ratings/market share and economically. Super Girl has attracted about 150,000 contestants in its five regional contest sites, and the TV audience for the finale of its four-month run has reached 400 million. The revenues from sponsorship, advertising, and SMS votings of the Super Girl 2005 have exceeded 100 million yuan.[187]

Besides the enormous success of Super Girl as an entertainment programme, however, what makes Super Girl a focus of numerous media observers, both domestically and internationally[188], came from a popular view that the programme was actually a rehearsal of democratic voting, or participatory democracy in the form of entertainment. It was the mass audience or the fans of contestants, not a handful of jury, who could decide who would be the winners of the contest by means of SMS voting via mobile phone. Hence this is of special significance due to the fact that there lacks an authentic mass participatory democracy in the political life of China.

In the conventional media argument, "entertainment" as a term seems to be contrasted to news on a political judgement, therefore it is news rather than entertainment being regarded as the source of public influence[189]. To this point, van Zoonen argues that the participatory television genres such as Big Brother or Pop Idol share several similarities with political activity and involvement: 1) both entertainment and political activity come into being as a result of performance; 2) both fan communities and political constituencies are concerned with activities like knowledge, discussion, participation, imagination of alternatives, and implementation; 3) both rest on similar emotional investments that are intrinsically

---

185 For the details of the ups and downs of Chinese television entertainment over the past two decades, see XIE and WANG.
186 The official title of Super Girl was 2005 Mengniu Yoghurt Super Voice Girl.
187 ZHANG Ying. *Super Girl: four million audience, over one million revenues from three sources* (in Chinese. 超级女声节目观众四亿 三大项收入数以亿计 or *chaojinüsheng jiemu guanzhong siyi, sandaxiang shouru shuyi yiji*). In *People Net* (on August 19, 2005). http://finance.people.com.cn/GB/42775/3628404.html. Last visited in January 2012.
188 A number of international media reported on the phenomenal success of the Super girl. Many of these media paid special attention to the SMS voting by fans throughout the whole process of the show. See reportages on USA Today, AP, BBC, ZDF, etc.
189 Simon Frith. Entertainment. In James Curran and Michael Gurevitch (eds.): *Mass Media and Society (2nd edition)*. London (a. o.): Arnold, 1996. pp. 160-78. p. 160.

linked to rationality[190]. Therefore, "the relevance of the main entertainment medium, television, should not be sought in its informative qualities, its appeal to cognitive capacities or its encouragement of rational deliberation", rather in fandom, which bears crucial similarity with political activity and involvement, namely, "in the emotional constitution of electorates which involves the development and maintenance of affective bonds between voters, candidates and parties".[191] It might be too early to conclude what kind of implications the participatory programmes like Super Girl would be brought to the democratisation process in China, nevertheless, the rise of fandom, the popularity of participatory programmes and the related discussions have brought a new perspective in understanding the role of audience in public sphere.

In contrast to the cheerful welcome to the emergence of entertainment democracy as a by-product of the successful participatory entertainment programmes, some scholars and journalists turned to criticise the vulgar aspects of entertainment programmes and their erosion of the public function of television. Under the provocative claim that "ratings are the fountainhead of all evils", a group of scholars and journalists sharply criticised the vulgarisation of television programmes, especially the entertainment programmes. They pointed out that many programmes were just inferior copies of successful formats and lacked of originality; the reliability of programmes and the needs of special interest minorities were sacrificed under market pressure; some programmes even used unfair means to manipulate ratings data; many programmes vigorously advocated sumptuous and lavish life style. Some scholars further argued that some genres of television programmes could not be commercialised, such as public opinion, information, high-brow culture, regional aids, and international communications.[192] These criticisms pointed out the fact that ratings data and advertising revenue have been the decisive indexes for the administrators of television stations to appraise programmes.[193] On the whole, the discussions on the public

---

190 Liesbet van Zoonen. Imagining the Fan Democracy. In *European Journal of Communication*, 2004, Vol 19(1): 39–52.
191 Ibid.
192 ZHANG Liwei. *Five genres of radio and television contents should not be commercialised (广播电视不能商业化的五种内容 or Guangbo Dianshi buneng Shangyehua de wuzhong Neirong)*. In www.academic.mediachina.net. Last visited in October 2005.
193 For example, in a reshuffle of the programmes of CCTV in 2003, many cultural programmes were cleared out from the screen because of their low ratings and low profit output. See XIA. In 2005, CCTV further took a series of measures to take both ratings and revenues of programmes as main indexes of appraisal. See *CCTV conducts a full-scale reform: ratings and revenue become hard indexes (in Chinese. 央视全面改革：收视收益成硬指标 or Yangshi Quanmina Gaige: Shoushi Shouyi cheng Yingzhibiao)*. http://news.xinhuanet.com/ent/2005-10/10/content_3600531.htm, accessed in February 2012.

functions of television were only in the initial stage and lacked systematic, in depth analyses.

While the scholars and journalists were attempting to figure out the connotation of "public television", the government has used the term "public" in the latest invention of provincial governmental channel. In 1999, SARFT started to abolish television stations at county level as programme generating broadcasters. Instead these televisions stations at county level became sheer transmission stations. This measure aimed to improve the efficiency and to enhance the quality of television programmes since many television stations at county level lacked the capability in programme production. However, this measure caused widespread discontent among county governments, because the television stations at county level were invested by county governments in the 1980s under the "four-level policy". The county governments deemed television stations as a governmental property which generated advertising revenue. As an expedient compensation, the State Council promulgated a "No. 82 Document" in 1999 to propose the establishment of "public" channels at provincial and municipal levels. According to the No. 82 Document, all provincial television stations and a few municipal television stations were permitted to establish a "public" channel. The newly established "public" channel is a full-programme channel whose programmes are provided by the provincial television stations, while a certain amount of broadcasting hours should be reserved for television stations at county levels to broadcast their self-generated programmes (mostly news and special reportages) in the respective regions.

The "No. 17 Document" co-promulgated by the Office of the Central Committee of CCP and the Office of State Council in 2001 furthered this "regional window" model of "public" channels throughout the country since 2002. However, under the long-standing confusion of "public" and "state" in Chinese political rhetoric,[194] these "public" channels actually functioned as the mouthpiece of county governments. This misleading usage of "public" makes the understanding of "public television" a more formidable task in China. The removal of television stations at county level was also criticised by overseas observers as a tightening up of media control, for this measure terminated the decentralised structure of Chinese television emerged in the 1980s.[195]

---

194 Cf. discussions in 2.3.3 *"The germination and a prolonged setback of the public logic in television"*, pp. 49 ff.
195 *The CCP further controls television (in Chinese. 中共进一步统管电视 or zhonggong jinyibu tongguan dianshi)*. www.kanzhongguo.com, accessed in October 2005. This web page was found to have been removed by the author's final check in February 2012.

2.5. At the Crossroads (since 2001)

The misleading usage of "public" has been taken further in a highly controversial reform of Chongqing[196] Satellite TV since early 2011. In January 2011, Chongqing Satellite TV started to broadcast "red culture" instead of popular TV series at the prime time, which comprised classic movies on the Chinese Revolution (before 1949) led by the CCP, songs and stories from the Revolution period, and documentaries with "contemporary mainstream values", etc.[197] In March 2011, Chongqing Satellite TV announced that it became an advertisement-free channel with the aim to establish a "mainstream medium and public interest channel" ("主流媒体，公益频道")[198], whilst the deficit (approximately half of the annual budget) was to be subsidised by the government. This reform was conducted under the guide of the Department of Propaganda of Chongqing municipal Party committee. The Party official explained that:

> The fact that television is now dominated by the government other than by the market embodies the character of public interest. In foreign countries, there is also a similar broadcasting system, such as the BBC in Britain, PBS in the USA, and NHK in Japan, where the state forbids these public interest television institutions from broadcasting advertisements... The aim of Chongqing is to remove the infection of commercial culture and to launch attack on vulgar culture.[199]

Critics see the launch of the "red channel" in Chongqing Satellite TV as part of the restoration of the radical left ideas led by BO Xilai, the secretary of Chongqing municipal Party committee, who is believed to achieve his personal political ambitions by provoking the struggle of routes against the dominant right wing. This misinterpretation of "public interest" television as "government controlled" television needs an urgent clarification, otherwise the concept of "public service broadcasting" would be instrumentalised in political struggles and cause misunderstanding among audience.

---

196 Chongqing is one of the four municipalities directly under jurisdiction of the Central Government besides Beijing, Shanghai, and Tianjin in China.
197 Press release of the Chongqing Satellite TV on January 1st, 2011. http://tv.cbg.cn/content/2011-01/01/content_5603367.htm. Last visited in September 2011.
198 Press release of the Chongqing Satellite TV on March 2nd, 2011. http://v.cqnews.net/first/2011-03/02/content_5807633.htm. Last visited in September 2011.
199 An interview with HE Shizhong, the Head of the Department of Propaganda of Chongqing municipal Party committee, on Chongqing Daily on March 3rd, 2011. http://fl.cqnews.net/html/2011-03/03/content_5811831.htm. Last visited in September 2011.

Chapter 3
Assessing the Transition of Chinese Television

Based on the theoretical frameworks illustrated in Chapter 1 and the descriptions of the transition of Chinese television over the past decades issued in Chapter 2, a working model of the transition of Chinese television reveals that Chinese television is undertaking an extrinsic transition over the past two decades, which is associated with the extrinsic transition of Chinese economy from plan to market. In the extrinsic transition of Chinese television, policy-makers remain the dominant player during the early stages of the transition process. However, the impacts of market powers and market mechanism are increasingly salient, especially the impacts from the television-correlative industries of advertising and audience research. This leads to a movement of the transition stages from a policy-maker-oriented stage towards market-mechanism-oriented stage, which means a forced adjustment undertaken by policy-makers. The current revenue structure of Chinese television further reinforces the inevitability of a transition towards market-mechanism-oriented stage, not to mention the subtle influences of commercial patterns of management and operation, which have been integrated into the day-to-day administration of television institutions.

This working model of the transition of Chinese television could be used, to a certain degree, to explain the self-commercialisation of Chinese television, which is manifested in the fact that Chinese television is transforming from non-commercial (state) television into commercial television voluntarily. This process of the self-commercialisation of Chinese television happened without opening Chinese television market to an external market segment, neither to domestic private television institutions nor to foreign media conglomerates. The reasons, which cause the self-commercialisation of Chinese television, are multifaceted – it is one of the ramifications of the ups and downs of the political and economic reforms over the past two decades, at the same time under the collusion of the ruling elites, along with a wide-ranging influence of the USA on Chinese society throughout the 1990s.

The consequences of the self-commercialisation of Chinese television, in the long run, tend to be perturbing. Under the duopoly of the state and the market, the public, which is the fundamental group that television serves, remains absent and underrepresented during the whole process. Neither the failure of the state nor the failure of the market comes under the supervision from the public. Furthermore, Chinese television is also confronted with bottlenecks in its further de-

3.1. A Working Model of the Transition of Chinese Television

velopment under the present reform scheme. For example, how can Chinese state-owned, party-controlled television become commercially competitive in an open television market without sacrificing its public functions? Can the administrative fiats guarantee that in the first place? And so forth.

This chapter ends with a discussion on the search for alternative reform scheme, which is deemed necessary when there exist obvious shortcomings with the present reform scheme.

3.1. A Working Model of the Transition of Chinese Television

3.1.1. Four stages of the extrinsic transition of Chinese television

As elaborated in Chapter 1, a model of extrinsic transition is suitably applicable for describing the transition of Chinese economy from plan to market over the past decades. Similarly, the transition of Chinese television from non-commercial to commercial, which is associated with the transition of Chinese economy as well as with the changes in Chinese society in general, also follows a model of extrinsic transition.

To go deep into this hypothesis, the transition of Chinese television gives sound evidences at least for the early stages of the transition. Following the four stages of the extrinsic transitions illustrated in Figure 1.1., the transition of Chinese television can be examined stage by stage as follows:

start of transition (before 1978)

Originally established as propaganda organs of the CCP, Chinese television was defined as "shiye" units and was exclusively financed by the state funds. This bears some similarities with the state-owned enterprises under a planned economy, which operate under a rigid planned allocation and distribution system.

complementary stage (1979-1991)

In 1983, after the state advocated a faster development of television as a modern means to facilitate the economic and political reform, an economic policy was also adopted to encourage television stations to "enhance economic benefits, to widen financial sources for the sake of supplementing the insufficient part of state funds" in order to supplement the insufficient investment by the state. Be-

Chapter 3 Assessing the Transition of Chinese Television

sides various means of "created income" by the television institutions, advertising revenue has since then become a fundamental financial source of television. The complementary stage of advertising industry evolved in parallel with, or more precisely, facilitated the development stage of both television sector and advertising industry as well. The increasing share of advertising revenue in the revenue structure of television stations is shown in the example of Shanghai TV in Figure 3.1, Figure 3.2, and Figure 3.3.

Figure 3.1 Revenue Structure of Shanghai TV in 1979 (in %)

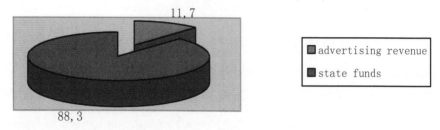

Figure 3.2 Revenue Structure of Shanghai TV in 1983 (in %)

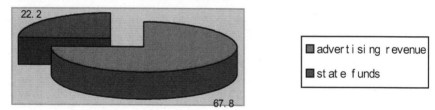

Figure 3.3 Revenue Structure of Shanghai TV in 1995 (in %)

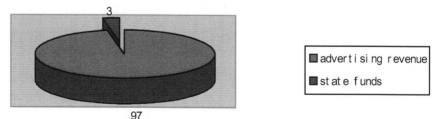

Sources of figure 3.1, 3.2 and 3.3: Lü, p. 204.

3.1. A Working Model of the Transition of Chinese Television

development stage (1983-1991)

With the affluent financial source generated from advertising revenue, Chinese television was able to proliferate throughout the 1980s, manifested with the fast increase of coverage rate on total population from 59.9% in 1983 to 81.3% in 1992. Television has become a highly influential mass medium in China.

voluntary adjustment stage (1992-2000)

In 1992, after the overall introduction of the market mechanism to Chinese reform scheme, television institutions have also taken voluntary adjustments to commercial-like television by reforming with market mechanism in a bottom-up manner. Starting from individual programme teams or programmes (*micro-level*) at the beginning of the 1990s, the voluntary adjustments gradually moved on to a entire television institution (*meso-level*) throughout the 1990s and to the whole television sector (*macro-level*) shortly before China's entry into the WTO in 2001.

a foreseeable forced adjustment stage (since 2001)

In recent years, after China's entry into the WTO and the power shift of the new leadership, the transition of Chinese television seems to present a less strong tendency towards the self-commercialisation in terms of policy-making, particularly with the restoration of television institutions as public service, and the evasive attitude of the SARFT towards the "conglomeration" (集团化 or Jituan Hua) of television institutions, which was eventually proved only a wishful thinking of some government officials who lacked sound understanding of television as an industry[200]. On the other hand, after a decade of voluntary adjustment to commercial-like television, Chinese television unavoidably continues its existing trajectory of development with market mechanism, when taking the present revenue structure into consideration, which is overwhelmingly dependent upon advertising revenue. On the whole, neither the policy-makers nor the market powers are able to play a decisive role in determining the future road of Chinese television. Nevertheless, if Chinese television continues developing with market mechanism as it currently does, at the same time more and more market players like domestic private investors and foreign investors are joining the game, it is foreseeable

---

200 LU (2005).

that the market powers will sooner or later take a more favourable position in the overall orientation of the transition of Chinese television.

This working model of the transition of Chinese television is to some extent an oversimplified version. Moreover, it also does not strictly follow the model of extrinsic transition of Chinese economy from plan to market. Some peculiarities of the transition of Chinese television will be examined more closely in the ensuing section. Nevertheless, this working model offers a concise point of view in understanding the intricate transformations of Chinese television throughout the past decades, especially when the transition seems to be a farrago of innumerable events parallel occurring in political, economic and social domains.

3.1.2. Peculiarities of the transition of Chinese television

In modelling the extrinsic transition of Chinese television with a reference to the model of the extrinsic transition of Chinese economy from plan to market, two peculiarities deserve further consideration.

First, there does not exist a market segment inside the television sector. It is the television-correlative industries like advertising and audience research which function as the motor of the transition. In other words, television as an individual industry was never directly open to external market powers, namely no external players were allowed to become television broadcasters. The television-correlative industries, such as advertising and audience research, facilitated the transition of Chinese television from non-commercial to commercial by creating spillover effects on television sector.

In comparison with television industry, which used to be included in the ideological domain, industries like advertising and audience research were imposed fewer limitations on market players during the economy reform. Take the entry of foreign capital into Chinese advertising market as an example, the first joint venture advertising company Dentsu Young & Rubicam was established in 1986, followed by many other major multinational advertising companies like Ogilvy & Mather (1991), McCann-Erickson (1991), Saatchi & Saatchi (1992). During the 1980s, advertising department within a television institution worked separately from programme production departments, so there still existed an "arm's length" between advertisements and programmes. In 1992, when Chinese television started to adopt a competitive mechanism inside television stations, whereby some individual programme teams were given the autonomy to raise funds through advertising revenue, in personnel recruiting, and foremost in making arrangements on formats and contents, the spillover effects of advertising started to penetrate into the smallest cell units of television institutions, i.e. the programme

3.1. A Working Model of the Transition of Chinese Television

teams. A fast development of advertising industry over the past two decades (1981-2001) with an average growth rate of 40.2% annually, whereby television advertising enjoyed a tremendous average growth rate of 51.7% annually in particular[201], facilitated the fast development in television sector. Besides financing television, the role of advertising incrementally expands into shaping programming and scheduling as it does in other Asian countries, for instance, in India.[202] Advertisers and their advertising agencies sponsor popular programmes, offer handsome prizes in game shows, "brand" programmes like Toshiba Zoo (《东芝动物乐园》 or Dongzhi dongwu leyuan) in Beijing TV, Lycra My Style My Show (《莱卡我型我秀》 or Laika wo xing wo xiu) in Shanghai TV, etc.

The audience research industry created similar spillover effects on television sector. Before the first professional audience research company CVSC was established by CCTV in 1995, audience researches were only occasionally conducted by CCTV in order to improve public service of television. After ratings data were regularly reported by CVSV and other professional audience research companies, advertisers gradually adopted ratings data as essential indicators when purchasing television advertising. This in turn forced television stations to react according to the market demands. In recent years, the impact of ratings data on the operation and administration of television institutions has been increasingly tremendous. They even manipulated the content and format of a programme, because many television institutions made decisions on whether to keep or "foul out" a programme exclusively according to the its ratings performance.

Second, as there lacks a market segment inside the television sector, it is the existed non-commercial (state) television institutions themselves that promote the transition process in a manner of self-commercialisation. Unlike the transition of Chinese economy from plan to market, by which there parallel exist a long established plan segment and a newly emerging market segment, and the plan segment is forced to act market-like under the increasing pressure from the market segment, the state-owned Chinese television voluntarily launched the process of self-commercialisation without any direct competition or pressure from a segment of commercial television.

As discussed in Chapter 2, most Chinese television institutions started to raise funds from advertising revenue since the mid 1980s. However, the commercial impact on television institutions remained insignificant at the beginning. Advertising revenues were principally gained for programme production or programme-related purposes, and the department of advertising worked separately from programme production departments. This means the autonomy of pro-

---

201 YU Guoming.
202 Kumar, Keval J. "Cable and Satellite Television in Asia: The role of advertising". In French and Richards (eds.), 2000. pp. 111-29. pp. 122-23.

Chapter 3 Assessing the Transition of Chinese Television

grammes was still intact from the commercial powers, notwithstanding was under the control of the Party. At the same time, television institutions still applied themselves to perform public functions. In one word, television remained largely not-for-profit in the 1980s. In 1992, after the institutions in the tertiary sector, including media institutions, were pushed by the new governmental policy to "operate independently and be responsible for profits and losses", television institutions moved to a for-profit stage. Through the reforms with market mechanism at the micro-, meso- and macro-levels, Chinese television became a lucrative industry and television institutions were enthusiastic about profit seeking. Besides advertising revenue, television practitioners drastically tried out many other complex economic means for the sake of profit seeking, such as bidding, capital performance, cooperation with foreign commercial media, etc. This crucial shift from not-for-profit to for-profit *(a process of commercialisation)* is, nevertheless, undertaken solely by Chinese television practitioners and within Chinese television institutions *(a process of self-commercialisation)*.

Chinese television practitioners not only voluntarily adopted commercial means in profit generating, but also voluntarily adjusted the patterns of day-to-day management and administration of television institutions to a commercial manner. More and more programme teams acted like a small enterprise: journalists were paid according to their workload and performance instead of a fixed salary; most journalists worked under short or mid term contracts. The same commercial principle was also applicable for the survival of a programme. Once the performance of a programme in the ratings war was not satisfactory, it would disappear from the screen – some of these "fouled out" programmes might have higher appreciation index[203] for their originality and informativeness.[204]

Bearing these two peculiarities of the transition of Chinese television in mind, it is fair to conclude that the extrinsic transition of Chinese television undergoes through a self-commercialisation of Chinese television institutions without the participation of a parallel market segment of commercial television. This is a distinguishing feature of the transition of Chinese television.

---

203 Appreciation Index is a method used by the audience research industry to measure audience satisfaction of a particular programme. See Nicholas Abercrombie. *Television and Society*. UK: Polity Press, 1996. p. 151.
204 According to the reportage on the Southern Weekend (《南方周末》 or nanfang zhoumo), ten programmes were "fouled out" from the full-programme channel CCTV 1 in June 2003 because of their poor performance of ratings. Five were cultural programmes, a famous cultural programme "Reading Time" included. See XIA.

3.2. Reasons, Consequences and Bottlenecks of the Self-commercialisation of Chinese Television

After modelling the four stages of the transition of Chinese television, it comes into question why market mechanism has been so dominant in the past decades, which eventually led to a self-commercialisation of Chinese television. It is also noticeable that during the reform of Chinese television with market mechanism there lacked a closer examination or critical reflection on the consequences of the self-commercialisation of Chinese television. Furthermore, there likewise lacked a cautious appraisal of other alternatives of reform scheme, which is indispensable before any crucial decision is made. If there were some aims of the reform when it was first started, can the present reform scheme with market mechanism achieve these aims? These questions are respectively discussed in the following sections. Some of these questions have been partially answered in historical review of the transition of Chinese television in the early chapter. Here, it attempts to present a compact and comprehensive analysis to the reasons, the consequences of the self-commercialisation of Chinese television, and the bottlenecks of the ongoing reform scheme.

3.2.1. Reasons of the self-commercialisation of Chinese television

When further exploring what brought about the drastic self-commercialisation of Chinese television, three reasons can be given to reveal the intricate context within which the transition of Chinese television over the past decades took place. These three reasons involve the macroscopical circumstances of Chinese society, the role of decision-makers during the transition, and an indirect external impact from the USA.

First, it is one of the ramifications of an uneven course of the economic and political reforms. In 1978, Chinese government started the economic and political reform simultaneously. This brought about both the fast development in economic sector and a relatively liberal political circumstance in the 1980s. In television sector, economic means like the introduction of advertising was adopted in order to generate the funds urgently needed for the fast development of Chinese television, while at the same time the democratic function of media in general was also hotly debated. With the advocacy of the "people principle" prior to the "Party logic", media (including television) actively promoted the emergence of the public sphere in Chinese society through far-ranging reportage on the political reform and other civic-related topics.

However, with the crackdown of the pro-democratic movement in 1989, the political reform was confronted with a severe stagnation. Deng's talk in 1992, which declared that the construction of the market economy was the central task of the country, restarted the once stagnated reform first in the economic sector, but the political reform went into a situation which was little better than a standstill. A very reluctant advance of political reform, if any, was strictly confined to the hold of the core group of the Party, which means any civic participation in political reform, even the elite groups, was absolutely out of the question. The outspoken dissidents would be suppressed with all forms of coercion like imprisonment, exile, purge, and unemployment.[205]

Under such macroscopical circumstances, which were economically relatively liberal but politically coercive, most elite groups chose to make use of their economic freedom: it is not only safer to reform with market mechanism for it fitted well with "political correctness", the authorities were also more tolerant towards the failures caused by bold measures of economic reform. The result was therefore the dominance of market mechanism as a means of reform in all social sectors, while the critical voices were keeping firmly suppressed. The ensuing boom of Chinese economy in the 1990s apparently further verified that market mechanism was highly effective. Market turned into a myth, a prevailing ethos of the time wholeheartedly favoured by political, economic and academic elites. The impact of the market myth in television sector was, then, the self-commercialisation of Chinese television – an outcome of a series of reform with market mechanism at all levels in the television sector, while a small amount of criticism was either too weak (from inside China) or being largely ignored (from outside China) during this process of self-commercialisation.

Second, decision-makers have played a crucial role in setting aims of a transition as well as in choosing the approach to achieve them. In an extrinsic transition, which is the case of Chinese television in question here, the impact of political choices of policy-makers on reform measures is highly active particularly at the early stages of the transition.[206] And again, the decision makers ought not to be confined only to the governing elite who constitute the decision makers in a narrow sense, but to include other elite groups like television practitioners as well as media academia, because the reform and the self-commercialisation of Chinese television is to a great extent a bottom-up process, whereby other elite groups (television practitioners in particular) are also deeply involved in.

---

205 Zhou He. "How do the Chinese media reduce organisational incongruence? Bureaucratic capitalism in the name of Communism". In Chin-Chuan Lee (ed.) *Chinese Media, Global Contexts*. London and New York: RoutledgeCurzon, 2003. pp. 198-214. p. 208.
206 See Section 1.1. pp. 21 ff.

3.2. Reasons, Consequences and Bottlenecks of the Self-commercialisation

As described in Chapter 2, three elite groups played a decisive role for the transition of Chinese television, namely the television practitioners, the governmental officials, and the media academia, while common audience largely conducted no direct participation in the process of transition. The aforementioned three elite groups, however, promoted the self-commercialisation of Chinese television out of different intentions.

Television practitioners, who have played an active role in promoting the self-commercialisation of Chinese television in a bottom-up manner, intended foremost to extend their autonomy both economically and editorially by making full use of their economic freedom. They were fairly successful at this point. They not only pushed Chinese television to become a lucrative industry, but also endeavoured to convert Chinese television from a sheer mouthpiece of the Party into an audience-oriented and market-oriented medium.

The governmental officials, gradually involved in a so-called model of state corporatism, reaped the benefits of the self-commercialisation both economically and politically. Economically, the government not only eased the financial burden of investing in the infrastructure of television industry by supporting the self-commercialisation of television institutions, but also benefited from that[207]. Politically, the government officials also improve their governance with the consequent achievements in television sector, such as a faster development of the industry, wider coverage, more choices of programmes, subsidising the construction of television infrastructure in economically backward areas, etc.

The media academia, which can be divided into the school of administrative research and the former pro-democratic reformists of the pre-1989 era, supported the self-commercialisation of television for respective considerations. The scholars from the school of administrative research applied themselves to pragmatic and business-oriented researches and raised no special concern about the political, social and cultural consequences of the self-commercialisation of television. The former pro-democratic reformists of the pre-1989 era, however, turned to support the market competition in media sector, if not to support the commercialisation of media straightly. These scholars[208], in resonance with some scholars outside China[209], believed that the market competition would provide the public pluralist perspectives beside the mainstream authoritarian voices with alternative viewpoints like environmentalism or consumer rights, which were es-

---

207 Through levy administration fees, broadcasting authorities at all levels also use the money to improve the welfare and working conditions of their staff members. See Lynch. pp. 53 ff.
208 Anonymous scholars.
209 Most of these scholars originate from a Greater China (including Mainland China, Taiwan, Hong Kong) but are trained and currently live in the Western. See Chin-Chuan Lee, Yuezhi Zhao, etc.

sential for the development of freedom of expression under an authoritarian regime and eventually helped the democratisation of some Asian countries and regions like Taiwan, South Korea.[210] At least in the meanwhile, this would help China to be a more open and justice society, whereby some form of evolving public sphere would empower the media to play a watch-dog function.[211] Both the scholars from the school of administrative and the former pro-democratic reformists, to various degrees, helped strengthening the buzz of a market myth, while the critical voices from the academia were repressed as always.

Third, an overwhelming influence from the USA in the 1990s also produced some inflammatory impacts that somehow stimulated the self-commercialisation of Chinese television. Despite the not always problem-free political and economic relations between the two countries as well as the demonisation of capitalism in the pre-reform years, the American model of business has clearly gained wide currency among Chinese economic elites in the 1990s under the impact of globalisation[212]. The diffusion of the American-style market economy was taking place through various channels – the establishment of American subsidies and joint-ventures in China, the frequent contacts across the Pacific Ocean, the wide-ranging reportage on Sino-American trade and business, not to mention an increasingly large number of Chinese students who have been educated in the USA and later returned China to develop their career.

Chinese television sector was also drastically affected by the US model of television in the 1990s. As the most active and most powerful exporter of media products worldwide, the USA has been admired for its success in media economy in Chinese media sector. When market mechanism became the dominant means of reform for Chinese television, no other country than the USA, which has a well-developed television industry, could be the best model to follow. Not only television practitioners, but also governmental officials and media academia, discussed enthusiastically the success of American media market.[213] American media conglomerates like AOL Time-Warner, Disney, News International and their ambitious plans of entering Chinese market were also widely concerned. This has become one of the rationale behind the industrialisation ("产业化" or chanye hua) of Chinese television, in that it was believed that Chinese

---

210 Chin-Chuan Lee. "Chinese Communication: prisms, trajectories, and modes of understanding". In Lee (ed.) *Power, Money and Media*. USA: Northwestern University Press, 2000. pp. 3-44. p. 35.
211 Feng (2003).
212 Barrett L. McCormick and Qing Liu. "Globalisation and the Chinese media". In Chin-Chuan Lee (ed.) *Chinese Media, Global Contexts*. London and New York: RoutledgeCurzon, 2003. pp. 139-58. pp. 150 ff.
213 When the world media economy was in discussion, most literature would "automatically" start to use the USA as a persuasive example. See discussions throughout the 1990s. Zhao(1998), pp. 186-88.

3.2. Reasons, Consequences and Bottlenecks of the Self-commercialisation

media could survive from the competition with foreign media conglomerates only when they could be just as "strong and big" as their foreign counterparts with the advantages of the economy of scale.

All these further affected the way of reforming on Chinese television. As American television is a purely commercial system, it is no surprise that Chinese television followed this model to commercialise itself. Regrettably, the strengths and weaknesses of the American model have never been comprehensively appraised during the self-commercialisation of Chinese television. Moreover, no alternative models have been included into the general discussion in the media sector either. Besides the fact that there lacked genuine critics under the sustaining political repression on freedom of expression, there also lacked sufficient knowledge about other models of television system. For example, there exists a misapprehension that the public service broadcasting system was similar to the state-owned television system under the planned economy.[214] Why did China need to use a "similar" system for reference when "reform" and "change" were being discussed?

3.2.2. Consequences of the self-commercialisation of Chinese television

Through the self-commercialisation over the past decades, Chinese television has transformed from a purely state television into a state-commercial television. The transition has caused profound changes in many aspects. Generally speaking, the consequences of the self-commercialisation of Chinese television are twofold, namely positive as well as negative sides.

In regard to the positive side of the self-commercialisation, the following points deserve a mention:

First, it enabled Chinese television to proliferate over the past decades. With the sufficient funding of commercial revenue (foremost with the funding of advertising revenue) under a state-led model of "social market", Chinese television was able to expand rapidly all over the country, including the economically backward remote and mountain areas, by which otherwise enormous difficulties in getting access to television only with state funds would be encountered. Today Chinese television has a coverage rate of 95%, which means more than 1.2 billion Chinese have access to the modern mass medium of television. This has far-reaching impacts on the diffusion of information, entertainment, knowledge and culture, which have made profound social impacts on Chinese society.

---

[214] Anonymous scholars.

Second, it enabled Chinese television programmes as well as the structure of Chinese television market to be more diverse and plural. The development of cable and satellite television throughout the 1990s made it technically possible by providing ample channels for the flourish of programmes in all genres. The affluent commercial revenue made this possibility in the end a reality. Among others, news programmes and entertainment were flourishing remarkably. News programmes expanded in terms of both broadcasting hours and forms. This helped the emergence of a state-led civil society in television sector, which means news programmes functioned in a way of "supervision by public opinion" under the direction of the Party. Notwithstanding a confined elbow room, the critical journalism played an indispensable role as watch-dog on social problems. The increasing demands for high quality entertainment programmes in a broad sense, including TV serials and various entertainment shows, have created opportunities for participants outside the state-owned television institutions, such as domestic and international investors, to enter the long-time closed Chinese television market. It is envisaged a gradual disintegration of the monopolistic status of the state-owned television stations. Although the conditions of competition were fairly unfavourable for the outside participants, and there still existed very strict controls of licensing, their participation has made the structure of Chinese television market more diverse than before.

Third, it freed (at least partially) Chinese television from a pure mouthpiece of the Party, which was originally regarded as the fundamental role of television. Started with the transfer of financial autonomy from central to local governments in the 1980s, this has changed the structure of Chinese television from a relatively centralised two-level structure into a decentralised four-level one. Local television institutions, which had strong incentives to generate advertising revenue, further strengthened the entertainment function of television other than the propagandist function. After the market mechanism was widely used to reform television in the 1990s, which accelerated the process of self-commercialisation of Chinese television, television practitioners made good use of their economic autonomy to enhance the informative as well as the entertainment functions of television. Today the Party still attempts to firmly hold its control over the "ideologically relevant" core area of news programmes, nevertheless, for many Chinese audience, television is no longer a pure mouthpiece of the Party, rather an informative and entertaining mass medium.

Although the positive consequences brought about during the process of self-commercialisation have facilitated a great proliferation and a wide diversity of Chinese television over the past decades, and this further contributed to the development of Chinese society, it also produced some uneasy consequences, which are largely ignored under the present reform scheme and need a closer ex-

3.2. Reasons, Consequences and Bottlenecks of the Self-commercialisation

amination. Five main negative consequences, namely for the programmes, for the audience, for the television market, for the professional ethic of journalists, and for the development of the public sphere, deserve a mention here without going deep into the details, for they have been painstakingly discussed in Chapter 2.

In regard to the negative consequences of the self-commercialisation of Chinese television for the programmes, it displayed a tendency towards entertainment, vulgarisation, and convergence, at the same time cultural and educational programmes stood in an inferior position. After advertising became the primary financial source of Chinese television, and ratings data became the decisive index of appraising a programme, television programmes turned to be extremely market-oriented and audience-oriented (but only those audience that are relevant for advertising sales). News programmes and entertainment programmes remain the safest genre of generating advertising revenue. For the reason that CCTV has the monopoly for national news programmes, many provincial satellite channels began to utilise entertainment programmes to widen their national market share. This led to a vulgarisation and convergence of programmes since many entertainment programmes were poor at innovation and remained plain clones of a small number of successful formats. Cultural and educational programmes often stood in inferior position because of their less successful performance in the ratings war. In some extreme cases, these programmes would be removed if they were economically unprofitable. In this way, the cultural and educational functions of television were gradually eroded.

Regarding the negative consequences of the self-commercialisation for the audience, the audience's interest received no equal attention any more. Due to their relevance to advertising, a relatively small number of wealthier urban inhabitants, instead of peasants who constitute the majority of Chinese population, became the target group of plenty of programmes. At the same time, audience of special interest and of minority groups were also strongly marginalised since they were also less significant in advertising market. Television audience were sold to advertisers in form of market share and ratings data, and were served discriminatively according to their consuming power. The "mass logic" of Chinese television, with which the state-owned television institutions gained their legitimacy by claiming their task of "serving the people", is therefore highly questionable.

The self-commercialisation of Chinese television has also caused some negative consequences for Chinese television market. On the one hand, the existing state-owned television institutions were confronted with an excessive competition. Owing to their single structure of financial sources, i.e. advertising revenue, the existing 47 satellite channels were in fact 47 commercial channels that competed fiercely with each other for national market share. The competition for advertising revenue was envisaged being intensified with the participation of numerous digital channels. Comparatively, the competition for regional market share was less fierce but faced a huge imbalance between economically advanced areas and economically backward areas, as well as between heartland and peripheral areas. On the other hand, the competition in television market was unfair between the existing state-owned television institutions and outside participants. During the process of the self-commercialisation of Chinese television, Chinese television market remained largely closed to outside participants like domestic and international investors. The state-owned television institutions often utilised their monopoly to oppress the development of the private production companies in television market. In short, although Chinese television has been largely self-commercialised, an open and fair mechanism of market competition has been far from being accomplished.

Concerning the consequences of the self-commercialisation of Chinese television for journalists, some negative ones also deserve a mention. In China, journalists were never endowed with full independence for their professional performance. The Party remained as always the paramount authority in the "ideological domain", which means all journalists were obliged to follow the guidelines and instructions of the Party and its Department of Propaganda. The journalists obtained some economic as well as editorial autonomy during the process of the self-commercialisation of television. However, without a clear separation of management and editorship, many journalists directly participated in economic activities, either forcedly or voluntarily, to "generate income" for their units. In the early stage of the self-commercialisation of Chinese television, many journalists engaged in "paid news" or "soft advertising", which led to an extensive ruin of the journalistic ethic and professionalism. In recent years, the economic activities in television sector were professionalised with the establishment of the market mechanism in television sector. Producers, the professional managers of television programmes, became the most powerful persons in a programme team. The producers were responsible for both the "political correctness" and the profitability of a programme, while the excellence of journalism turned a less primary concern for them. This indicates that Chinese television journalists were currently working under the manipulation of two powers – the Party and the market. While the press freedom has not been essentially improved through the self-commercialisation of television, the journalistic ethic and professionalism were facing erosion from the market.

Last but not least, the negative consequences that the self-commercialisation of Chinese television brought about also affected the development of the public sphere in Chinese society. The reform in television sector was in principle led by

3.2. Reasons, Consequences and Bottlenecks of the Self-commercialisation

a small group of elites, including the governmental officials, television practitioners and media academia, while the mass of audience as the general public remained largely inactive during the whole process of transition. It is true that in many countries the reforms in television sector were also led by a small group of elites, however, the odd thing in China was that so far there lacked an extensive discussion about the public functions of television under the authoritarian state-corporatism. In other words, the public was most of the time either absent or underrepresented during the process of transition. With the proposal of a shift towards a "public service government" put forward by the new HU-WEN regime, some improvements might be made. Nevertheless, it would be over-optimistic to expect a comprehensive discussion about the relationship between television and the public sphere, for the HU-WEN regime revealed no intention to loosen their control over "ideological domain".

3.2.3. Bottlenecks in the ongoing reform process

In 1992, as the architect of Chinese reform DENG advocated to restart the once stagnated economic reform, he said: "No debate is one of my inventions"[215] ("不搞争论是我的一个发明" or "bugao zhenglun shi wode yige faming") so as to avoid the endless conflicts of routes inside the Party over whether the reform was following the route of socialism or capitalism. This has later become a tacit agreement inside the Party when extremely controversial issues came forth during the process of reform. Chinese reform, especially after the crackdown of the Tian'anmen movement, was conducted in such a pragmatic manner of "doing" rather than "discussing" the ends of a policy. The reasons that there lacked sufficient public discussions during the reform process were not only the tacit agreement of "no debate" inside the Party, but also the expedient nature of Chinese policy-making. As HONG pointed out, the Party preferred to "have an implicit policy rather than a clearly defined policy" so as to execute a highly flexible and extensive control over the interpretation and implementation of a certain policy.[216] In other words, the Party could interpret the elusive policies according to the provisional needs, while the bureaucrats at the basic levels could only conjecture about what was the real intention of the Party behind these elusive policies. It is therefore not surprising that many bureaucrats would only discuss about the positive impacts of policies in trade journals in order to be "in unanimity" ("保持

---

215 DENG Xiaoping Quotes. http://zg.people.com.cn/GB/33839/34943/34978/35419/2664977.html.
216 HONG, p. 112-114.

一致" or "baochi yizhi") with the Party, for "political correctness" was always the top criterion in state-led discussions.

Under such circumstances, there lacked necessary examination of the ends of policies. The Party and government would adapt new policies aimed at new problems or new situations whenever necessary instead of conducting a series of consistent policies. Without debate, examination as well as efficient regulations, however, television institutions, especially those at basic levels, often went beyond the limits, which was described as "disorder" ("乱" or "luan") and "overrun" ("滥" or "lan") when a certain policy was "too loose". Then new policies would then be urged to tackle the problematic situations of "luan" and "san", such as "the spiritual pollution of Western bourgeois ideology" in the 1980s, or "an excessive construction of infrastructure" in the 1990s, which often means a tightening of control. In this way, Chinese television developed in company with a fluctuation of loose and tight policies.

However, the inconsistent policies finally led to a disorientation of the fundamental goals of the television reform. It is little better than impossible to list the ends of Chinese television reform for two reasons: First, the ends were seldom clearly stated in official documents, and if there were any, they would also keep varying from time to time for the inconsistent nature of Chinese policy-making.[217] Second, some claimed ends were actually duplicitous for the Party has always been facing a dilemma of keeping or giving up Communism as a belief system since the reform started. As HE pointed out, "giving up Communism completely would destroy its mandate to rule, but keeping it as it is would challenge and shackle what the Party is actually doing".[218] The Party attempted to expediently overcome the dilemma through the claim of constructing "socialism with Chinese characteristics". Despite the difficulties of clearly defining the fundamental ends of Chinese television reform, a number of salient ends of Chinese television reform over the past two decades are still noticeable in three different domains (See Figure 3.4). In view of the risk of an oversimplification, this table only serves – 1) to display to what degree some most often claimed ends have been realised, neglected or virtually discarded, and 2) to question whether the current reform scheme can fulfill these ends – in order to briefly evaluate Chinese television reform.

---

217 See authors like HE, PAN, HONG etc.
218 He. p. 199.

3.2. Reasons, Consequences and Bottlenecks of the Self-commercialisation

Figure 3.4 Ends and Realities of Chinese Television Reform

Claimed ends of reform	Realities (evaluated with ++, +–, – –)*
Political ends	
– serving as the Party/government's mouthpiece to promote its interest, policies and ideology.	– the Party/government still holds the control over television, but the impact is gradually confined to particular areas like news sector or to the bureaucratic competence like licensing. (+–)
– facilitating modernisation and improving people's lives.	– proliferation of television all over the country throughout the past decades. (++)
– serving "the people" (as mandate to rule).	– "the people" is indeed a politically sensitive term for it often triggers off discussions on democratisation; therefore the related public discussions are generally repressed. (– –)
Economic ends	
– establishing television market with market mechanism.	– fast development of television market but lack of a sound market mechanism. (+–)
– profit-seeking.	– heavy dependence on advertising revenue and polarisation between television institutions. (+–)
– enhancing the competitiveness against international media conglomerates after China's entry into the WTO.	– lack of real competitiveness; at the same time no guarantee of wins for Chinese television industry in an open competition with foreign counterparts. (– –)
Public ends	
– supervision by public opinion;	– state-led and state-controlled, no real supervision of public opinion. (– –)
– providing social, cultural and educational functions.	– fairly informative but heavily entertainment-oriented; an obvious erosion of cultural and educational functions. (– –)

* For a brief evaluation, ++ indicates that the ends are fully or largely realised; +– indicates that the ends are partially realised; – – indicates that the ends are not realized, or being largely neglected or even discarded.

Figure 3.4 shows that the current reform scheme has satisfactorily fulfilled the political ends of the reform. The Party played a dominant role during the reform process. Even in the relatively liberal period of the mid and late 1980s, it was also the Party that led the public debates on political and economic reforms, only in the end the situation was out of control. The reform also achieved the target of enhancing most people's access to television as a modern mass medium. In recent years, however, the impact of the Party is declining in many programme genres except news due to the increasing impact of the market. The Party/government also helped the market powers to get strengthened in order to consolidate its own power through good governance. Although "serving the people" was and kept being the source of its mandate to rule, the Party was still extremely cautious about discussing it openly. Therefore, the reform did not really represent the benefit of "the people" rather than that of the Party.

The economic ends also belong to the main target of Chinese television reform. They have even become the focus of the reform in the past decade after the political reform was stagnated. Without consideration of the potential negative consequences of the current reform scheme, dominated with market mechanism, and lack of necessary public criticism at the same time, however, Chinese television has been greatly commercialised during the reform process. Although a television market has been established and kept a phenomenal growth, it also brought about some hidden troubles for the future development of Chinese television market, such as no sound market mechanism has been established due to the administrative manipulation of the state and the stable monopoly of state-owned television institutions, excessive competition for advertising revenue among television institutions, etc. Such a television market lacks real competitiveness in the international competition. In other words, Chinese television market and the main players, namely the state-owned television institutions, are developing under the umbrella of protectionism instead of in an open and fair competition. It is therefore fair to conclude that the economic ends are only partially achieved.

What have been largely neglected during the reform process are the public ends. Deriving from the Party's claim of "serving the people", the public ends of reform nominally existed so as to legitimise the Party's mandate to rule. The current reform scheme has to some extent promoted the development of public sphere in forms of state-led supervision of public opinion, a clear expansion of informative news programmes, a diversification of programme landscape, etc. However, these improvements are not achieved for the public's own sake; instead, they are rather the side products of the commercialisation of Chinese television. Without an explicit setting of public ends for the reform, the cultural and educational functions of television were neglected and even eroded during the reform process. Regrettably, the erosion of the cultural and educational functions of television has not received any serious concern so far.

Overall, the current reform scheme has facilitated the development of Chinese television in the past decades and enabled television to become an influential mass medium in Chinese society. This has consequently helped to consolidate the Party's governance, promoted the fast development of television industry, and to a limited degree stimulated the evolution of public sphere. However, closer attention needs to be paid to the failures caused by the current reform scheme, foremost in the insufficient realisation of the economic ends, the negative consequences brought about by the self-commercialisation of Chinese television, and a severe negligence of the public ends. Based on the aforementioned findings of this brief examination, it is imperative to search alternative measures so as to remedy the existing failures of the current reform scheme.

3.3. In Search of an Alternative

On the grounds that there are obvious and salient failures caused by the current reform scheme, it is therefore necessary to search alternatives so as to remedy these failures. A wide-ranging enquiry and debate should be included and alternatives need to be assessed.

Two approaches are adopted when alternatives are being searched: the inductive approach and the deductive approach. Richard Collins elaborates these two approaches when he tries to sort the definitions of the public service broadcasting.[219] The inductive approach defines the pubic service broadcasting through codifying what the public service broadcasting "is" on the base of its historical practices, while the deductive approach concerns on the theoretical systematisation of what public service broadcasting "ought" to be. In other words, the inductive approach focuses on what the public service broadcasting's actual conditions were and are, and the deductive approach concerns an ideal state of the public service broadcasting which may not be fully realised in the reality but inspires the practitioners. Actually, the policy makers in many countries have widely adopted these two approaches in the process of broadcasting system innovation. On the one hand, in the empirical aspects, the experiences and practices of other countries are studied and compared in an inductive way, with the aim to obtain useful ideas for system innovation; but on the other hand, in the theoretical aspects, the process of a system innovation is also a process of approaching the ideal state of a system, which is based on those theoretical frameworks that reflect the values of the policy makes and the society as well. That is to say, if the policy makers of one country imitate a certain model of broadcasting system,

---

[219] Richard Collins. "'Ises' and 'Oughts': public service broadcasting in Europe". In Robert C. Allen and Annette Hill (eds.) *The Television Studies Reader*. London and New York: Routledge, 2004. pp. 33-51.

they also directly or indirectly accept the values and ideals which this model pursues.

Thus, several influential broadcasting systems – the emergence and the development – are to be briefly assessed with an inductive approach, while the deductive part of a system – the ideas and theoretical frameworks – are also to be analysed.

It appears a convoluted task to complete because there seems to exist numerous broadcasting systems in the world. In actual fact, it dose not offer many alternatives to be assessed when only the main broadcasting systems are under discussion and when the history of Chinese television is taken into consideration. In Chapter 1, Kops' geometric exposition of broadcasting systems has displayed the three basic types of the world broadcasting systems, namely the public service broadcasting, the state broadcasting, and the commercial broadcasting, according to their revenue structures.[220] Most countries have more or less mixed broadcasting systems in that the various (and also numerous to date) separate broadcasters in those countries have diverse financial resources. However, the overall broadcasting system of a country is still determined by aggregating the weighed revenue structure of all separate broadcasters of the country. In this way, the broadcasting systems in the world are categorised into different distinct types: the countries like the Soviet Union and China have (had) a government broadcasting system, the broadcasting system in the USA is purely commercial, and the countries like Britain and Germany have a mixed dual broadcasting system which is a combination of the public service broadcasting system and the commercial broadcasting system.

It becomes easier to find an alternative when there are only three main broadcasting systems under discussion. Moreover, the history of Chinese television further clarifies the issue. In retrospect, Chinese television has imitated two models in its history. It was first established under the impact of the Soviet Union model in the 1950s, by which television was clearly defined as propagator, educator and mobiliser. Then it followed the model of America in the 1990s (but only pragmatically in the economic aspect) in order to develop television as a profitable industry, while trying to maintain television as the mouthpiece of the Party at the same time. The first two models have been profoundly studied in China when they were imitated, thus they are not unacquainted to Chinese policy makers and should be excluded as "alternatives". And the third model, namely the dual system, whose heartland lies in Europe, has not received sufficient attention and systematic study in China. Therefore, the focus of searching an alternative here is to learn about the dual system in order to discover the useful experiences

---

[220] See Section 1.2, pp. 25-27. Compare with Head; and Robert L. Hilliard, Michael C. Keith. *Global Broadcasting System*. USA: Focal Press, 1996.

3.3. In Search of an Alternative

and ideas for the further reform of Chinese television. The other two models, especially the American model, remain in the background for comparison and further discussion.[221]

---

221 Even as a background for comparison and further discussion, the Soviet model and the American model are analysed in different scope in this book. After the collapse of the Soviet Union in 1991, the broadcasting system in Russia and in the Eastern European countries have radically transformed, so the Soviet model has faded into historical terminology in broadcasting studies. It hence does not serve as a model for the future system innovation for China and receives relatively little discussion here. With regard to the American model, there still remains a great deal to be made clear – although it has been lavishly discussed and keenly imitated in China in the late 1990s, the core ideas of the American model like the press freedom or the monitor of democracy were (and to a large extent are still) carefully evaded by Chinese policy makers. Therefore, the ideas of the American model are to be examined when compared with the dual system.

Part 2
The Dual Broadcasting System and its Inspirations

Chapter 4
The Purely Public Service Broadcasting System: the predecessor of the dual broadcasting system

Unlike being ignored in China, the public broadcasting system was the pride of its cradleland Britain and was especially appreciated among media academics worldwide.[222] The British pubic service broadcaster, the BBC, was widely imitated in many countries after WWII, from Europe (Germany, Spain) to Asia (Japan, Korea), not to mention the former colonies of the British Empire like New Zealand, Australia, Canada. In fact, the public service broadcasting has been, argued Humphreys, a characteristic element of Western European broadcasting systems (except Luxemburg).[223] Therefore, the research of the dual broadcasting system, whose predecessor and one of the current fundamental pillars is the public service broadcasting system, will start with a historical review of the development of the public service broadcasting system. The later development and transition of the public service broadcasting system to the dual system also reveals how contentious the views of different players on the future of broadcasting system were. Moreover, it is also interesting to observe that a comparative approach to other broadcasting systems has always been adopted during the emergence and the development of the dual system, for instance, the negation or the adoration of the American purely commercial system, and the vehement criticism of state broadcasting in Germany after WWII. The analysis is by and large limited to the broadcasting systems in Britain and West Germany. Apart from the fact that British broadcasting system as the prototype and the pioneer of the public service broadcasting system is historically significant while West German broadcasting system is known as a successful imitator with its own adjustments, the status quo that both countries possesses a sophisticated public service broadcasting sector and an active private sector also makes them important object countries for researches on the dual broadcasting system. Naturally, the relatively convenient access to the research resources also contributes to this limitation of the research scope.

---

222 See, for example, Wolfgang Hoffmann-Riem, *Rundfunkaufsicht im Ausland: Großbritannien, USA und Frankreich*. Düsseldorf: Presse- u. Informationsamt d. Landesregierung Nordrhein-Westfalen, 1989. p. 3. Burton Paulu. *British Broadcasting*. USA: University of Minnesota Press, 1956.
223 Peter Humphreys. *Mass Media and Media Policy in Western Europe.* Manchester and New York: Manchester University Press, 1996. p. 111.

Chapter 4 The Purely Public Service Broadcasting System

The prototype of the pubic service broadcasting is the British Broadcasting Corporation (the BBC). It was first established as a private company – the British Broadcasting Company (the BBC) – by a couple of leading British radio manufacturers in 1922. Because the share of waveband in Europe was very limited, the BBC was granted a de facto but not de jure monopoly by the Post Office, which was the responsible government department for the issues of telegraphy and telephony services, merely for the administrative convenience. The first general manager of the BBC was John Reith, who has been widely regarded as the founding architect of the public service broadcasting. With his advocacy, the British Broadcasting Company was transferred five years later to the British Broadcasting Corporation, which was a publicly funded quasi-autonomous organisation established under a Royal Chart. It has been the first public service broadcasting institution in the world and was seen as a "sociological invention of immense significance" and a "breathtaking administrative innovation"[224].

The public service broadcasting system was a single system in Britain for about three decades from 1927 to 1954. Afterwards it was substituted by a dual broadcasting system of coexistence of the public service broadcasting and the private broadcasting until today. In West Germany, the public service broadcasting system was also for decades a single system from the 1950s till the 1980s, and it shifted to a dual broadcasting system in 1984. The analysis to the public service broadcasting system here focuses on its periods as a single system.

4.1. The principles and characteristics of the public service broadcasting

In Britain, where the public service broadcasting originated, no one has ever given an exact or widely accepted definition of the public service broadcasting system in numerous related literatures. The practitioners and the scholars usually compile a list of principles and characteristics to demonstrate what the public service broadcasting is or ought to be. This is, in Richard Collins' words, the "ises" – what the public service broadcasting is in the real practice – and "oughts" – what the public service broadcasting should be in an optimal state – of the public service broadcasting system.

The current principles and characteristics of the public service broadcasting have to be traced back to the advocacy of its founding architect John Reith. When Reith envisaged the scope and conduct of broadcasting in 1925, he advocated that broadcasting ought to be a public service with the following characteristics as Scannell summed up:

---

[224] William Robson, cited by Seaton. James Curran and Jean Seaton. *Power without Responsibilities (5th Edition).* London and New York: Routledge, 1997. p. 113.

4.1. The principles and characteristics of the public service broadcasting

First, the service must not be used for entertainment alone. It should be a cultural, moral and educative force for the improvement of knowledge, taste and manners. Broadcasting should give a lead to public taste rather pander to it. Second, broadcasting should be a national service. Everyone should be provided access to broadcasting so that they can share public events and ceremonies as part of a public, corporate, national life. Third, broadcasting should be free to offer information and to help the formation of public opinion. This is the core element of the concept of pubic service in a mass democratic society. Fourth, the BBC should be granted monopoly as an essential means of guaranteeing the BBC's ability to develop as a public service in the national interest. Fifth, the BBC should change its status from a company in the private sector to a corporation in the public sector in order to give broadcasting a greater degree of freedom and independence in the pursuit of the ideals of public service. The BBC should be free from both commercial pressures and the interference and pressure from the state, so that broadcasting could develop its educational, cultural and political role as a public service.[225]

The Post Office supported Reith's advocacy and then changed the BBC from a private company into a public corporation in 1927. Since then, the BBC has developed under these Reithian principles to be a public service broadcasting institution. With the establishment of a universally accessible national service and a provision of mixed programming ranging from news, drama, sport, religion to music (light to classical) and light entertainment, Reith's ideals were largely, if not completely, realised in the ensuing years. The BBC successfully won the reputation for itself both domestically and internationally as "purveyor of moral and cultural 'uplift' ... for the masses"[226] for its high-quality educational and cultural programmes. The public service broadcasting system became an influential type of broadcasting system worldwide after WWII.

In the ensuing 30 years after WWII, the public service broadcasting system and the ideals it represents were stably entrenched in most western European countries (except Luxemburg, Monaco and Andorra), until it was drastically challenged by commercial powers in the 1980s. In Figure 4.1, Humphreys reproduced a table which contains two similar models of the contemporary European public service broadcasting which precisely indicate some of the most fundamental characteristics of the public service broadcasting system.

---

[225] Paddy Scannell. "Public Service Broadcasting: the history of a concept". In Edward Buscombe (ed.) *British Television: A Reader*. Oxford: Oxford University Press, 2000. pp. 45-62. pp. 47-49.
[226] Ibid. p. 50.

Figure 4.1 Characteristics of public service broadcasting: two similar models (reproduced by Humphreys)[227]

Blumler's criteria	The Broadcasting Research Unit's criteria
Ethic of comprehensiveness	Geographic universality – equal access to same service
Generalised mandates	Catering for all interests and tastes
Diversity, pluralism and range	Catering for minorities
Cultural vocation	Catering for national identity and community
Non-commercialism	Universality of payment: system funded by users (i.e. licence fee)
	Competition to produce good programming rather than audience size
	Guidelines to 'liberate' programme makers, rather to restrict them
Place in politics	Independence from vested interests and government

Humphreys' table is surely helpful in obtaining some first impression of the public service broadcasting before going into details. According to these principles, a short profile of the public service broadcasting system, in terms of organisation, programming, programmes standards, targeted audience and finances, could be outlined as following:
– the institution of the public service broadcasting is (legally) independent of the state and other vested interests;
– it has a mixed programming with a wide range of genres and caters for demographically and ethnically various groups;
– the programmes are of high quality with a main focus on the remit of culture;
– the service is accessible to everyone within the national territory;
– the public service broadcasting is financed with license fee and non profit-oriented.

However, it seems less explainable when more sophisticated analyses (rather than the generalisation of principles and characteristics) are needed. For example, how to differentiate the ideas of the public service broadcasting from other systems when some similar principles are alleged, such as the "geographic universality" and "national identity" which also exist in the government broadcasting, and principles like diversity, pluralism which are also among the values of

---

227 Humphreys, p. 118.

the purely commercial broadcasting. Moreover, the rough generalisation of principles and characteristics also makes the fact less visible that some of the principles of the public service broadcasting are actually historical accidents "without any ideological rationale"[228]. An example is the licence fee. The licence fee is regarded as one distinguishing feature of the uniqueness of the public service broadcasting; nevertheless, it was first collected by the British Post Office in the early days of broadcasting as a lucrative source of revenue-producing[229].

Further questions remain to be answered beyond the generalisation of the principles and characteristics: Where do these principles come from? Which kind of ideas do they imply? And what differentiates the public service broadcasting system from the other broadcasting systems of purely commercial and government controlled? Answers to these questions probably lie in the different perspectives of the understandings of broadcasting – its role and function in a society, its relationship with state and market, its property, what it conveys to the audience and the way it achieves this. The uniqueness of the public service broadcasting could be best presented when in comparison with the understandings of broadcasting in other broadcasting systems. This will be discussed at length in the next section.

4.2. The understandings of broadcasting in the PSB: the BBC as the prototype

The establishment of the first public service broadcasting system in Britain in the 1920s is often seen as an initiative full of Britishness. The British public service broadcasting was indeed the only one of its kind in terms of broadcasting system in the first half of the 20th century. Meanwhile, most other western countries have chosen two other types of broadcasting system which seemed self-evident from a practical viewpoint of the policymakers: the countries where the free market philosophy was dominant and the control of the government was relatively weak, for example the United States, have chosen the purely commercial broadcasting system; some other countries like Germany, the then newly formed Soviet Union and even France, where the power of the government was much more overwhelming, have chosen a state-directed broadcasting system.

As McQuail argues that the principles of (modern western) mass media often coincide with the core values of modern western society[230], it is reasonable to

---

228 Paddy Scannell and David Cardiff. *A Social History of British Broadcasting (Vol. 1 1922-1939): serving the nation*. UK and USA: Basil Blackwell, 1991. p. 5.
229 Ibid.
230 Denis McQuail. "Mass Media in the Public Interest: towards a framework of norms for media performance". In James Curran and Michael Gurevitch (eds.) *Mass Media and Society (2nd ed.)*. London: Arnold, 1996. pp. 66-80. pp. 70 ff.

Chapter 4 The Purely Public Service Broadcasting System

say that the principles of the public service broadcasting also conform to the values of the societies that adopt it. It goes without saying that modern western society has a different set of values to that in authoritarian countries. Nevertheless, the set of values within modern western societies is also not necessarily identical. Britain, Germany and the USA all belong to modern western society; however, some of their values, at least in the area of broadcasting, still show wide discrepancies. This is to say, the difference of broadcasting system in fact implies the differences of values in the domain of broadcasting, or, their (largely historically) different understandings of broadcasting, especially at the emerging age.

The values, which the British public service broadcasting aimed to convey when it was first established and consolidated, will be analysed from five aspects: broadcasting as public utility, broadcasting as culture, and the relations of broadcasting with market, state, audience. As the very prototype of the public service broadcasting, the British public service broadcasting (or more precisely the BBC) and its prehistory will be the focus of the analysis.

4.2.1. Broadcasting as a public utility

When the British broadcasting system was still in the initial stage of the 1920s, wavebands were defined by the very first British broadcasting committee[231] – the Sykes Committee – as a "valuable form of public property".[232] This has set the crucial starting point for the future development of broadcasting as public service in Britain, that is to say, broadcasting was understood for the first of time as a public service other than private business or state apparatus.

What prompted the Sykes Committee to define wavebands as public property was originally out of technical considerations, in that air wave was an extremely scarce resource at that time in Europe. Dozens of countries in the Continental Europe had to negotiate for sharing the limited air wave resources, and then the allocated air waves in each country had to serve other prior tasks with military and marine purposes. Consequently, the air waves available for broadcasting were little better than rare. When enthusiasm of broadcasting was booming in Britain at the beginning of the 1920s, it was impossible to provide adequate frequencies to numerous license applicants. The regulators of broadcasting had to solve this conflict. In such a situation, the Sykes Committee defined air waves as

---

231 British broadcasting committee is an independent consulting body which is called and appointed by the Parliament every few years (usually before the renewal of the BBC Royal Charter). It works to examine and evaluate the important issues of broadcasting in Britain, and offers the Parliament suggestions for the future policy making.
232 Cited by Scannell, p. 46.

4.2. The understandings of broadcasting in the PSB: the BBC as the prototype

"public property", whose control "ought to remain with the state" when broadcasting as "a potential power over public opinion and the life the nation"[233] was taken into consideration.

However, the impact of this definition of air waves as "public property" went soon beyond its technical considerations and was far-reaching. Like a chain reaction, it fundamentally impacted the ensuing development of British broadcasting system. From this starting point of air waves as "public property", broadcasting has been deliberately developed into a public service. The missions of broadcasting to serve the public, the relations of broadcasting with market, state and audience, have all been reinterpreted under this innovative basic philosophy. These again forged the regulation, structure, organisation, programming and financing model of British broadcasting system as a public service system: the private company – the BBC – was transferred to a public corporation by Royal Charter in 1927; the public service broadcaster BBC was granted a status of monopoly; it adopted a mixed programming and was financed through license fee… All these arrangements were made to achieve one aim – to establish a broadcaster that can best serve the public.

Under the superior value of serving the public, other broadcasters may choose arrangements which are different from those of the BBC in achieving their aim. For example, besides licence fee, the German public law broadcasters[234] do not exclude advertising as a means of raising revenue. The principal concern is that the respective arrangements must not hurt the value of serving the public.

In short, in the public service broadcasting system, public service and public interest have been among the highest rank of values for broadcasters. This has already made an essential difference from the values of commercial and state-owned systems, where making profit or serving the interests of the state is the top priority of their broadcasters.

4.2.2. Broadcasting as culture

What should or does broadcasting convey to its audience? The purely commercial broadcasting system and the state-owned broadcasting system seem to give straightforward answers to this question. For the US commercial broadcasters, it is foremost **entertainment**, along with information and others; for Chinese state-owned broadcasters, **propaganda** was and is their essential mission, which was

---

233 Ibid.
234 The public law broadcasting (der öffentlich-rechtliche Rundfunk) is the German variant of the public service broadcasting.

Chapter 4 The Purely Public Service Broadcasting System

true at least before the commercialisation of broadcasting and remains the rhetoric of the present broadcasters.

However, the same question would not seem to get the same straightforward answer in the public service broadcasting system. Before the BBC became a public corporation in 1927, Reith has been convinced that the contents of radio programmes must be more than entertainment and should be "better programmes".[235]

Reith had strong convictions on the social and cultural functions of broadcasting. Regrettably, as the general manager and director general of the BBC, he did not have enough freedom for the programming of "better programmes" in the early days. For fear of loosing their readers and revenue, the newspaper industry put pressure on the government to forbid the BBC from news reporting; while the Post Office was also reluctant to allow the BBC to handle "controversial issues", such as political commentary and talk.[236] Therefore, the overwhelming efforts of the BBC for "better programmes" were put into the cultural and educational programmes, which have always belonged to Reith's firm belief of improvement of knowledge, taste and manners of the masses through broadcasting.

In the early days of the BBC's programming, cultural and educational programmes have made up the majority of the airtime. These programmes had a rich diversity of genres, ranging from music, theatre, talk to lectures and sport, and catered for both the general public and the widely various demographic and ethnic groups, such as children, women, senior citizens and minority groups. Most of the programmes were of high quality in terms of programme production. For example, many lectures were given by the most influential British intellectuals of that time. For the music programmes, the BBC had either signed contracts with the most excellent British performers or even established its own orchestra. The expenses spent by the BBC on cultural and educational programmes would be incomparably higher than its US commercial counterparts, which heavily depended on the low-cost gramophone records for their music programmes. As early as in 1925, British broadcasting was praised by a neutral witness in a memorandum for the Crawford Committee for its better quality of programme contents and its mature role as "an instrument of culture", when in comparison with the US broadcasting where "programmes were poor" and radio was still like "a scientific toy" for every boy.[237] Although the programmes of the BBC were sometimes criticized as elitist or highbrow for their preference for classical works, the contribution of the BBC to cultural and educational programmes were widely re-

---

235 Asa Briggs. *The History of Broadcasting (Vol. 1): the birth of broadcasting*. Oxford and New York: Oxford University Press, 1995 (reprint). p. 228.
236 Ibid. pp. 150-67.
237 Ibid. pp. 317-18.

4.2. The understandings of broadcasting in the PSB: the BBC as the prototype

spected. Engagement with culture remained a core merit of the public service broadcasters even after they won more significance in news reporting and handling controversial matters.

A new dimension of culture developed by the BBC was "a national culture"[238], which was forged through the broadcasts of various events which could attract nationwide interest or were of national significance, such as "royal occasions, religious service, sports coverage, and police series"[239]. Listening to these programmes became a shared experience of the nation, and further promoted "the sense of belonging to our country, being involved in its celebrations, and accepting what it stands for"[240], i.e. a process of forming and strengthening the national identity. The national monopoly of the BBC reinforced its image as "arguably the most important single cultural institution in the nation"[241].

In Germany, it was cleared as early as in 1926 (the Weimar Republic) that the affairs of broadcasting in terms of programmes were placed within the domain of culture on a federalist basis (Kulturhoheit der Länder)[242]. After the notorious centralist propagandist NAZI time throughout the 1930s and the 1940s, this tradition of placing broadcasting within the domain of culture and federalism was re-established in the public law broadcasting (der öffentlich-rechtliche Rundfunk) of post-war Germany in 1961 through "the television case" ("das Fernsehurteil"[243]).

In fact, the understanding of broadcasting as culture exists for a long time as part of the European perspectives on broadcasting. This has later caused fierce disputes between the European Union and the USA on the issue of broadcasting in the recent two decades. For example, in the GATT Uruguay Round (1986-1994), both sides could not reach consensus in the Service Trade Agreement on whether audio-visual service (broadcasting, television and film etc.) should follow the principle of free trade or rather be given a cultural exemption. Nevertheless, in the new UNESCO Convention on Cultural Diversity adopted in 2005 principally supported by Canada and France, the international community acknowledges for the first time both the economic and cultural nature of the cultural activities, goods and services (including television, film, etc.).[244] However, as the USA and Israel are the only two countries that voted against the Conven-

---

238 Scannell, p. 57.
239 Annan Committee (1977), cited by Scannell. Ibid.
240 Ibid.
241 Ibid.
242 Albrecht Hesse. *Rundfunkrecht: die Organisation des Rundfunks in der Bundesrepublik Deutschland (3. Aufl.)*. München: Verlag Franz Vahlen München, 2003. p. 3.
243 Ibid, pp. 16-18.
244 UNESCO. *Convention on the Protection and Promotion of the Diversity of Cultural Expressions*. 2005. http://unesdoc.unesco.org/images/0014/001429/142919e.pdf.

tion while 148 countries approved it, whether the trade-culture dispute between the USA and the European Union has been really settled remains in question.

4.2.3. Broadcasting and market

The establishment of the public service broadcasting in Britain entirely denied market forces in the sector of broadcasting and preferred a public monopoly of the public service broadcaster the BBC. This proceeded in opposite direction of the US commercial broadcasting.

Broadcasting as a mass medium first started booming in the USA in the 1910s. The US broadcasting system developed under the market mechanism from the very beginning. In the USA, broadcasting does not differ tremendously from other industries dominated by the free market principles, such as free competition for market share, profit-oriented, etc. The ownership of broadcasters remains in private hands. Any organisation can be licensed by the government so long as it states to operate broadcasting in "the public interest, convenience, and necessity" (Communications Act of 1934).[245] In short, broadcasting is as commercial as other mass media, such newspaper or magazine, of which advertising has been their vital financial resource.

As a latecomer of broadcasting at the beginning of the 1920s, Britain once regarded the USA as an important model to follow. Some British government officials visited the USA in the early 1920s in order to learn from US broadcasting. However, British decision makers decided not to follow the US commercial broadcasting system after they knew more about it. Instead, Britain established a commercial monopoly of the BBC in 1922, and further transferred the BBC to a public corporation in 1927. The commercial means of operating broadcasting was since then strictly forbidden in Britain, where broadcasting was solely financed by licence fee. The denial of market mechanism in Britain was reached by a small group of policy makers under various considerations.

Because of the aforementioned technical condition of broadcasting, namely the scarcity of air waves which were inadequate for all license applicants, air wave was defined as "public property", whose allocation under market mechanism was excluded. And because of the (potential) salient significance of broadcasting on public life, the control of it was in the hand of the state. Then the broadcasting committees were established to make decisions on British broadcasting policy. Debates undertaken by three groups of forces in the Sykes Com-

---

245 David Ostroff. "United States of America". In Leen d'Haenens and Frieda Saeys (eds.) *Western Broadcasting at the Dawn of the 21st Century*. Berlin and New York: Mouton de Gruyter, 2001. pp. 409-33. pp. 413-14.

4.2. The understandings of broadcasting in the PSB: the BBC as the prototype

mittee (1923) and the Crawford Committee (1925) have finally reached the consensus on the denial of the market mechanism in broadcasting.

The first group of forces was the newspapers. They strongly opposed the new medium broadcasting adopting advertising as a means of raising revenue in order to protect their own interests in advertising market. The second group of forces was British governmental officials, who had shared the opinion for a long time that a copy of the go-as-you-please method of the USA would only result in the "chaos of the ether" in Britain.[246] They further argued that advertising "would lower the standard"[247] and preferred license fee funding, which, as Scannell and Cardiff point out, was foreseen by the Post Office as a possible means to increase the highly lucrative revenues[248].

Nevertheless, the most eloquent argument against market mechanism came from Reith, who represented the interests of British broadcasting and keenly advocated a public monopoly in broadcasting. In his opinion, only a monopoly of public service broadcasting could maintain high standards of programmes, efficiency of management and planned growth of broadcasting. A public corporation also enjoyed a greater degree of freedom and independence. A profit-oriented broadcasting would most likely incline to serve the populous urban areas instead of the whole nation. As the form of public corporation was widely regarded as an efficient way to operate public resources, such as forestry, water and electricity, and the dissatisfaction with the industrial competition was prevailing among the British society in the 1920s, Reith's advocacy of a non-profit public monopoly of broadcasting gained general support and turned into reality in 1927.[249]

The general denial of market mechanism in broadcasting, if not completely[250], later became a common feature of (western) European broadcasting (except Luxemburg), summarized by McQuail as the traditional "non-commercialism" of

---

246 Asa Briggs. *The BBC: the first fifty years.* Oxford and New York: Oxford University Press, 1985. pp. 17-20.
247 Briggs (Vol.1, 1995). p. 150.
248 Scannell and Cardiff, pp. 5-6.
249 Curran and Seaton (1997), pp. 111-13.
250 Although German public law broadcasters did not completely exclude advertising from their funding (radio since 1948, television since 1956), the advertising time was strictly limited in terms of the total length and the specific air time. On an annual basis, no more than 20 minutes of advertising per day is allowed, with a maximum of 25 minutes. Advertising on television is allowed only before 8:00 p.m. The proportion of advertising revenue in the whole public law broadcasting revenue was also considerably smaller than that of the license fee (advertising 23.6 per cent, license fee 76.4 per cent in 1985). See Guido Ros, "The Federal Republic of Germany," in Leen d'Haenens and Frieda Saeys (eds.), *Western Broadcasting at the Dawn of the 21st Centry.* Berlin and New York: Mouton de Gruyter, 2001.pp. 275-306. p. 276. Heinz-Werner Stuiber. *Medien in Deutschland (Band 2): Rundfunk (2. Teil).* Konstanz: UVK Medien, 1998. p. 952.

European broadcasting[251]. Non-commercialism in broadcasting was regarded as a positive value in Europe in serving the public interest, ensuring high standards of programme quality, and providing a positive discrimination for cultural and educational contents. However, it also brought about an attitude towards market mechanism in commercial media, such as advertising and sponsoring, as negative for a danger of indirect manipulation on programming and programme contents.[252]

4.2.4. Broadcasting and state

The relationship between broadcasting and state in the public service broadcasting system is an interesting case to observe. The establishment of the public service broadcasting was founded on a rejection of politics, so claims Seaton[253]. However, it has taken a long way before the real independence of broadcasting from state was achieved. And the interrelationship between broadcasting and state was never unproblematic, especially in some critical crisis situations like wartime.

British civil servants started to control the order of telegraphs and the related activities since very early years, which could be traced back to the 19th century. The 1869 Telegraph Act had conferred power on the Postmaster-General to control telegraphs; and the 1904 Wireless Telegraphy Act, the first of its kind in the world, extended the power of the Postmaster-General to further control wireless telephony. Between 1905 and 1914, the Post Office has developed a licence system for wireless enthusiasts, which was six years earlier than a similar licence system issued in the United States, and issued the first printed licence in June 1905.[254]

Therefore, it was not surprising that the British Post Office also attempted to put broadcasting beneath its control at the founding stage of broadcasting. However, the attempt was eventually in vain. The Sykes Committee (1923) denied both an unrestricted commercial monopoly[255] and direct government control of broadcasting[256]. Instead, a Broadcasting Board to organize the broadcasting in the "public interest" was recommended. Two years later, the Crawford Commit-

---

251 Denis McQuail. "Commercialization and Beyond". In Denis McQuail and Karen Siune (eds.) *Media Policy: convergence, concentration and commerce*. London: Sage, 1998. pp. 107-27. pp. 109-10.
252 Ibid. See also Hesse, pp. 192-93.
253 Curran and Seaton (1997), p. 113.
254 Briggs (1985), pp. 10-11.
255 Paulu. pp. 11-12.
256 Scannell, p. 47.

4.2. The understandings of broadcasting in the PSB: the BBC as the prototype

tee (1925) further recommended that the BBC should be left to public control through "setting up a corporation with a widely representative governing body" other than controlled by the Post Office or any other government department.[257] The corporation was set up by Royal Charter instead of by special statute or by the Companies Act, thus the corporation was even under no parliamentary direct control and connected least possibly with political activities. The Charter also endowed the BBC with higher status (than a company) and much more freedom, for "a corporation incorporated by charter could do anything which the charter did not specifically prohibit it from doing", while a company under the Companies Act could "only do what it was specifically authorized to do by its memorandum and articles".[258]

The transfer of the BBC from a private company to a public corporation under Royal Charter in 1927 manifested the independence of broadcasting from commercial and political powers, at least as the ideal of public service broadcasting. Which factors have enabled the BBC to achieve this formal and partly substantial independence from state, while in some other European countries (like Germany) the state control on broadcasting was still predominant?

The denial of broadcasting as a government department was the direct result that most members of the Sykes Committee[259], especially the representatives of the three main parties, refused to use broadcasting as a partisan medium. Obviously, if the reporting of the BBC was in favour of one party, this would cause enormous dissatisfaction from other parties. Moreover, the Post Office also did not want to conduct a day-to-day administration of broadcasting; therefore, it even forbade the BBC from undertaking the "controversial matters" of political reporting, for this would easily cause "controversy" and the Postmaster-General might have to face questions in the House of Commons. Out of these considerations, to establish a Broadcasting Board to organize the broadcasting in the "public interest" would be a better solution for the Post Office to control broadcasting indirectly.[260]

If, as mentioned above, the attitudes of the main British parties and the government department itself – the Post Office – have more or less made a contribution to the independence of the BBC from state through the recommendation of establishing an independent Broadcasting Board, other opinion groups in the British society opposed a direct government control of broadcasting almost unanimously when public inquiries were made by the broadcasting committees.

257 Briggs (1961), p. 300.
258 Ibid, pp. 322-23.
259 The ten members of the Sykes Committee were representatives from the Parliament, the Post Office, the Press, the Radio Society, the BBC, and one "for good measure". Briggs (1961), p. 164.
260 Briggs (1961), pp. 150 ff.

Chapter 4 The Purely Public Service Broadcasting System

In other words, there existed a general consensus in British society that broadcasting should be independent from state. Among others, two factors helped in achieving this consensus in British society.

First, along with the capitalist development of the press, the struggles for press freedom from the late eighteenth to the mid-nineteenth century were foremost struggles against the state.[261] The newspapers, most of which appealed to the bourgeois and proletarian public, actively claimed universal political and civil rights – the right to vote, to free speech and free assembly. During this long-lasting process of winning press freedom, the so-called "Fourth Estate" – the commercialized and gradually depoliticized liberal Press – arose, which featured as political independent and scrutinized the state through open criticism. In the 1920s, the idea of press independence from state and a disconnection of press and party politics had gone deep into most people's minds, especially in the Press itself. Therefore, it is not surprising that the Press strongly opposed the dangers of bureaucracy in Department control and preferred keeping broadcasting in public hands as the BBC was about to transfer from company to corporation in 1926[262]. Otherwise it usually appeared less friendly to broadcasting because of the conflicts of interests between broadcasting and the Press.

The second factor is the resolute endeavour of Reith in winning autonomy in the execution and administration of the BBC to be free from state and political impacts. In the 1920s, there pervaded a reflection of party politics and dissatisfaction with free unplanned Capitalism among different British political allegiances, from the extreme right, to the centre and the left. Party politics were sometimes obstructive in social development, while neither state nor commerce was capable and efficient enough in organising public affairs. A better possibility was to let "the elite of clever and disinterested public servants" manage public affairs.[263] Reith was a prime mover of these ideas. He was extremely confident of his understanding of broadcasting, and believed that he was leading the BBC in the correct direction of development. Therefore, he disliked policy decisions made by the Post Office, for he thought the Post Office officials knew little of the problems of programme building but concerned more about technical matters. He preferred a loose parliamentary control instead of tight state administration by the Post Office. The establishment of an independent and non-partisan corporation would safeguard the political independence of the BBC and thus could best serve the public. Even within the public corporation, Reith expected a

---

261 See James Curran, Part I: Press history, chapters 1-5, and Part IV: Theories of the media, chapter 21, in Curran and Seaton *Power without Responsibilities (6th ed.)*. London and New York: Routledge 2003; Scannell (2000), pp. 57-58; Ralph Negrine, *Politics and the Mass Media in Britain (2nd ed.)*. London and New York: Routledge, 1994. pp. 39 ff.
262 Briggs (1961), p. 319.
263 Curran and Seaton (2003), pp. 113-14.

4.2. The understandings of broadcasting in the PSB: the BBC as the prototype

clear division of work between the Board of Governors and the Director General. In his opinion, the Governors, who had the de jure authority of controlling broadcasting, should be no "experts" of broadcasting and no representatives of particular interests, but "persons of judgement and independence, who would inspire public confidence by having no interests to promote other than the public service"[264]. Their responsibilities were "general not particular", above all to watch programme policy and to discuss major matters of policy and finance with the Director General. The de facto control of the BBC – the execution of the policy and the general administration of the BBC – should be left to the Director General, namely Reith himself, and his officers.[265] The Director General was the person to "manage the BBC, to co-ordinate the various activities of broadcasting, and take responsibility for the daily conduct of affairs"[266]. As a person of strong personality and with profound understanding of broadcasting, Reith successfully convinced most members of the broadcasting committees and many other principal figures involving broadcasting policy decision, like the witnesses of the inquiries of broadcasting committees, Governors of the Corporation. His efforts were finally rewarded – the BBC was guaranteed independence from state by Royal Charter, and his interpretation on the division of work between Governors and the Director General was written into a statement on the functions of Governors, which was circulated to all new Governors from 1930 until 1952.[267]

In practice, the relationship between the BBC and the Government was not always easy. There were occasional tensions between both sides, especially in times of charter renewal or government in crises like the General Strike in 1926, not to mention the restrictions on political reporting and controversial matters in the early years of the BBC. As the idea of the political independence of the BBC gained wider currency by policy makers and the general public, these restrictions were gradually lifted. And the BBC also developed an ethic of political neutrality in political reporting. Anyway, the fact that independence of state has been legally set down as a principle is a clear endorsement of the ideals of the public service broadcasting.

---

264 Asa Briggs. *The History of Broadcasting (Vol. 2): the golden age of wireless.* Oxford and New York: Oxford University Press, 1965 and 1995 (reprint). p. 393.
265 Ibid, pp. 399-400.
266 Ibid, p. 394.
267 Ibid, pp. 300-400.

4.2.5. Broadcasting and audience

The name of "public service broadcasting", if understood literally, refers to broadcasting that serves the public. Who are the public as audiences of broadcasting? How does broadcasting define its relationship with the public? What makes the public service broadcasting different from other sort of broadcasting, like commercial or state-owned, if it claims to serve the public?

When the BBC was still a company, it was stated by Reith in 1926 that "the policy of the Company was to bring the best of everything into the greatest number of homes"[268]. In the Reithian conception of "the public", it is everyone within a nation state. Broadcasting should be universally accessible to all members of the nation, especially to those in the remote area of the country where broadcasting meant more for the people.[269] Moreover, Reith further expounded his views on audiences: the (living) audiences are "composed of individual people" and are "capable of growth and development", so that they should not be treated as "nameless aggregates with statistically measurable preferences, targets for the programme sponsor".[270]

Thus, for Reith, the audience of broadcasting is everyone in the nation; they are highly various individuals in terms of age, sex, interest, career, religion, education, and region. The function (or rather the mission) of broadcasting is, though providing "the best of everything" (high quality programmes), to contribute to the personal growth and development of the audiences, as well as to their participation in the national cultural life. The Reithian understanding of the audiences of broadcasting had in turn impacted the programming philosophy of the public service broadcasting, which is summarized by Crisell as to provide "something (best) for everyone" and to provide "everything for someone".[271] The former principle refers to the adoption of "mixed programming". The variety of programmes ranges from classic and light music, drama, news, talks, religion, to sport, light entertainment; and the targeted groups of audience include children, women, and people of various careers and from various regions. Everyone can find his or her favourite parts of programmes. The latter principle concerns the scheduling of various programmes. To avoid selective listening or viewing, no regular or "fixed point" scheduling would be adopted except news

---

268 Briggs (1961), p. 218.
269 Briggs (1965), p. 237.
270 Briggs (1961), p. 218.
271 Andrew Crisell. *An Introduction History of British Broadcasting (2nd Edition)*. London: Routledge, 2002. p. 29.

4.2. The understandings of broadcasting in the PSB: the BBC as the prototype

bulletin.[272] The intention is to encourage the audience to expand his or her interest in the full range of programmes.

Though not explicitly stated by Reith himself, another conception of "the citizen" was later used as an equivalent to the Reithian conception of "the public" in political and academic debates on broadcasting policies in Britain. During the process of mass democratisation in Britain throughout the 19th century and the 20th century, citizens were granted more and more rights and obligations in civic, political, social and cultural domains. Many key elements of the ideal of "citizenship", such as active participation in social life, individual and collective identities, common knowledge and pleasures in a shared public life, representation of the community, had been adopted in the ideal of public service broadcasting. Civil society as an area of society which fought to be independent from political influence also corresponds to the BBC's efforts to gain independence from political (and commercial) influences.

Reith did take some measures to develop a democratic programming policy, as well as try to establish a good relationship with the audiences. For example, soon after the Company was established in 1922, Reith employed from 1923 onwards a number of outside advisory committees to give advice on programmes in various subjects – religious, educational, language, music, women and children, provincial, etc.[273] The critics and advisers were experts in the respective fields. Furthermore, a magazine which targeted the general audience of the BBC and conceived by Reith as "the connecting link of the service"[274], the *Radio Times*, was also launched in 1923. By providing audience with contents of editorial comment, programmes, (and surprisingly, large proportion of advertisements), the *Radio Times* soon became a great success, which passed the million mark of circulation in 1928.[275]

Nevertheless, all these measures did not save the BBC from the criticism of being elitist, paternalist, even dictatorial to its audience. These condemnations seemed ostensibly not completely arbitrary. The BBC lagged behind American broadcasters in undertaking systematic audience studies.[276] Unlike their US commercial counterparts, the preference of audience has not been officially acknowledged as an indicator of programming policy by earlier BBC programme execu-

---

272 This principle was substituted with regular programme scheduling during the Second World War on the grounds that both the audiences and the BBC needed the predictability of daily broadcasts in the wartime. Curran and Seaton (2003), pp. 146-47.
273 Briggs (1961), pp. 219 ff.
274 Ibid, p. 271.
275 About the launch of the *Radio Times*, see ibid, pp. 270 ff.
276 Not until 1936 did the BBC start to set up a department to do listener research. A decade later, the BBC finally established a fully functioning Audience Research Department in 1946. See Paulu, p. 342.

tives. Instead, the BBC reserved it a privilege for itself to determine which programmes were the best for audience. An often mentioned example for accusing of the elitism of the BBC was that the BBC staff, many of whom were middle class graduates of Oxbridge, preferred broadcasting serious music, drama and lectures, which were intellectually demanding and more informative, to popular music and light entertainment. Unfortunately, the stereotype of the arrogant public service broadcasters was eventually exacerbated by Reith's much misunderstood comments on the audience of broadcasting: "It is occasionally indicated to us that we are apparently setting out to give the public what we think they need – and not what they want – but few know what they want and very few what they need."[277]

Yet Reith's comments should also be understood in the historical context when fine culture and high education were still luxury for ordinary people in Britain in the 1920s.[278] What deserves to highlight here is that the public service broadcasting has developed a democratic understanding of audience, by which broadcasting claimed its mission to solely serve the interests of the public, to cater for the individual growth and development of everyone in the nation, and to facilitate the formation of national and regional cultures. In short, it equated the audience of public service broadcasting as "the citizen" of a nation state. The understanding of broadcasting audience as citizens gradually became a general consensus in British society which had profound influences on defining the role of broadcasting in a modern democratic society. This consensus lasted for nearly five decades, until a different interpretation of audience as consumer arose to prevail in Britain in the 1980s.

From the above analysis, it is cleared that broadcasting is understood in the public service broadcasting system:
– as a *public utility* which serves the public interest;
– as *culture* rather than entertainment in the commercial broadcasting, or propaganda in the state broadcasting;
– to *reject market mechanism* like advertising and sponsoring, and to be non-profit oriented;
– to be *independent from state control* with high autonomy;
– to *regard audience as citizen* of a modern society.

Under these basic understandings of broadcasting, the very first public broadcaster, the BBC, was set up as a public corporation with specific commitments to education, culture, and later information. It was exclusively funded with licence fee instead of advertising revenue or state subsidy. The independence of the in-

---

277 Briggs (1961), pp. 217-18.
278 Briggs (1985), p. 54.

stitution was guaranteed with a Royal Charter, according to which the governing body of the BBC was no governmental department but an independent Broadcasting Board whose members were "the trustees of the national interest". Broadcasting's targeted audience was every citizen in the nation, while the function of broadcasting was to cater for citizen's individual growth and development, so as to enable his or her participation in national affairs.

After learning about the understandings of broadcasting in the public service broadcasting set by its founders, it becomes palpable to understand the background of the characteristics and principles summarized by Blumler and The Broadcasting Research Unit, such as "geographic university" and "catering for all interests and tastes", which comes from the understanding of audience as citizens in the nation, and "cultural vocation", which implies the understanding of broadcasting as culture.

It is noteworthy that the principles and characteristics of the public service broadcasting are not static. As the society developed and technologies advanced, some new principles and characteristics were brought into the existing set of principles to enrich the understandings of broadcasting. After the Second World War, the public service broadcasting system was involved in two major changes: domestically, it expanded the economic and democratic commitments of broadcasting which led to the transition of the monopolistic PSB to a dual broadcasting system in Britain, namely the coexistence of the public service broadcasting and the commercial broadcasting; internationally, the PSB was widely acknowledged as a model broadcasting system and was imitated by many other countries for its achievements in enhancing the cultural and democratic functions of broadcasting. The next section will analyse these changes in depth.

4.3. The British model of PSB after WWII: domestic criticism, international imitation and European consolidation

After getting through the teething troubles in the emerging stages of the 1920s, the PSB was successfully consolidated in Britain throughout the 1930s. At the same time, the British system started to serve as a model in some foreign countries, while being appreciated by many others.[279] The public esteem for the BBC reached a climax during the Second World War. When speed, accuracy and punctuality were essential for people in wartime, and there was a shortage of newsprint, broadcasting (or more precisely, the BBC) became a highly influential medium during the war. In contrast to the propaganda of German Nazi

---

279 Briggs (1961), p. 468.

broadcasting, by which false or glamorised information was often utilized as weapons in "the phoney wars", the BBC persisted in "telling the truth, nothing but the truth, and near as possible the whole truth"[280] in a calm and neutral manner. This has made the BBC almost the only reliable information source for many people in the occupied European countries. The world-wide coverage of the BBC Forces Programme as well as its Overseas Service, broadcast in 45 languages by the end phase of the war, also greatly enhanced the international reputation of the BBC as a world service. The programmes of the BBC in wartime, which consisted of light music, humorous drama, serious talks, war reports with both hard facts and soft human touches, had also helped in improving the morale of both the British citizens and people in occupied countries.[281]

Despite the fact that the BBC was enthusiastically admired by both domestic and overseas audiences in wartime, it was confronted with antithetic attitudes in the post-war period: domestically, the monopoly of the BBC was fiercely criticised and it finally ceased in 1954 with the introduction of the commercial television into the British broadcasting system; internationally, the British model of public service broadcasting was widely admired and imitated – partly or entirely – by numerous countries in the world, ranging from the former colonies of the British Empire to newly democratised countries after the Second World War.

4.3.1. Domestic criticism and change of the PSB

In the 1940s and at the beginning of the 1950s, British audience were generally satisfied with the programme output of the BBC.[282] The unprecedented success of the televising of Queen Elizabeth's Coronation in 1953 was seen as a perfect "television's coronation"[283], since television was by then still a quite new medium to Britons. For the audience, it might be a good idea to have some more choices of programmes when the launch of a second television channel was under discussion in the Parliament.

However, there were wide discrepancies in the issue of broadcasting (inter alia television) among the political elite, media practitioners, and broadcasting

---

[280] The aspiration of "telling the truth" for news was initiated by the News Division of the Ministry of Information, which was founded after the war broke out. Nevertheless, this has been the motto of the BBC for its war reports. See Briggs (1985), pp. 178 ff..

[281] On the history of the British broadcasting as well as the BBC, see Asa Briggs, *The History of Broadcasting in the United Kingdom (Vol. 3): the war of words*. London and New York: Oxford University Press, 1970; Briggs (1985), pp. 173-238; Curran and Seaton (2003), pp. 126-48; Crisell, pp. 49-71.

[282] Asa Briggs. The History of Broadcasting in the United Kingdom (Vol. 4): sound and vision. Oxford and New York: Oxford University Press, 1995. p. 207.

[283] Briggs (1985), p. 275.

policymakers. Although the so-called "television wars" at the beginning of the 1950s seemed a dazzling drama of "defending" or "attacking" the BBC with plenty of committee reports, written polemics on the press and parliamentary debates, there were basically three types of critics targeted at the BBC. The first group of critics were the anti-monopolists, who did not necessarily resent the BBC and its performance, but regarded monopoly as a negation of freedom. They, therefore, preferred competition. The second group were the critics of the BBC, who disliked both the BBC and it programme output. The BBC was criticised as a gigantic bureaucratic organisation with top-heavy staffs, lack of efficiency, a place of complacency, and the programme output of the BBC was often didactic and mostly London-based. Similar to the anti-monopolists, the critics of the BBC also believed that monopoly was the cause of these ill facets of the BBC.[284] The third group of critics were some Conservative MPs who needed whatever proposal that would help the Conservative Party to win the general election of 1955. Since the major political rival of the election, the Labour Party, openly declared its support for the BBC as well as its monopoly, the Conservative Party had to seek alternative routes on the issue of broadcasting policy. To introduce commercial television in Britain came out as a counter proposal of the Conservative Party in such circumstances. Being directed against the support of the Labour for the monopolistic status of the BBC, an idea of "competitive television" which was indeed an embellishing formulation of "commercial television" became a fundamental principle of conservative policy. The pro-Conservative business interests also actively joined in pressing their political spokespersons for change.

It was eventually the political rivalry between the Conservative and the Labour that directly led the transition of British broadcasting system from the PSB to a dual system. The governing party, the Conservative, issued a series of White Paper in 1952 and 1953 to elaborate the idea of establishing a second Authority to supervise the commercial system. Based on this idea, the Television Bill 1954 was published and the new supervisor of commercial television – the Independent Television Authority (the ITA) – was brought into being, which marked a milestone of the introduction of commercial television in Britain. The Conservative finally won the 1955 election, and this further consolidated the idea and institutionalisation of "competitive television" in British broadcasting system.

Despite the decisive role of political reasons which terminated the monopoly of the BBC and introduced the commercial television, there were profound technological, economic and social reasons which also contributed to the break of the

---

284 Briggs (Vol. 4,1995), p. 208.

Chapter 4 The Purely Public Service Broadcasting System

"no advertising" tradition of public service broadcasting. On the technological level, the airwaves used for military purposes in the wartime were now gradually released for public use after the war. Nevertheless, the reason that advertising was first allowed exclusively in television section[285], not both radio and television, was above all economic. On the one hand, television was a medium of extremely high costs in comparison with radio. Many broadcasting practitioners have realised that the existing licence system could not finance the future of television[286]. On the other hand, television advertising was of enormous business value to many industries. Television was even deemed "a natural selling medium" in the United States.[287] The business interests, including the potential television licence applicators who wanted to profit from advertising revenues, the consumer goods manufacturers who needed television advertising to promote their products, as well as the television manufacturers who would anyway benefit from the television boom, all urged the introduction of a commercial television. However, it has to be pointed out that the impact of the industry lobby on policy-making was fairly limited before the Conservative MPs turned to adopt the idea of "competitive television" to counterattack their political rivals.

The social reason for the introduction of commercial television into the public service broadcasting was the willingness of the whole British nation to thoroughly bid farewell to the war and the emergence of a consumer society in post-war Britain. The beginning of the 1950s in Britain was the years of full employment and "the age of affluence". People had aspirations to own more durable consumer goods and make a fuller use of their leisure. They were keen on expending money on housing, television sets, cars and telephone, which used to be luxury for many families. A consuming society was coming.[288] In such an optimistic and hedonistic social atmosphere, the words which related to the miserable wartime, such as rationing, national planning or nationalisation, and austerity, became unpopular among people, especially among the young generation. The change of the Zeitgeist also spilt over into the area of broadcasting. The BBC was criticised by some back benches of the Conservative for its monopolistic status as well as the didactic and propagandistic inclinations in its programmes. Another change in public attitudes to broadcasting was the increasing demand for entertainment and information rather than education in broadcasting service. Actually, the BBC has also enhanced the entertaining and informative functions of broadcasting in the post-war programming.[289] However, it seemed that the idea

---

285 The commercial radio appeared a decade later in Britain.
286 Briggs (Vol. 4, 1995), p. 399.
287 Briggs (Vol. 4, 1995), p. 926.
288 Ibid, pp. 391-95.
289 Briggs (1985), pp. 288 ff.

of commercial television would better cater to the public demand for more entertainment in broadcasting.

Regardless of the change in the Zeitgeist and in public tastes, the BBC, the majority of television and film producers, the press and many politicians (especially those of the Labour) stood up for the traditions and values of the public service broadcasting during the "television wars". They rejected the introduction of commercial television in particular. In their opinion, the programmes of the BBC were much better both in quality and in variety than the programmes from many other countries, including the programmes produced by the leading commercial broadcasters from the United States. Moreover, a former BBC official refused to equate "commercial" with "free". The BBC even firmly insisted that it would not change its principle of not "selling time", nor would it accept any form of sponsorship.[290]

The Conservative draftspersons of the White Paper seemed to share most of the core values of the British public service broadcasting, which could also be seen as part of the consensus politics of the 1950s in Britain. The constitution of the ITA borrowed heavily from the BBC model.[291] And it was remarked by Sepstrup three decades later as "commercial public broadcasting"[292] on the grounds that the British commercial television had very high standards for programme quality and the sponsors had few direct controls over the programmes. This means that the British commercial broadcasting still bore the ethos of public service broadcasting despite its commercial funding with advertising revenues.

The promulgation of the Television Act 1954 not only declared the existence of commercial broadcasting in Britain, but also marked a new phase of British broadcasting, i.e. the dual broadcasting system.

4.3.2. The international imitation of British public service broadcasting and its consolidation in Europe

During the Second World War, the BBC not only made great achievements in improving the morale of the British nation, but also built a worldwide reputation as a reliable and impartial broadcaster. By the end of 1943 the BBC was broad-

---

290 Briggs (Vol. 4, 1995), pp. 801ff.
291 Briggs (1985), p. 287.
292 Sepstrup (1989), p. 32, cited by Chien-San Feng. *The Political Economics of Broadcasting Capital Movement: an anlysis to the traditions of Taiwanese broadcasting media in the 1990s (in Chinese. 《广电资本运动的政治经济学》 or Guangdian Ziben Yundong de Zhengzhi Jingjixue).* In a research series of Taiwan (Taipeh): *A Radical Quarterly in Social Studies (in Chinese, 《台湾社会研究》丛刊 or Taiwan Shehui Yanjiu)* 05, 1995. p. 74.

casting in 45 languages, ranging from German, French and Greek to a large number of Asian languages like Cantonese and Kuoyu[293], Malay, Thai and Japanese.[294] The BBC's foreign services had covered many parts of the world and were received by millions of foreign audience, which made the BBC a real global medium.

Besides the world-wide reputation of the BBC among global audiences, public service broadcasting system also attracted enormous attention from broadcasting policy-makers globally in the early post-war period. As a distinctive model of broadcasting system, public service broadcasting had already been adopted by a couple of countries before the Second World War. Nevertheless, most of them were the Commonwealth countries like Australia, Canada and South Africa, which traditionally had deep political and cultural connections with Britain. A noticeable exception was Japan, which has adopted the model of the BBC (by then the British Broadcasting Company) very early – the main Japanese public broadcaster NHK was established in the year of 1926. In the early post-war period, the influence of the British model of public service broadcasting went beyond the sphere of the British Empire and was widely recognized as a main broadcasting system alongside commercial broadcasting system and state-controlled broadcasting system.[295] The ideas and principles of public service broadcasting had attracted broad attention worldwide and made a profound impact on other national broadcasting policy-makings, though at different levels.[296] The base camp of public service broadcasting system was eventually consolidated in the post-war Europe (except Andorra, Luxembourg, and Monaco) with national variations on institutional structures or revenue systems. Humphreys makes two classifications of European public service broadcasting system according to the revenue systems and the patterns of politicisation respectively.

293 Kuoyu refers to Mandarin Chinese.
294 Briggs (1985), pp. 224-25.
295 See, for example, the American broadcasting researcher Burton Paulu. *Radio and Television Broadcasting on the European Continent*. Minneapolis: University of Minnesota Press, 1967.
296 Feng differentiates the adoption of public service broadcasting in various countries into three levels: as system, as channel, or as programme. He categorises the public service broadcasting in Western and Northern European countries as the example of "system", the PBS in the United States as the example of "channel", while a small number of public service programmes on the commercial television in Taiwan as the example of "programme". See Feng (1995), pp. 68-76. Robert W. McChesney also analyses the difference between the public service broadcasting in the USA and in other countries like Canada, Britain and Germany. The latter is full-service broadcasting with education, entertainment, and public affairs aimed at the entire population of the country, while the PBS in the US is a marginal compensation for the failures of the corporate media system in educational and cultural provision. See Robert W. McChesney. "Public Broadcasting: past, presemt and future". In Michael P. McCauley et al. (eds.) *Public Broadcasting and the Public Interest*. Armonk an New York: M.E. Sharpe, 2003. pp. 10-24.

4.3. The British model of PSB after WWII

Figure 4.2 Types of European broadcasting systems according to revenue systems[297]

Pure public	Belgium, Denmark, Norway, and Sweden
Mixed revenue	Austria, France, Germany, Greece, Ireland, Netherlands, Portugal, Spain, and Switzerland
Dual system	UK (private sector established in 1954), Finland (in 1959), and Italy (from 1976 onwards)
Pure commercial	Luxembourg, Monaco, Andorra

Figure 4.3 A classification of some Western European public broadcasting systems according to patterns of politicisation[298]

Executive or single party dominated	France, Italy (until 1975), Italy (1994), Greece
Arm's length influence	Britain, Sweden
Multiparty/group dominated	Germany, Austria, Italy (post-1975), Denmark, Netherlands, Belgium

The reason that the public service broadcasting was consolidated in early postwar Europe was that broadcasting was now endowed with a new value – the democratic function of broadcasting – besides other existed values and principles initiated in the emerging age of the BBC[299], whilst the existed values and principles have also been strengthened now.

The first decade after the Second World War was the years of democratisation in Western Europe and of independence movements in Africa, Asia and Latin America. During the post-war reconstruction of democracy in Western European countries, the function and role of broadcasting in modern democracy were put in the foreground during the process of policy making. Moreover, airwaves remained a scarce resource in the densely populated Europe at that moment, although some more airwaves were released from the military for civil use. How to manage the scarce resource of airwaves was a practical problem which the policy makers had to confront. An optimal broadcasting system should give consideration to all these factors.

Public service broadcasting was chosen as Europe's solution to realise the democratic function of broadcasting when airwaves were still scarce. The Euro-

---

297 Humphreys, p. 125.
298 Ibid, p. 157.
299 Values of the public service broadcasting at its emerging stage see pp. 118 ff.

pean policy makers believed that the public service broadcasting is superior to other broadcasting systems for it had performed four key roles in the extension of citizenship rights in the first half of the twentieth century. These are, first, provision of a public space of information and debate; second, a mechanism of accountability and power holders; third, fostering national culture; and fourth, connecting the private (domestic) and the public.[300] The organisation, financing and range of programmes of the BBC model strengthened the advantages of public service broadcasting in terms of accordance with the principles of democracy: it kept the state at arm's length; and was funded by audiences through licence fees; it provided programmes of high quality on information, entertainment and education by highly qualified, independent journalists; the diversity and plurality of programmes, especially the needs of minority groups, were deliberately taken into consideration; etc. The democratic role of media, especially of public service broadcasting, is later academically legislated through Habermasian theory of "public sphere", which is conceived as:

> ... a 'space' where access to information affecting the public good is widely available, where discussion is free of domination and where all those participating in public debate do so on an equal basis. Within this public sphere, people collectively determine through rational argument the way in which they wish to see society develop, and this shapes in turn government policy. The media facilitate this process by providing an arena of public debate, and by reconstituting private citizens as a public body in the form of public opinion.[301]

Two other main broadcasting systems, i.e. the state-owned and the commercial broadcasting systems, did not gain a general recognition by European countries. They first rejected a state-controlled broadcasting system on deep reflections of the notorious misuse of broadcasting as an instrument of propaganda by the Nazis during the Second World War. A state-operated broadcasting service became later part of the ideology of the adversarial Communist countries. Most European countries also fully or partly refused a purely commercial broadcasting system. Motivated by notions of social justice, European policy makers believed that broadcasting might be best left to the public hands instead of to state or to commercial powers on the grounds that broadcasting was regarded as scarce and influential "public good". The informational, educative, cultural purposes of broadcasting and its potential as tool in the construction of the nation state were strongly emphasised in the early post-war period. Broadcasting as a place for informed public debate and unified nation was prior to it as a marketplace for pri-

---

300 Graham Murdock. "Citizens, Consumers and Public Culture". In Michael Skovmand and Kim Christian Schroder (eds.) *Media Cultures: Reappraising Transnational Media*. London: Routledge, 1992. pp. 17-41. p. 33.
301 James Curran. *Media and Power*. London and New York: Routledge, 2002. p. 233.

vate capitals. Therefore, public regulation and even public ownership were seen as necessary in Europe.

The pan-European technical cooperation, programme exchanges and personnel training among the main European public service broadcasters have further consolidated the position of public service broadcasting in Europe. The European Broadcasting Union (EBU) was formed at a conference at Torquay in 1950. The Major-General Sir Ian Jacob, Director of Overseas Services of the BBC, was elected as the first President of the EBU. The majority of the active members of the EBU are European public service broadcasters. The first Eurovision exchange of programmes started with eight participating countries (United Kingdom, Belgium, Denmark, France, Netherlands, Italy, Switzerland, and West Germany) in 1954. Besides the cooperation and exchange among broadcasting organisations, the missions of the EBU today include ensuring that the crucial role of public service broadcasters is recognised and taken into consideration by decision-makers at EU level and promoting the public service values in the global debate on media policy by working with UN, UNESCO and World Broadcasting Unions.[302]

4.4. Theoretical development of public service broadcasting: the case of West Germany

As one of the numerous worldwide imitations of the BBC model in the post-war time, the broadcasting system of the Federal Republic of Germany (often called West Germany) was regarded as typical public service broadcasting for nearly three decades until the introduction of commercial broadcasting in West Germany in the 1980s. Nevertheless, the adoption of public service broadcasting system in West Germany was not purely voluntary, but rather the consequence of the defeat of "the Third Empire" in the Second World War and the establishment of a democratic Germany, i.e. West Germany, under the control of the Western Allies.

In such a historical context, the establishment and development of public service broadcasting in West Germany underwent two phases. The first phase was the reconstruction of broadcasting under the control of the Allies from 1945 to 1949, namely right after the unconditional surrender of "the Third Empire" in 1945 till the establishment of West Germany in 1949. In this phase, a number of (German Federal) Land-based broadcasting institutions were first established by the American, French and British military governments in their respective occu-

---

[302] See Paulu, pp. 137-39, and the official website of the European Broadcasting Union: http://www.ebu.ch/en/about/index.php (visited in June 2008).

Chapter 4 The Purely Public Service Broadcasting System

pation zones[303]. Some of the paramount values of broadcasting in a democratic modern society, like the belief in freedom, the principle of distance from the state (staatsfern), and the organisation of the public law broadcasters were first ascertained by the Allies in the Western occupation zones, and then inherited by the newly founded Federal Republic of Germany a few years later. In other words, the reconstruction of broadcasting in West Germany was rather "a medium of democratisation and, in a narrow sense, of re-education"[304].

The second phase was the sovereign development of broadcasting after the establishment of West Germany in 1949. In this phase, juridification (Verrechtlichung) of the problems in broadcasting sector became an important mechanism of broadcasting policy development. A few significant examples are, among others, the West German Basic Law of 1949, more precisely Article 5, Section 1, Sentence 2, guarantees freedom of reporting by broadcasting as well as freedom of opinion and freedom of press, whilst freedom of information was noteworthy guaranteed for the first time by a German Basic Law; individual Land-based broadcasting institutions as well as federal broadcasting institutions – *Deutsche Welle* and *Deutschlandfunk* – were founded on the base of public law; the cooperation of individual Land-based public-law broadcasters was realised through various treaties; the rulings of the Federal Constitutional Court (Bundesverfassungsgericht) have far-reaching impacts on settling disputes or dealing complaints relevant to the development of broadcasting policy at constitutional level, especially when political approaches fail to work.

As an imitator of British public service broadcasting, West German public-law broadcasting has a lot in common with the British prototype in terms of the understandings of broadcasting. Nevertheless, West German public-law broadcasting has its specific characters due to the historical context and the actual conditions of the country. As mentioned above, the reconstruction of broadcasting in

---

303 The Americans set up one system in each Land of their zone: Radio Frankfurt (to be renamed Hessischer Rundfunk, HR, in 1948), Radio Stuttgart (from 1949 Süddeutscher Rundfunk, SDR), Radio München (renamed Bayerischer Rundfunk, BR, in 1948) and Radio Bremen. The British established one centralised broadcasting institution, the Nordwestdeutscher Rundfunk (NWDR), for their whole occupation zone (including Nordrhein-Westfalen, Schleswig-Holstein, Niedersachsen, Hamburg and the British sector of Berlin), which served more than half of the German population. In 1954-55, the NWDR was split up into Norddeutscher Rundfunk, NDR, with its office in Hamburg, and Westdeutscher Rundfunk, WDR, based in Cologne. The French established the Südwestfunk (SWF) in Baden-Baden and Radio Saarbrücken in Saarland, which was renamed Saarländischer Rundfunk (SR) in 1952. In West Berlin the United States Information Agency set up RIAS (Rundfunk im amerikanischen Sektor) in 1946, which was joined by the Sender Freies Berlin (SFB) in 1953. See Guido Ros, The Federal Republic of Germany, in Leen d'Haenens and Frieda Saeys (eds.), p. 275, and Stuiber, p. 188.
304 Heinz-Werner Stuiber. *Medien in Deutschland (Band 2): Rundfunk (1. Teil).* Konstanz: UVK Medien Verlagsgesellschaft mbH, 1998. p. 192.

4.4. Theoretical development of public service broadcasting: the case of West Germany

post-war West German was rather "a medium of democratisation and, in a narrow sense, of re-education", or more exactly, the reconstruction of values. American, French, British occupying powers all attempted to impose their own understandings of broadcasting upon German broadcasting institutions in their occupation zones, at the same time German politicians attempted to return to the pre-war Weimarian traditions of broadcasting. Despite these discrepancies, one critical factor in the post-war reconstruction of West German broadcasting was that all sides have reached a general consensus, which was a purposive reaction to the misuses of broadcasting by the Nazis during the Second World War.

Roughly speaking, West German public-law broadcasting was affected by *three strands of ideas*, namely *freedom of broadcast, broadcasting as a cultural matter*, and *the organisational form of the public service broadcasting*. Theses ideas were either promoted (not without resistance from the German side) by the Allies, such as the ideas of freedom of broadcast and of the organisational form of the public service broadcasting; or were defended by German politicians as the pre-war Weimarian traditions of broadcasting, such as broadcasting as a cultural matter. It took about three years (from 1945 to 1948) for the Allies to help Germans in setting up the legal framework of independent public service broadcasting, whereas the internalisation and consolidation of the ideas of the public service broadcasting in Germany were not completed until the beginning of the 1960s, with the milestone of the first broadcasting ruling of the German Federal Constitutional Court.

4.4.1. Freedom of broadcast

Under the profound impact of liberalism and laissez-faire business principles in American culture, the broadcasting system of the United States emerged in the 1920s as a purely commercial one, by which broadcasters were organised as for-profit private enterprises supported by advertising revenues. The values behind were a faith in property rights, the market and mini-government[305], which were believed quintessential for the liberal culture of freedom and democracy.

---

[305] Thomas Streeter discusses the emergence of corporate liberalism from the 1880-1920 period, by which the meanings of "freedom", "markets", "rights" and "property" have deviated from those of the classic liberalism in the 19th century, and the impact of corporate liberalism on the emergence of the purely commercial broadcasting system in the US. Instead a mini-government in classic liberal meaning, Streeter argues that the US government, accompanied by corporate elite, had actually played an active and crucial role for the formation of American purely commercial broadcasting system. See Thomas Streeter. *Selling the Air: a critique of the policy of commercial broadcasting in the United States.* Chicago & London: The University of Chicago Press, 1996.

Chapter 4 The Purely Public Service Broadcasting System

The values of freedom and democracy were therefore first principle of the reconstruction of broadcasting in the US occupation zones. They were clearly stated at the very beginning of a fundamental document of the broadcasting policy in the US occupation zones, *American Draft for an Explanation about Freedom of Broadcast in Germany, May 1946 (Amerikanischer Entwurf zu einer Erklärung über Rundfunkfreiheit in Deutschland, Mai 1946)*. The document claimed that

> "On the way to establish a free, democratic and peaceloving Germany, (...) German broadcasting sector (...) must devote itself to the human ideals of truth, tolerance, justice, freedom and respect for the rights of the individual personality. (...) To this end, the henceforward established independence of the German broadcasting sector must be sustained."[306]

The document further pointed out that an independent German broadcasting sector must be non-partisan and "plays neither directly nor indirectly chessmen of government, nor instrument of a particular group or personality". It would instead "only serve the whole people in a free, equal, open and fearless way". Ten general principles of programmes for broadcasters and for the future broadcasting institutions, ranging from the representation of the widest variety of opinions to measures that guaranteed the objectivity of the comments and news, were stated for the sake of the independence of broadcasters. These principles were later called "The Ten Commandments" of the American broadcasting policy (die "Zehn Gebote"), which were regarded as the initial legal framework for post-war German broadcasting statues.[307]

In the opinion of the US military government, an independent broadcasting sector must not be a state-controlled broadcasting on the grounds of the negative experience of the Nazi-controlled broadcasting during the war. This became another principle of German broadcasting, the principle of *distant from the state (staatsfern)*. British occupation power had the similar opinion on the independence of broadcasting. Hugh Greene, the leader of the BBC German Department since 1940 and the crucial figure of the post-war broadcasting policy of British Military government, fought "against German state institutions, against parties, and against 'what they called the democratic control of broadcasting'"[308]. The conception of the Allies was therefore to establish the broadcasting which was as independent as possible from the government and from the influence of the parties. It should be organised as a public organisation as "the service of the general public for the general public"[309].

---

306 Hans Bausch. *Rundfunkpolitik nach 1945 (Erster Teil: 1945-1962)*. München: dtv, 1980. p. 72.
307 Ibid. pp. 72-77.
308 Ibid, pp. 54-55.
309 Bausch.

4.4. Theoretical development of public service broadcasting: the case of West Germany

This conception deviated greatly from the German perception of broadcasting, by which broadcasting was understood by German politicians as governmental organisation since the Weimarian time, or more exactly, as the properties (including the radio transmitters, studios and the licence fees) and competence of the Ministry of Post. Even some most sincere German democrats, according to the American military governor Lucius D. Clay, were "blind for the importance of the free press and free broadcasting"[310]. Therefore, in the first post-war years of reconstructing broadcasting, the Ministry of Post fought hardly for its previous rights on broadcasting. The Allies, meanwhile, insisted that the principle of *distant from the state* was a fundamental policy (foremost of the US military government), and broadcasting must be separated from the Post ("Trennung von Rundfunk und Post"). In the end, the functions of the German Ministry of Post in the US occupation zones were restricted to: a) collection of licence fees by order of the Länder-governments as the central toll gate; b) on-standby service for the cable which was necessary for the operation of broadcasting; c) maintenance service of fault clearance in broadcasting.[311] Due to the establishment of a Combined Economic Area in 1947 by the British and the US occupation zones (the "Bizone"), both the British and the US Military governments kept pace with each other in many issues of policy making. So, similar restrictions to the functions of the Ministry of Post also happened in the British occupation zone[312]. The French military government also followed similar broadcasting policies in its occupation zone. Shortly before the establishment of West Germany in 1949, the Ministry of Post has lost the control over many areas of competence in the sector of broadcasting, including its properties of radio transmitters and studios, and its discretion of freely allocating licence fees. In this way, the intervention of the state in broadcasting was to a large extent eliminated under the supervision of the Allies.

Concerning the concrete organisation of the independent broadcasting institutions, the Americans chose the BBC model of public corporation as the organisational form of independent broadcasting[313]. The achievement of establishing independent broadcasting in American occupation zones was treasured by American expert Clark Foremen as "the real triumph of democracy" in Germany.[314]

The idea of broadcasting freedom was eventually endorsed by the West German Basic Law of 1949 as one of the highest values of German broadcasting.

---

310 Ibid. p. 23.
311 Ibid. p. 33.
312 Ibid, p. 37.
313 This will be discussed in length in the next section of "the organisational form of the public service broadcasting" on page 149.
314 Bausch, p. 247.

4.4.2. Broadcasting as a cultural matter

As early as in the time of the Weimar Republic of the 1920s, broadcasting has been regarded as a cultural matter which was within the competence of the Länder in cultural matters (die Kulturhoheit).[315] In the post-war period, however, there existed at times conflicts between the Bund and the Länder over the competence in broadcasting since there lacked a clear consensus between the two sides. This matter was not clarified and consolidated until 1961 in the form of the first broadcasting ruling by the Federal Constitutional Court.

Although the reconstruction of broadcasting was mainly organised by the Allies in their respective occupation zones after 1945, German politicians also played an active role in the whole process. The main claim of German politician to broadcasting was to return to the pre-war Weimar traditions, by which the first principles of German broadcasting were set in the 1920s. Among others, these principles included:
- the Post Office of the Reich possessed the competence of technical infrastructures and equipments of broadcasting (die Funkhoheit), for whose use must be paid by programme producers. This did not include studio equipments;
- broadcasting should be non-partisan; therefore the cultural side of broadcasting was in the foreground. Broadcasting served no private interests but the generality as "public responsibility";
- the Länder (Federal States) possessed autonomy in cultural matters, by which the control of broadcasting programmes was included;
- the landscape of German broadcasting was a regional one for technical reason instead of in virtue of federalism;
- there was a clear tendency towards centralisation in terms of 1) the supervision of programmes, for only materials offered by the news agency "DRADAG" were allowed to be used in news service. The DRADAG was mainly controlled by the Ministry of the Interior; and of 2) the organisation of broadcasting companies under company law. The individual broadcasters must cede 51% of their company share to the RRG, which was an umbrella company controlled mainly by the Post Office of the Reich;
- a parallel model of supervision committees: one committee was responsible for the news and comments service in connection with politics. This committee was composed of three members, one from the Reich and two other from the Länder. Another committee was a cultural advisory committee, which

---

315 Compare p. 114.

4.4. Theoretical development of public service broadcasting: the case of West Germany

should influence the arrangement of programmes in the fields of arts, science, and the education of the people;
- broadcasting was financed through the licence fee paid by individual listeners as well as advertising.[316]

Based on these principles, German politicians suggested reconstructing broadcasting with following rules: "the Post Office takes charge of the technical operation of broadcasting; the transmission stations return to the hands of the Reich; the state ministry takes the political responsibility, and the director or directorate for the arrangement of programme will be set up under a centralised control (but no Ministry of Propaganda)"[317]. The Americans refused these suggestions on account of the tendency of state-controlled broadcasting. Although Americans established several Land-based public law broadcasters according to their preference for federalism, Britons and Frenches established contrariwise centralised broadcasters in their respective occupation zones. After the foundation of West Germany in 1949, the conflict between the Bund (the federal government) and the Länder (the federal states) over the competence of broadcasting resurfaced, especially after Germany obtained the full sovereignty from the Allies with the German Treaty (der Deutschlandvertrag) in 1955, for the Allies still had a greater influence on broadcasting institutions than the Bund before the Germany Treaty. The main conflict was several (unsuccessful) attempts of the Bund to establish national broadcasting institutions which were envisioned to be under direct control of the Bund in the 1950s.

This conflict between the Bund and the Länder in broadcasting sector was finally resolved by the first broadcasting ruling of the Federal Constitutional Court, the Ruling of Television, in 1961. The Court clarified the competence in broadcasting according to Article 5, Article 30, and Article 73 No. 7 of the West German Basic Law, and declared that the Bund had competence only in transmission technology of broadcasting, while the other aspects of broadcasting were accordingly a matter of the Länder, including programme, organisation of broadcasting and studio technology.[318]

The Ruling of Television 1961 originated from the practice of steering public and social development in West Germany by the judges of the Federal Constitutional Court outside political approach, especially when political approach defected. This first broadcasting ruling was regarded as "the Magna Charta of broadcasting" in the history of German broadcasting because of its far-reaching influence on the future development of German broadcasting. Besides its imme-

---

316 Hesse. pp. 1-5.
317 Stuiber, p. 193.
318 Stuiber, pp. 425-29. Other contents on the first broadcasting ruling, see also Bausch, pp. 430-38; Hesse, pp. 16-17.

diate achievement of resolving the long-time existing conflict between the Bund and the Länder over the competence in broadcasting through this particular case, the much more profound significance of the first broadcasting ruling lied in achieving consensus about broadcasting among all relevant groups in multi-faceted aspects. One significant point was that the Court reiterated the principle of *distant from the state (staatsfern)*. The Court pointed out that, in the current special situation ("Sondersituation") of insufficient spectrums, the public law broadcasters were suitable institutions for realizing the broadcasting freedom which was guaranteed by Article 5 of the German Basic Law. This not only provisionally assured the oligopolistic status of the regional public law broadcasters in a fairly long period of three decades (till the beginning of the 1980s), but also led the full withdrawal of the Bund from the broadcasting policy making and a moderate manner of the Bund in other areas of culture policy as well.[319]

Another significant point was to confirm the relationship between broadcasting and culture. As Stuiber points out, to allocate all aspects – but transmission technology – of the competence in broadcasting to the Länder was to be understood as the extension of the competence of the Länder in cultural matters ("Ausfluß der Kulturhoheit der Länder").[320] This understanding has indirectly defined the property of broadcasting as a cultural matter. It was a decisive point for the future broadcasting policy making in Germany. Since then, the development and policy making of broadcasting largely happened within the realm of culture. It also significantly differentiated German understanding of broadcasting from, for instance, the American understanding of broadcasting as product to be consumed and sold, and from the understanding of broadcasting in communist countries as propaganda instruments of the state. This marked a grand distinction in the standpoint on broadcasting in respective broadcasting systems.

4.4.3. The organisational form of the public service broadcasting

The Allies chose the BBC model of the public service broadcasting as the organisational form of the broadcasting institutions in their respective occupation zones in Germany. This was an interesting decision when the organisational forms of the broadcasting system in these three countries were paid closer attention to, in that they adopted three typical broadcasting systems of the world respectively: the public service broadcasting system in Britain, the purely commercial broadcasting system in the USA, and the governmental broadcasting system in France. The choice of public service broadcasting for post-war Germany did

---

319 Bausch, p. 429.
320 Stuiber, p. 427.

4.4. Theoretical development of public service broadcasting: the case of West Germany

not happen by chance. All the three occupation powers had their own considerations on this issue.

Although the public service broadcasting or rather the BBC model originated from Britain, British military government did prudentially think over the purposes that the broadcasting system should serve in post-war Germany. This, according to the crucial figure of broadcasting policy in the British zone of Allied occupied Germany Hugh Carlton Greene[321], was "to integrate (broadcasting) with the political life in post-war Germany, to deepen and to further support the traditions of freedom and independence which have been already achieved."[322] However, Britons had two worries in achieving their purposes. First, they did not want to impose these ideas on German through regulations. The most ideal result was that Germans would like to accept the ideas as their own. The second worry of Britons was the continuity of British broadcasting policy after the handover of broadcasting institutions to Germans. The Chef of the "Public Relations/Information Services Division" of the British military government, Major General Sir Alex Bishop, clearly stated that "we do not want to leave a government controlled machine, nor do we want commercial broadcasting".[323] Therefore, the BBC model of public service broadcasting became an obvious alternative for Britons.

Under the leading of Hugh Carlton Greene, a centralised public service broadcaster of BBC pattern – the Nordwestdeuscher Rundfunk (NWDR, the Northwest German Broadcasting Corporation) – was established as an institution of public law in British occupation zone. During the process of organising the NWDR with a legal basis, Greene tried to speak as wide as possibly to German opinion groups: governments of the Länder, the Zonal Advisory Council (Zonenbeirat[324]), the representatives of the parties, the churches, the cultural organisations, the trade unions, the employers, etc. In the end, the organisation of NWDR and the related statutes were rather a compromise of British ideas of public service broadcasting to German mentality and history. Greene struggled hard for independent broadcasting against the state and political influence on broadcasting, "which is called 'the democratic control of broadcasting by them (the Ger-

---

[321] Hugh Carlton was Head of BBC German Service since 1940. After the war, he became the organiser of NWDR under the title of Chief Controller and first General Director of the NWDR from 1946-1948. Greene was regarded as the person who nearly alone influenced the broadcasting policy in the British occupation zone.

[322] Hugh Carlton Greene, cited by Stuiber, p. 188.

[323] Bausch, p. 23.

[324] Der Zonenbeirat was an advisory German organ in the British occupation zone which was established under the arrangement of the British military government in 1946. It consisted of representatives from the governments of the Länder, the trade unions, the parties, and the trade associations and was appointed by the British military government. See http://de.wikipedia.org/wiki/Zonenbeirat.

mans)'"[325], also part of the Weimarian traditions of German broadcasting. Through intricate negotiations with his German colleagues, Greene did succeed in establishing a broadcaster of the BBC pattern under the Ordinance No. 118 of British military government on 1st January 1948. However, Greene did not completely fulfil his goals for the organs of the NWDR – the main committee (Hauptausschuss) and the administrative board (Verwaltungrat) – consisted of a majority of political party members, whilst the Board of Governors of the BBC comprised independent personalities by English convention. Nevertheless, Greene's effort contributed to the establishment of a tradition of independent broadcasting in Germany, which is still alive till today. Or perhaps the label of "public service broadcasting" alone has already exerted far-reaching influence on the theoretical development, legislation and practice of German broadcasting.

The US military government, on the contrary, did not have any concrete concept for the organisation of broadcasters in its occupation zones. What the US military government clearly adhered to was that the new German broadcasting system must be distant from the state and decentralised. With these ends in view, the US military government considered several possible organisational forms of broadcasting. State-controlled broadcasting was out of the question. But it was also impractical to copy the US form of the purely commercial broadcasting in Germany on technical and economic grounds. Other than the fact that the resources of spectrum were fairly abundant in the US, there were no enough free airwaves available for private use in the densely populated Continental Europe. And the poor economic situation of post-war Germany was also unfavourable for a purely commercial broadcasting. Therefore, the US military government decided to establish several decentralised, independent public law broadcasters according to the BBC model to safeguard freedom of broadcast from state control.

During the drafting of broadcasting law in individual Länder of the US occupation zones, which organisational form of public law broadcasting should be chosen was also a focus in the related discussions: the organisational form of public law corporation (Körperschaft des öffentlichen Rechts), or of public law institution (Anstalt des öffentlichen Rechts)?[326] In German legal system, both these two organisational forms under public law are a form of self-administrated, special purpose fund. The difference is that the public law corporation has members, while the public law institution instead has users. The last draft of Hessian broadcasting law decided for the organisational form of public law institution (Anstalt) on the grounds that an institution (eine Anstalt) "may be more suitable than a number of public law and private law organisations in their grouping into a corporation (eine Körperschaft)", when the public purpose that broadcasting

---

325 Bausch, p. 55.
326 See Bausch, pp. 82-85.

4.4. Theoretical development of public service broadcasting: the case of West Germany

served was taken into consideration.[327] The concrete arrangements of the institution included:

a) the legal status of the institution was a public law institution with the right of self-administration;
b) the institution had normally three governing bodies[328], namely the broadcasting council (Rundfunkrat), the administrative council (Verwaltungsrat) and the director general (Intendant). As the representative organ of the general public and the highest decision-making body, the broadcasting council was set up in accord with the principle of pluralism and consisted of members from the relevant political and cultural groups such as political parties, churches, universities, trade unions, associations of employers, artistic and cultural organisations, but no single group should obtain dominance over others. The administrative council had the function of supervision in order to keep broadcasting free from the influence of government, as well as checking the personnel and financial issues of the institution. The director, voted by the broadcasting council, took the responsibility for programming and represented the institution towards the outside world;
c) the programming should follow the principles in "The Ten Commandments", such as fair balance, non-partisan, objectivity and etc;
d) the institution would be financed predominantly through license fees (Rundfunkgebühr[329]) in order to guarantee the financial independence of broadcasting from state influence. The license fees should be exclusively spent for the purpose of broadcasting.

On the whole, the organisational form of the public law institution and its concrete arrangements stated in the Hessian Broadcasting Law met the conditions of

---

327 Ibid, p. 85.
328 After the dissolution of the NWDR in 1955, the newly established NDR (Norddeutscher Rundfunk, the North German Broadcasting) and WDR (Westdeutscher Rundfunk, the West German Broadcasting) had both an extra Programmbeirat (Advisory Council of Programme) besides three normal governing bodies. This was because the Rundfunkrat of the both broadcasting institutions were originally established according to a parliamentary model, which largely mirrored the proportional representation of the parties in the Landtage (Parliaments of the Länder). This extra Programmbeirat therefore took over the representation of the socially relevant groups. See Stuiber, p. 210.
329 It is noteworthy that German drafters of broadcasting law were ordered by the US military government to give "broadcasting fee" ("Rundfunkgebühr") a new expression through legislative means. The "broadcasting fee", according to an instruction of the US military government on 21 November 1947, should "be charged for a service, and not for the possession of an electrical appliance, like it is called in the law on telecommunication facilities in the year of 1928." See Bausch, p. 75. This indicates an important shift in the understanding of the "broadcasting fee" from the technological aspect (broadcasting as the possession of an electrical appliance in the traditional licence fee) to the journalistic and social aspects of broadcasting (broadcasting as a service for the users in the new expression of broadcasting fee).

the US military government in safeguarding free broadcasting and a clear separation between broadcasting and the Post. Under the support of the US military government, the Hessian broadcasting law became later a model for other Länder in the US occupation zones, so the organisation of broadcasting institutions in the US occupation zones was broadly in a similar way. In the French occupation zones, a public law institution similar to those in the American occupation zones, the Südwestfunk (SWF, the Southwest Radio), was established through an ordinance of French military government in October 1948.

Shortly before the establishment of West Germany in 1949, West German broadcasting system had completed its first stage of reconstruction from state-controlled, propagandistic broadcasting of the Nazi period to independent public law broadcasting under the supervision of the Allies. As the work of reconstruction during this period was done in individual occupation zones of Britain, the US and France, the coordination of the newly established public law institutions and further integration of these individual institutions within a national framework were therefore conducted after the establishment of West Germany in 1949. In the second phase of the sovereign development of broadcasting system since then and especially after its coming into effect of the German Treaty in 1955 which claimed the full sovereignty of West Germany, *juridification (Verrechtlichung)* of the problems in broadcasting sector became typical for the development of West German broadcasting system.[330]

The juridification of the problems in broadcasting sector was so comprehensive that many aspects of West German broadcasting system were involved. The first important aspect of the juridification in broadcasting sector was the fundamental principles of broadcasting. Some most fundamental principles concerning problems in broadcasting sector were normalised by the constitution, namely the Basic Law (Grundgesetz) of West Germany, which was regarded as the highest norms of the country. One central principle was the freedom of individual and public communication as a whole which was guaranteed in Article 5 of the West German Basic Law of 1949. The content of Article 5 of the West German Basic Law was:

Article 5 (Freedom of opinion and Freedom of the press; Freedom of art and science)

(1) Everyone has the right freely to express and to disseminate his opinion by speech, writing and pictures and freely to inform himself from generally accessible sources. Freedom of the press and freedom of reporting by radio and motion pictures are guaranteed. There shall be no censorship.

---

330 Stuiber, p. 19.

4.4. Theoretical development of public service broadcasting: the case of West Germany

(2) These rights are limited by the provisions of the general laws, the provisions of law for the protection of youth and by the right to inviolability of personal honour.

(3) Art and Science, research and teaching are free. Freedom of teaching dose not absolve from loyalty to the constitution.[331]

In the frame of freedom of opinion and freedom of the press normalised by Article 5 of the West German Basic Law, broadcasting as a means of mass media serves as an indispensable element for the generation of individual and public opinions during the overall process of communication. The freedom of broadcasting was accordingly normalised and guaranteed by Article 5 Section 1 Sentence 2 of the West German Basic Law, which became later the most important constitutional basis for the interpretation of the function and role of broadcasting in the rulings made by the Federal Constitutional Court (Bundesverfassungsgericht).

Another essential part of principles normalised by the West German Basic Law was the competence in the broadcasting sector. Article 30 of the West German Basic Law was of particular importance for the allocation of competence in the broadcasting sector between the Bund and the Länder, by which broadcasting fell within the competence of the Länder as part of cultural affairs. Furthermore, the question of competence in the broadcasting sector involved a number of other problems such as the relationship between broadcasting and telecommunications, overseas broadcasting services, etc. These were to be normalised in respective articles of the West German Basic Law, for instance Article 70 ff. of the West German Basic Law concerning the legislation of the Bund and Article 87 f of the West German Basic Law concerning the competence of the Bund, and Article 32 of the West German Basic Law concerning the foreign relationships.

The second important aspect of the juridification in broadcasting sector was that many important issues in the broadcasting sector were regulated through legislative means. The Land-based public law broadcasting institutions were set up under respective broadcasting laws of the Länder. As institutions of public law, these Land-based broadcasters were obliged by law to carry out extensive public tasks, whilst they were also guaranteed the right of self-administration by law as well. Moreover, the trans-regional cooperation and coordination between the Länder on broadcasting issues or regulations of broadcasting issues at national level were usually achieved through treaties between the Länder (Staatsverträge). The treaties between the Länder would become binding Land law, when they were ratified by the respective Land parliament through acts of sanctioning or constitutional resolutions of sanctioning. These treaties between the Länder con-

---

331 See http://www.constitution.org/cons/germany.txt, visited on October 26, 2010.

Chapter 4 The Purely Public Service Broadcasting System

cerned numerous issues in the broadcasting sector, ranging from the founding of the ZDF (Zweites Deutsches Fernsehen, Second German Television) jointly by all the Länder in 1961, the programme cooperation and coordination among Länder members of the ARD[332], and the regulation of the national radio DeutshclandRadio, to the financial and technological issues of broadcasting such as the collection, amount and use of the license fees (Rundfunkgebühren), financial balance (Finanzausgleich) and the view data system (Bildschirmtext) and so on.[333]

The third important aspect of the juridification in broadcasting sector was the significant role that the rulings of the Federal Constitutional Court (Bundesverfassungsgericht) played for the theoretical and institutional developments of the West German broadcasting system. Although Article 5 Section 1 Sentence 2 of the West German Basic Law has literally guaranteed "the freedom of reporting by radio and motion pictures" at the constitutional level, it was the interpretations of the Federal Constitutional Court through rulings that attempted to make a clear definition of "the freedom of broadcasting" (Rundfunkfreiheit) and to further clarify the principles relevant to the guarantee of the freedom of broadcasting in practice. This was of special significance in regulating the broadcasting sector especially when the problems on broadcasting had a tendency of increasing complexity along with the advancements of technology and economy. It has not only helped in resolving, or more important, in preventing political conflicts regarding the broadcasting order such as the Bund-Länder Conflict in the first ruling on broadcasting in 1961, but also further concretising the frameworks of broadcasting system by means of demanding the legislature to detail the structure of broadcasting order by statute.

Before the change of West German broadcasting system from the purely public law broadcasting system into the dual broadcasting system in 1983, there were three rulings on broadcasting made by the Federal Constitutional Court. The first and second rulings on broadcasting, i.e. Ruling of Television (Fernseh-Urteil) in 1961and Ruling of Value Added Tax (Mehrwertsteuer-Urteil) in 1971,

---

332 The full name of ARD is Arbeitsgemeinschaft der öffentlich-rechtlichen Rundfunkanstalten der Bundesrepublik Deutschland, which means the "Consortium of public-law broadcasting institutions of the Federal Republic of Germany". It is a joint organisation of Germany's Länder public law broadcasting institutions and was founded in 1950 to represent the common interest of the decentralised Land-based broadcasters at national and international levels. It also offers a full-programme television channel for the national audience.

333 The treaties between the Länder were originally a group of individual treaties with specific themes which were signed during the development of West German broadcasting over the decades. At the reunification of Germany in 1991, these individual treaties between the Länder were replaced by one collective treaty – the "Staatsvertrag über den Rundfunk im vereinten Deutschland vom 31. August 1991" (Treaty between the Länder over the broadcasting in the reunified Germany from August 31 1991). Stuiber, p. 329 ff.

4.4. Theoretical development of public service broadcasting: the case of West Germany

were regarded as two important milestones for the broadcasting freedom in West Germany[334]. As discussed earlier, the first ruling on broadcasting – the Ruling of Television – has for the first time used the term of "freedom of broadcasting", which was convenient for the future discussions among the constitutional jurists when they needed such a term analogous to the freedom of press (Pressfreit). In fact, the "freedom of broadcasting" was and kept as the core in the future rulings on broadcasting made by the Federal Constitutional Court. To guarantee the freedom of broadcasting has been the highest norm for the theoretical developments and practices in German broadcasting sector. With this end in view, the first and second rulings on broadcasting made by the Federal Constitutional Court had developed following important principles on broadcasting:

The first ruling on broadcasting: *Ruling of Television (1961)*
- the principle of distant from the state (Staatfernheit).
- as one of the indispensable means of modern communication which influence the formation of the public opinion, broadcasting is more than a "medium" of the formation of the public opinion; it is an eminent "factor" of the formation of the public opinion. The involvement in the formation of the public opinion limits itself by no means to news reporting, political commentary, serial programmes on political problems of the current, the past and the future; the formation of the public opinion also happens in radio dramas, musical performance, transmission of cabarets, until into the scenic designs of a performance.
- the arrangement of broadcasting is the legislative competence of the Länder (Article 30 of the West German Basic Law).
- the competence of the Bund is exclusively for the transmission technology, not for the content (Article 73 No. 7 of the West German Basic Law).[335]

The second ruling on broadcasting: *Ruling of Value Added Tax (1971)*
- broadcasting institutions assume public responsibility, undertake the tasks of the public administration and fulfil an integrated function for the whole state. Their activity is therefore not "commercial or professional" ("gewerblich oder beruflich") in the sense of tax law.

---

334 Soon after the second ruling on broadcasting by the Federal Constitutional Court, the Federal Administrative Court made a ruling on broadcasting in 1971. This is the third ruling on broadcasting with constitutional significance for the organisation of broadcasting and the protection of the freedom of broadcasting. It was also the first time for the jurists to apply the general principles publicised in the Ruling of Television and the Ruling of Value Added Tax in an important practical case. See Bausch, pp. 443-46.

335 The ruling of the Federal Constitutional Court on February 28, 1961, BVerfGE 12, 205-64. See http://www.servat.unibe.ch/dfr/bv 012205.html, last visited in November 2010.

Chapter 4 The Purely Public Service Broadcasting System

– broadcasting is not allowed to be left to the free play of the forces, but is a matter of the general public (Sache der Allgemeinheit).[336]

The public law broadcasting system was greatly consolidated in West Germany along with the process of juridification in broadcasting sector. Especially the rulings of the Federal Constitutional Court enormously helped in resolving existed conflicts as well as preventing potential conflicts between socially relevant forces, among others the political parties, the economic forces and the Press. The pattern of public law broadcasting as a system and the monopoly of the Land-based public law broadcasting institutions were gradually accepted as a general consensus in West German broadcasting sector under the special technical conditions of the time – the scarcity of frequencies. The ensuing developments of broadcasting in the 1960s and the 1970s were thereafter forwarded within such a consensus in favour of public law broadcasting. In 1963, the second television programme in West Germany – Zweites Deutsches Fernsehen (ZDF, Second German Television) – was launched as part of the indirect consequences of the Ruling of Television two years before. Different from the federally organised ARD broadcasting institutions, ZDF was a centrally organised public law institution serving the whole West Germany. It was established with the participation of all Länder through a state treaty of ZDF (ZDF-Staatsvertrag) and the content of the ZDF programme should be contrasted with the programmes provided by the ARD institutions. ZDF was also financed by the license fee by sharing this financial source with the ARD institutions in the proportion 30:70.[337] Since 1964, the Land-based public law broadcasting institutions further expanded themselves with the establishment of the so-called "third television programme"[338], which should provide programmes with more specifically regional aspects in contrast to the nation-wide programmes provided by the First Programme (ARD) and ZDF. At the starting time, all of these "third television programme(s)" emphasized their main concern on information and formation of public opinion, which was a key characteristic of the public law broadcasting system. Later the "third television programme" gradually developed from education-focused programmes to full programmes with more mass-appealing contents, while the regional aspects still well maintained.[339]

---

336 The ruling of the Federal Constitutional Court on July 27, 1971, BVerfGE 31, 314-57. See http://www.servat.unibe.ch/dfr/bv 031314.html, last visited in November 2010.
337 Stuiber, pp. 225-27.
338 For financial reason or for reasons of cultural identity, not every Land-based public law broadcasting institution produced its own third television programme. Some broadcasting institutions of the Länder provided a joint programme together. "N3" was provided jointly by Norddeutscher Rundfunk (NDR), Radio Bremen (RB), and Sender Freies Berlin (SFB); "Südwest 3" was provided jointly by Saarländischer Rundfunk (SR), Südwestfunk (SWF), and Süddeutscher Rundfunk (SDR). See Stuiber, p. 229.
339 Stuiber, pp. 228-30.

Chapter 5
The Dual Broadcasting System in Britain and Germany

The dual broadcasting system, featured with the coexistence of public service broadcasting and private broadcasting, first emerged in Britain in 1954. Nevertheless, it has not been adopted by the majority of the European countries until three decades later, namely since the 1980s.[340] In most European countries, the public service broadcasting and its similar variants enjoyed a status of monopoly throughout a relatively long period of nearly three decades. The reasons for the monopoly of the public service broadcasting lied largely in the post-war social political consensus in Europe on the democratic and cultural role of broadcasting in a modern democratic society, and in the special technical situation of scarce spectrums from the 1940s till the 1980s as well. Triggered by the advancement of transmission technologies such as cable and satellite since the 1960s, the wishes from the private sector for participation in broadcasting became imperative. During the process of introducing the private broadcasting which led to the collapse of the monopoly of the public service broadcasting, the function and role of broadcasting were again the focus of rethink of broadcasting policy among the policy makers. This time, market and competition have been the buzzwords in the related discussions. The existing ideas on broadcasting have been challenged and revised in the new context of related discussions, while the discrepancies in the understandings of broadcasting between the public and the private "camps" were sometimes so big that the post-war consensus was seriously under threat. This did not only happened in the countries which were still lying in the process of establishing the dual broadcasting system like West Germany, but also happened in Britain during the 1980s, where the public service broadcaster – the BBC – and the private broadcasters – ITV – have achieved a peaceful state of coexistence in the past three decades.

Besides the divergence of ideas, policy makers and practitioners were also confronting with problems arising in practice, such as the competitive relationship between the public broadcaster(s) and the private broadcasters, the increasing demand for regulations aroused by the active business activities in private

---

340 The co-existence of the public service broadcasting and commercial broadcasting started in Britain in 1954, in Italy 1972/1974, in West Germany in 1984, in France in 1985, in Belgium (French community) in 1987 and (Flemish Community) in 1989, in Denmark in 1988, in Greece, Holland and Spain in 1989, in Ireland in 1990, in Luxemburg in 1991, in Portugal and Sweden in 1992, in Finland in 1985/1993, and in Austria in 1995/1997/2001. See http://wapedia.mobi/de/Duales_Rundfunksystem. Last visited in January 2011.

broadcasting sector like concentration of ownership or media convergence, new challenges to the dual broadcasting system triggered by the latest social and technological development such as European integration, globalisation and digitalisation, etc.

Therefore, the analysis on the dual broadcasting system in this section is focusing on the ideas and practices in the dual broadcasting system, by which there appeared to exist more conflict of ideas and more uncertainty in practice than in the previous period of the purely public service broadcasting system. This has, in turn, showed the richness and complexities of the fundamental values of the dual broadcasting system which distinguished it from other broadcasting systems. For example, the dual broadcasting system constantly refers to the American purely commercial broadcasting system during its development. Nevertheless, it remains somehow quite critical (the degree varies in Britain and Germany) of American model of broadcasting at the same time. These criticisms of American purely commercial system by the dual broadcasting system, either from the ideological perspective of the British decision makers before the 1980s, or from the constitutional perspective of the German Federal Constitutional Court, are highly insightful for a subtle cognition of the ills of the purely commercial broadcasting.

Two other concerns of this chapter include some of the most often raised questions related to the dual broadcasting system. One concern is whether the dual broadcasting system, in particular its public service sector, has become obsolete in the era of Internet. Another topic involves the extensive imitation of the dual broadcasting system by many Central and Eastern European countries (CEECs) after the fall of Communism in 1989. Yet it proved largely a failure a decade later. A host of scholars try to find out the reasons for the failure, whilst the historical and cultural legacies of the old institutions or of a wider context of culture are some of the frequently mentioned reasons. A counter-argument will be made here with the relative success in Eastern Asia (Japan and Korea) in order to point out that the incomplete process of democratisation, rather than cultural and historical factors alike, is the real reason for the failure of establishing a democratic broadcasting system in the CEECs.

5.1. Dual broadcasting system: the advent of the market logic and its impact

Broadcasting in public service system was once free, if not totally, from the participation of market forces and the impact of market logic.[341] With the introduction of commercial television in Britain in the 1950s and private broadcasting in Germany in the 1980s, market forces and market logic entered the sector of broadcasting. This has, inevitably, brought an enormous impact on the understanding of broadcasting and market. Nevertheless, the impact of market forces and market logic on British broadcasting was significantly different in the first years from 1950s to 1980s and the years from 1980s onwards. This will be respectively analysed here.

5.1.1. The first encounter with the market logic in Britain: from the 1950s to the 1970s

In order to gain access to the television industry, the market forces and their supporters first used the concept of "competition" to support their legitimacy in the television industry at the beginning of the 1950s in Britain. The campaign for commercial television set the goal to terminate the monopoly of the public service broadcaster, the BBC, which had enjoyed this privilege since its establishment in the 1920s.

Historically, the BBC obtained its status of monopoly at its forming stage in the 1920s for various grounds. The Post Office merely deemed it administratively convenient to deal with only one licensed broadcasting service than several. Reith, the founder of the BBC, held the viewpoint that the monopoly of broadcasting was the essential means to guarantee the BBC's ability to develop itself as a public service in the national interest. According to Reith, the monopoly was

---

341 Cf. the earlier discussion on "broadcasting and market" in the era of public service broadcasting on pp. 122 ff. The British public service broadcasting system is to be theoretically totally free from the impact from the market – no advertising and no sponsorship are allowed to be broadcast on public service broadcasting. Unlike in Britain, there was no strict ban on broadcasting advertising in Germany in the public law broadcasting system. Some German public law broadcasters have begun to broadcast radio advertisements since 1948 and television commercials since 1956. The discussions on television advertising in Britain at the beginning of the 1950s have also played a part in the acceptance of partial advertising financing for broadcasting in Germany. Nevertheless, advertising revenue just played a complementary role for the broadcasting financing (less than 10% of the total revenue) on the grounds of maintaining a friendly relationship between the Press and broadcasting, by which the public law broadcasters were voluntarily bound to the weekday limit of advertising time to 20 minutes before 8 p.m. and broadcast no local advertisement. See Bausch, *Rundfunkpolitik nach 1945 (Zweiter Teil: 1963-1980)*. München: dtv, 1980. pp 531-66.

not only technically efficient and economical in organising a universally available broadcasting service for the whole nation in the public interest, it was also ethnically important to maintain homogeneous policy and standards throughout the country.[342] Competition, on the contrary, was not favoured by "the large number of important people and a large number of the interested public" because the consumers could only buy what was offered in a free market, but not necessarily the most advantageous. The industrial competition could be inefficient in comparison with a centralised control based on the principle of justice.[343] The first experience of American commercial broadcasting system in the 1920s, described as "chaotic" by some British high officials, also did not give the British policy makers any positive impression. The BBC was thereafter granted the status of monopoly as a public service broadcaster for the British nation until the end of the 1940s. Market forces and market mechanism, including the financial means of advertising and sponsoring, were entirely excluded from participation in arranging and organising broadcasting in the British public service broadcasting system.

However, the attitudes towards "monopoly" and "competition" changed after the Second World War. The first post-war committee of inquiry into broadcasting – the Beveridge Committee (1950) – made the question of monopoly in its central concern. Beveridge criticised the four scandals of monopoly: bureaucracy, complacency, favouritism and inefficiency. Although the report recommended a renewal of the BBC's licence, it was just because the alternative, American-style commercial television, seemed far worse.[344]

The advocates of commercial television, largely supported by the industrial interests of advertising and entertainment, took advantage of these criticisms in the campaign for commercial television and criticised the monopolistic public service broadcaster, the BBC, for being expensive, inefficient, ridden with oversized crews and oversized administration, paternalistic, self-righteous and arrogant, and as well as elitist and metropolitan, vulnerable to political pressure, etc. They further claimed that competition instead could counteract the shortcomings of the monopoly. From the point of view of the post-war liberals, any monopoly of broadcasting was inevitably the negation of freedom, no matter how efficient it ran. The democratic values of diversity and choice, which were believed to be promoted by a competitive broadcasting system, gained wide currency in the post-war British society.[345]

---

342 Scannell, pp. 48-49.
343 Curran and Seaton (2003), p. 112.
344 Ibid, p. 160.
345 Cricell, p. 83.

5.1. Dual broadcasting system: the advent of the market logic and its impact

Although it remained questionable that competition must not necessarily be commercial or a natural virtue of the free market, the market forces eventually achieved their goal of entering the sector of television largely thanks to the political struggle between the Conservative and the Labour.[346] However, this was less than a triumph of the market logic in broadcasting. Instead, as Crisell states, the commercial television was set up as an extension of the public service concept.[347] Not only was the commercial television supervised by a BBC-like public body, the Independent Television Authority (ITA)[348], there were also many fairly cautious arrangements and regulations on commercial television which aimed to "safeguard this medium of information and entertainment from the risk of abuse or lowering of standards"[349]. In other words, the British commercial television carried the same motto of the BBC as to inform, educate and entertain. The programmes made by ITV contractor companies had to meet the same high standards as the BBC did. In order to avoid the potential negative influence of commercial advertising on programme, the ITA set very strict separation of advertising from programme content and controlled the nature, quality and total length of advertising. Programme sponsorship was forbidden.[350] In some respect, the commercial television was more limited than the BBC. For example, the ITA was not allowed to originate any political broadcasts apart from relaying in their entirety of the BBC political broadcasts. Programme contractors were also not allowed to present religious or fund-raising broadcasts without prior permission from the Authority.[351] It came out that the first encounter of broadcasting with the market forces resulted in an integration of market mechanism – advertising funding – with the existed public service values. The ITA and its contractor companies were de facto none other than public service broadcasters, except for being financed by advertising revenue. They were what Sepstrup refers to as "commercial public broadcasting".

Although the commercial television in Britain was hardly revolutionary, the era of competition did come. Not only was the competition between the BBC and ITV quickly started as expected, the internal competition within the different

---

346 For details see my analysis in the "domestic criticism and change of the PSB" (Section 4.3.1), pp. 132 ff.
347 Crisell. p. 90.
348 According to the Television Act 1954, the British commercial television, Independent Television (ITV), was comprised of the authority, the ITA, and its contractors. The ITA owned and operated the television transmitters, but did not make programmes and did not sell airtime. The contractors were various programme-making companies on regional basis. The programme-making companies were financed by advertising revenue and had to support the ITA through a levy raised on their revenue. See Crisell, pp. 90-91.
349 The white paper on broadcasting policy 1952. Cited by Paulu, p. 48.
350 Crisell, pp. 90-91.
351 Paulu, p. 54.

Chapter 5 The Dual Broadcasting System in Britain and Germany

sections of the BBC as well as the competition between ITV companies also became increasingly intensive.[352] The outcome of the competition in the first years was fairly positive and fruitful. It promoted technological developments in television throughout the 1950s and led to an enormous flowering of talent and inventiveness in programme-making in the 1960s. ITV made great contribution in developing a format for the television news as well as developing television journalism in a new direction. Different from the tedious BBC news bulletin read by an unseen newscaster accompanied by still photographs, Independent Television News (ITN) were presented by newscasters with their own personality, used a large quantity of film in the bulletins, and incorporated quite much informed comment. This attracted an immense audience. In other genres of programmes, such as drama, comedy and light entertainment, pop music shows and sport, both the BBC and ITV have made various progresses under the impact of competition.[353]

Due to the post-war affluence and the emergence of a consumer society, the number of television sets owned by the British households rose from 1 million in 1951 to 13 million in 1964. Television became undoubtedly an influential mass medium in Britain. Along with the emergence of commercial television, the mood of broadcasting was tremendously changed from the solemn BBC style to a populist, audience-oriented one. But some political elites, represented by the Pilkington Committee of 1962, were quite sceptical of these changes brought about by commercial television, especially the alleged manipulative power of advertising over the public, and accused ITV of vulgarity. The Pilkington Report reiterated the cultural purposes of broadcasting and reinforced the status of public service broadcasting by giving the third channel to the BBC.[354] The relationship between the BBC and ITV in the 1960s, as Crisell puts, seemed complementary: "the commercial television had won the lion's share of the audience, but the BBC retained a moral and cultural superiority".[355] This has been described as "a comfortable duopoly" of the BBC and ITV in the British history of broadcasting.

On the whole, the direct consequence of the first encounter of the market logic with broadcasting was the introduction of commercial television without eroding the fundamental values of the public service broadcasting. Furthermore, British commercial television inherited the motto of the BBC as to inform, educate and entertain, and tried to integrate with the values of the existed public service broadcasting. Actually, many members of ITV staff were former BBC staff, so it

352 See Curran and Seaton (2003), p. 163. And Seymour-Ure, p. 91.
353 Cricell, pp. 90 ff.
354 Curran and Seaton (2003), pp. 171-77.
355 Ibid, p. 109.

5.1. Dual broadcasting system: the advent of the market logic and its impact

was unsurprising that they were inclined to share the common values of public service broadcasting. What commercial television strained for was, above all, to make a fortune in broadcasting, but it gained its legitimacy by claiming to bring competition into broadcasting so as to counteract the shortcomings of monopoly. The establishment of the ITA guided the commitment of British commercial television to public service instead of merely to profit. Although few of those claims from the commercial television campaign were fully realised, it appeared fair to say that the BBC, ITV, and British audience all benefited from the competition – a competition of programmes for audience and quality, but not for finance. The co-existence of commercial television and public service broadcasting remained comfortably complementary and fairly stable until the end of the 1960s.

In the 1970s, along with the collapse of the post-war consensus caused by a series of political and economic crises, new ideas on broadcasting also emerged to challenge the existed understandings of broadcasting. Most notably, the Annan Report (1977) developed a pluralist viewpoint on broadcasting, according to which broadcasting should cater for the full range of groups and interests in society rather than to serve the universal interest or the national interest. Broadcasting should also not seek to offer moral leadership but to offer opportunities for various opinions.[356] "Pluralism" has since then become an important principle for the organisation and arrangement of British broadcasting. The initiative for establishing a publisher-broadcaster Channel 4, whose aim was to offer greater freedom of choice (both for producers and for audience) outside the BBC and ITV and to serve the marginalised minorities in society, obviously followed the principle of pluralism developed by the Annan Report. Nevertheless, as Goodwin points out, pluralism in broadcasting developed by the Annan Report should be regarded as the extension of public service broadcasting values.[357] A radical break with the public service broadcasting values took place in the 1980s, when the market liberals rose to political and economic dominance and sought to redefine broadcasting with the market logic.

5.1.2. To redefine broadcasting with the market logic: from the 1980s onwards

At then end of the 1970s, the broadcasting policy in Western Europe was confronting the pressure for change. The direct imperative first came from the technological advancements of cable and satellite throughout the 1970s, which envisaged the transmutation of broadcasting from a single delivery system (broadcast

---

356 Curran and Seaton (2003), pp. 194-96 and p. 365.
357 Peter Goodwin. *Television under the Tories: broadcasting policy 1979-1997*. London: bfi publishing, 1998. p. 92, see note 1.

air waves) with a small number of channels into a multi-channel system of broadcasting. Policy makers in most EU countries felt a particularly urgent need of responding to these latest technological advancements mainly because the USA and Japan have made a leap in the research and application of cable and satellite broadcasting services in the 1970s.

In the debates on the future broadcasting policy triggered by the technological advancements, the discrepancies among the policy makers in most EU countries were extremely large: some of the policy makers, especially the technocrats, were enthusiastic about the ensuing "broadcasting revolution" brought about by the new technologies, while some others were pessimistic about the "decline and fall of public service broadcasting"[358]. One after the other, EU countries finally all chose to introduce private broadcasting into the traditional public service television system, the same as the case in Britain three decades before. The process of establishing the dual broadcasting system has always been accompanied by numerous wide-ranging debates on rethinking broadcasting, by which new ideas (the market logic among others) joined battles with the existed ones. How could the newly established dual system become a compatible system for the adversarial set of ideas of public service broadcasting and commercial broadcasting? Although Britain has introduced commercial broadcasting as early as in 1954, the imperative for changes in policy-making caused by the latest technological advancements was as urgent as in other European countries of the traditional public service broadcasting system. The experience of Britain and West Germany in the 1980s and the 1990s present us with two different approaches to respond to the market logic within a whole complex of social, political and technological changes.

5.1.2.1. Britain: Mrs. Thatcher's reform and the demise of public commercial broadcasting

From the point of view of many broadcasting scholars in Britain, the public service broadcasting and its values have been seen attacked by an alliance of political and economic forces, particularly from Thatcher government. However, what happened to British broadcasting throughout the 1980s and the 1990s should first be placed in a wider context of the economic and political climate during these periods. In fact, broadcasting was just one of the many public sectors which were

---

[358] This is the title of a book written by Michael Tracey, which best describes the deep anxiety over the constant state of crisis faced by European public service broadcasters throughout the 1980s and the 1990s. Michael Tracey. *The Decline and Fall of Public Service Broadcasting.* UK: Oxford University Press, 1998.

5.1. Dual broadcasting system: the advent of the market logic and its impact

to be "reformed" or "deregulated" by the neo-liberal government under Mrs. Thatcher, whilst the conflicts between the BBC and the Thatcher government were especially fiercer than in other sectors.

After two decades of rapid development and affluence in the post-war period, Britain began to confront with a series of political and economic crises in the late 1960s and throughout the 1970s: strikes, sit-ins, lock-outs, demonstrations, and acts of terrorism caused by the escalation of the conflict in Northern Ireland. The mood of the general public became darkened, and elsewhere of the world was also experiencing a great upheaval after the Cold War and Vietnam War started in the 1960s. When the Oil Crisis finally broke out in 1973, Britain was confronted with its greatest crisis after the Second World War: one million working days were lost in strikes in 1977 alone. Britain became the "sick man of Europe" for its severe industrial stoppages and rampant inflations.[359] The post-war welfarism and state-intervention were in question.

The first female leader of the Conservative Party, Mrs. Thatcher, who has the personality of decisiveness, forcefulness, strong-will and self-assurance as just what Britain needed, won the general election in 1979 with a comfortable overall majority when Britain was at a hard time. Her manifesto was to bring economic progress to the country and renew the spirit and solidarity of the nation. She has adopted a series of radical concepts, which were thought to be influenced by the Austrian school, to deal with the severe domestic problems in Britain. The main ideas of the Austrian school involve reducing the state intervention and allowing the "market forces" to rule the economy. As a neo-Conservative, therefore, she distinguished from her predecessors Macmillan and Heath by bidding farewell to post-war welfarism and mixed economy and returning to "economic liberalism". And the typicality of the public policies under Mrs. Thatcher, the so-called Thatcherism, was generalised by Norman Lowe as follows:
a) the role of the state in society must be reduced;
b) monetarism was the best way to make Britain prosperous again;
c) self-help and individualism;
d) a strong element of British nationalism; and
e) Thatcherism was radical and anti-establishment.[360]

This had the goal, in short, to adopt policies of the market logic to privatise the public sector and to deregulate the private sector under the Thatcher government. This had not only a far-reaching impact on the economic and political spheres, but also has changed British government's policy to cultural affairs. Thatcher government cut public expenditure in huge amount to reduce "state intervention"

---

359 Crisell, pp. 194-95.
360 Norman Lowe. *Mastering Modern British History*. London: Macmillian Press Ltd, 1998. p. 567.

and treated arts and cultures without difference to other business. Many cultural institutions were forced not to depend on state subsidy but to finance themselves from a free market. Film and theatre all suffered a continuous decline of audience and lack of constant income.[361]

Mrs. Thatcher determined to reform British broadcasting, in particular the BBC, with the same set of market logic for some good reasons: the ideological, editorial as well as economic ones.[362] Firstly, from an ideological perspective, the BBC was like any public institution in the public sectors that should be reformed anyway on the grounds that public service was inefficient and uncompetitive. As criticised by the advocates of commercial television four decades before, the criticism of the BBC for being over-staffed, over-protected, and over-bureaucratic resurfaced.[363] Market, on the contrary, would generate the proper outcome through the free market choice.

Secondly, from an editorial perspective, the journalistic values of the BBC did not fit in with Mrs. Thatcher's political viewpoints. Not only was the BBC against Mrs. Thatcher's general principle of "anti-establishment", she was particularly resentful of the BBC's reporting of the Falklands War and the Northern Ireland issues. The BBC's approach to deal with controversial issues with impartiality and objectivity seriously irritated Mrs. Thatcher as disloyal and offensive, for the members of the terrorist groups like the IRA were interviewed by the BBC. Mrs. Thatcher censored the BBC for "misusing its freedom" and this had to be changed.

Thirdly, from an economic perspective, commercial interests were also clamouring for government's reform in public service broadcasting for their own ends. The most aggressive commercial lobby was conducted by the international media conglomerate News International and its affiliated newspapers (The Sun, The Times, and The Sunday Times). The owner of News international Rupert Murdoch was an old friend of Mrs. Thatcher and her most influential supporter in the press. The BBC and the BBC's World Service, whose programmes had world-wide reputation for quality and diversity, stood in the way of the satellite services from Sky Television (the subsidiary of the News International) in the domestic British and international broadcasting markets. Therefore, "Aunty Must Go", The Sun shrilly demanded.[364] Other market powers such as advertising industry and the right-centre think-tanks were also keen on putting advertising on

---

361 On the impact of Thatcherite policies on British cultural affairs, see John Hill, *British Cinema in the 1980s*, Oxford and New York: Oxford University Press, 1999; and Lester Friedman (ed.), *Fires Were Started: British cinema and Thatcherism*, USA: University of Minnesota Press, 1993.
362 Crisell, p. 233.
363 Curran and Seaton (2003), p. 219.
364 Ibid. pp. 207 ff.

5.1. Dual broadcasting system: the advent of the market logic and its impact

the BBC as well as supporting new channels with more advertising or sponsor opportunities. In fact, people in the advertising business led a remarkably successful lobby campaign to influence broadcasting policy-making in the 1980s.[365]

Although Mrs. Thatcher acted more like an opportunist in broadcasting policy without producing any coherent project against the established institutions[366], the initiatives, appointments and policies of her government based on the market logic affected British broadcasting in an all-around manner which covered nearly all important fields of broadcasting: the newly developed cable and satellite broadcasting services, the existed public service broadcasting and public service commercial broadcasting as well.

First, the Thatcher government heavily deregulated cable and satellite broadcasting market in Britain during her first term in office (1979-1983). Being deemed as a purely technological infrastructure for new information services by the Thatcher government, the establishment of the cable system was directed by the Information Technology Advisory Panel (ITAP), whose members had obviously a better understanding of electronics but few of broadcasting. And Britain was also the only country in Europe to fully depend on private investment – namely by the industry and the audience – in cable system, while state investment was the major funding for cable system in West Germany, France and Japan.[367] Yet the feedback from the industrial side and the audience side was not really positive. To promote cable and satellite broadcasting by the market logic eventually proved to be futile.

A second attempt of Mrs. Thatcher to reform British broadcasting was to appoint Peacock, a professor of economy with a distinctive free-market persuasion, to review the financing of the BBC with a consideration of introducing advertising into the BBC in her second term in office (1983-1987). Although the Peacock Report in 1986 surprisingly rejected the Thatcher government's intention of introducing advertising into the BBC, it produced three paramount consequences for British broadcasting: it redefined broadcasting with the market logic that replaced the public service understandings of broadcasting as the dominant rhetoric in discussions on British broadcasting thereafter; it led to an instant and yet more grandiose reform on the commercial sector of the British public service duopoly – ITV and Channel 4 – with an ever clearer separation from the public service values; and it shifted British broadcasting from public service towards a more market-oriented direction in the long run.

---

365 Tom O'Malley. *Closedown? The BBC and government broadcasting policy 1972-92*. London: Pluto Press, 1994. pp. 22-23.
366 Peter Goodwin, "The Role of the State", in Jane Strokes and Anna Reading (eds.) *The Media in Britain: currant debates and developments*. London: Macmillan Press Ltd, 1999. pp. 130-42.
367 Curran and Seaton (2003), pp. 197-201.

Professor Alan Peacock, who has never pursued media before his appointment as Chairman of the Committee on the Financing of the BBC[368], adopted a free market approach in the analysis of the problem of financing broadcasting. The Peacock Report stated that:

> "British broadcasting should move towards a sophisticated market system based on consumer sovereignty. This is a system which recognises that viewers and listeners are the best ultimate judges of their own interests, which then can best satisfy if they have the option of purchasing the broadcasting services they require from as many alternative sources of supply as possible."[369]

By framing the future of British broadcasting as a whole in terms of market, the Peacock Report used a set of languages and terms, which were methodologically as well as ideologically seriously different from those of the public service broadcasting, for redefining broadcasting. Whereas broadcasting was now handled as a market rather than public service, accordingly, viewers and listeners were consumers, and programmes were products in a broadcasting market. The Peacock Report was in principle a purely economic analysis of the demand-provision relationship in a broadcasting market, and an evaluation of various financing possibilities involved in this market, ranging from the existing means of funding broadcasting such as public funds and advertising, to other potential means such as subscription and direct payment. It first analysed the status quo of British broadcasting from an economic perspective, which was far from a sophisticated broadcasting market as the Peacock Report stated, and then made recommendations on how to achieve this aim in the long-term.[370]

The Peacock Report further explicated its understandings of broadcasting with the market logic philosophy. Broadcasting should be first and foremost a direct consumer market, whereby only the consumer choice and direct payment could reflect the real needs and financial preference of the consumer. Public service, consequently, still could find a modest place in the free broadcasting market as a supplementary factor by providing a range of types of programmes which were "suitable for public patronage" like the public-funded National Galleries. These types of programmes would include news, current affairs, documentaries, programmes about science, nature and other part of the world, educational programmes, high quality programmes on the Arts, and critical and controversial programmes, etc. This has been the rationale for retaining the licence fee and not

---

368 Sir Alan Peacock. "The 'Politics' of Investigating Broadcasting Finance", in Tom O'Malley and Janet Jones (eds.) *The Peacock Committee and UK Broadcasting Policy*. UK: Palgrave Macmillian. 2009. pp. 84-100. p. 84.
369 Peacock Report 1986, p. 133. Cited by Goodwin (1998), p. 78.
370 For details on the analysis of a three-stage-development of free broadcasting market and the corresponding recommendations on each stage in the Peacock Report, see Goodwin(1998). pp. 69-92.

5.1. Dual broadcasting system: the advent of the market logic and its impact

introducing advertising onto the BBC. In order to support its ideas of a free broadcasting market, the Peacock Report also revisited the theme of free market as the free marketplace of expression which was by then only dominant in the press, and the theme of efficiency of resource allocation which led to the notorious initiative of ITV franchise auction system.

Although the economic approach of analysis adopted by the Peacock Report has provoked a very hostile response from many politicians (especially those of the Labour) and broadcasters right after its publication, this set of market logic languages and terms gradually achieved a sort of cross-party consensus about the reform of British broadcasting in the following two years. The direct consequence of the Peacock Report was the governmental publication of the White Paper 1988 under the title of *Broadcasting in the 90s: Competition, Quality and Choice*, and the royal assent of the Broadcasting Act 1990 based on the proposals of the 1988 White Paper. These two documents followed the market logic initiated by the Peacock Report: broadcasting was now a market which should be more open and competitive through the costs and efficiency based reforms. The main focus of the White Paper 1988 and the Broadcasting Act 1990 was to deregulate the public service commercial broadcaster ITV and Channel 4. A new regulator for terrestrial commercial television, the Independent Television Commission (ITC), was established to replace the IBA[371]. The ITC was a licensing body rather than a broadcasting authority, in that it did not provide programmes services and would no longer control the qualities and standards of the ITV programmes like the IBA did. The competence of the ITC expanded to cable and satellite services. Two other radical market-driven measures of reform were the auction of the ITV franchises and that Channel 4 was to sell its own advertising in the name of efficiency. All these reforms indicated a complete break of British commercial broadcasting with its public service commitment.

The third field of broadcasting, which Mrs. Thatcher attempted to reform with the market logic, was the core of the British establishment as well as British broadcasting – the gigantic public service broadcaster of the BBC. Although the official commercialisation of the BBC through introducing advertising into it was rejected by the Peacock Report, the public service broadcaster was still seriously impacted by other means of the market logic. As Seaton observed, the BBC has been enveloped in a new style of institutional administration – managerialism – since the later half of the 1980s. By appointing persons with strong business background and conservative inclination as the Governors and Director General, it led to a dramatic power shift inside the BBC: the managers and the

---

371 The Independent Broadcasting Authority (IBA) was the reconstitution of the ITA in 1972, when the Sound Broadcasting Act 1972 gave the ITA responsibility for organising commercial radio in the UK.

idea of efficiency became dominating and fashionable, whilst the programme makers were marginalised. Working as programme makers in the BBC meant not only less-fashionable and less-privileged under the new managerialist ethos in the 1980s, but also meant less-recruited and less-paid in the organisation. The traditional journalistic values of public service broadcasting of being critical and highly creative (sometimes rebellious) were discouraged both inside the BBC by the managers, and outside the BBC by the government and the pro-conservative press. Under pressure from both inside and outside, the BBC and the programme makers started to move towards more efficiency-conscious. Managerial measures with market logic were introduced at the BBC, whereby the most notable example was Producer's Choice, which was a trading system designed around an internal market to make costs transparent.[372] The programme makers were now more like a trinity of programme makers, accountants and managers, who had to watch the costs carefully and sought to buy services with the cheapest price either from the internal market or outside the BBC besides programme making.

To sum up, under the reform conducted by the Thatcher government throughout the 1980s and the 1990s, British broadcasting has experienced a radical shift in the understandings of broadcasting from the perspective of traditional public service to a perspective of the market logic. The cable and satellite broadcasting services were regulated from the very beginning of their development with the market mechanism. The legislation of the Broadcasting Act 1990 led to a sudden break of the British commercial broadcasting sector (by then ITV and Channel 4) with their public service commitment since the introduction of commercial television in the 1950s. The public service broadcaster, the BBC, though luckily escaped from the official commercialisation of financing, could not avoid an indirect commercialisation of the institution, in this case the business-style of administration and management interpenetrated and dominated the BBC as a result of the reshuffle of the Board of Governors and Director General through Mrs. Thatcher's appointments.

5.1.2.2. British dual broadcasting system in the post-Thatcher eras

Besides the instant impact of reform of broadcasting conducted by the Thatcher government as above mentioned, the profound and lasting impact of this reform should probably be better assessed in a much longer term. The Peacock Report on British broadcasting went particularly far beyond the prompt reform on British commercial broadcasting guided by the Broadcasting Act 1990. The mar-

---

372 Curran and Seaton (2003), pp. 217-27.

5.1. Dual broadcasting system: the advent of the market logic and its impact

ket logic philosophy, with the help of the redefinition of broadcasting according to this set of market logic developed by the Peacock Report, has since then dominated the discourses on broadcasting in the following decade. The market logic rose to reshape the British broadcasting policy landscape and changed the way of thinking about the provision of broadcasting in society. About two decades later, the market logic finally reached its peak in 2003 with the establishment of a new FCC-style regulator for British commercial broadcasting and telecommunications, the Office of Communications (Ofcom). This new regulatory body was in the tradition of Peacock so as to address itself to promote competition and unnecessary regulations across the areas of broadcasting and telecommunications, whose latest development involved a new phase of technological advancements in Internet and digital broadcasting. Ofcom has hence been dubbed the "child of Peacock".[373]

Not only in Britain, the public service broadcasting was caught in crisis worldwide since the 1980s. The public service broadcasting lost its ground in Canada, New Zealand, and was marginalised in some other countries such as Austria. It was unable to be established in central and eastern Europe despite the effort from the publish service broadcasting heartland.[374]

Under the circumstances, another strand of thinking – treasuring the values of public service broadcasting – had to struggle hard (at the beginning rather impotently) to defend itself, for the legitimacy of financing the BBC with license fee kept being questioned throughout the years. The supporters of the public service broadcasting, especially the "left" academia[375], kept elaborating new theories of public service broadcasting to counterbalance the overwhelming dominance of the market logic. In contrast to the politically unfavourable situation of the public service broadcasting, researches on the public service broadcasting blossomed vigorously among academia with the best intentions to save it. These researches were mainly focusing on two themes. One theme was to criticise the defects and drawbacks of the commercial broadcasting, particularly the failure of market. Since broadcasting was a business requiring enormous start-up and running costs, the ownership of commercial broadcasting had a strong tendency of concentration. A concentration of broadcasting ownership was very likely to threat the diversity of opinions because of the domination of few voices as well as the power to propagate a single political viewpoint[376]. It was also likely to threat the

---

373 Janet Jones, "PSB 2.0 – UK Broadcasting Policy after Peacock", in O'Malley and Jones (eds.), pp. 187-206. p. 193.
374 Collins. p. 33.
375 The "left" academics in the area of public service broadcasting are led by British scholars such as John Keane, James Curran, Nicholas Garnham, Richard Collins, Graham Murdoch.
376 Gillian Doyle. *Media Ownership*. London: Sage Publications, 2002. p. 12.

diversity of cultures because the programmes of the commercial broadcasting with mass appeal were unable to deliver a full range of programme provisions[377]. Another theme was to go deep to analyse the functions of broadcasting, first and foremost its democratic function in a modern society. This was inspired and supported particularly by the theory of discourse (Diskurstheorie) and the concept of public sphere (Öffentlichkeit) of Jürgen Habermas. The public sphere was understood as "a realm of social life where the exchange of information and views on questions of common concern can take place so that public opinion can be formed".[378] The mass media were the modern institutions of the public sphere. As citizens of a civil society, viewers and readers were comprehensively informed through mass media on the one hand, while on the other hand, the mass media also offered space for discussions on questions of common concern in an organised form, which helped to generate topically specified public opinions in the public debates.[379] Since the process of discourse in the public sphere was so indispensable to modern democracy, so that the democratic function of broadcasting should be the prior concern in broadcasting politics. This democratic argument of broadcasting was strongly emphasised by its supporters after the scarcity of spectrum was no longer an argument for the legitimacy of public service broadcasting along with the rise of cable and satellite broadcasting.

After years of yells and struggles, recently the BBC was witnessed the end of the crisis in the 1990s, for the BBC retained a fairly stable status in the British broadcasting market largely thanks to its programmes with both popularity and quality.[380] Today, it often displays tripartite audience shares in British broadcasting market, whereby the BBC, the terrestrial commercial broadcasting (ITV, Channel 4, and Channel 5), and the other types of commercial broadcasting (cable, satellite, and IPTV etc.) have approximately one third of the audience shares each (see Figure 5.1).

---

377 James Curran (2002). pp. 227 ff.
378 Peter Dahlgren. *Television and the Public Sphere: citizenship, democracy and the media.* London: Sage Publications, 1995. p. 7.
379 James Curran (2002). pp. 232 ff.
380 Curran and Seaton (1997), pp. 229-31.

5.1. Dual broadcasting system: the advent of the market logic and its impact

Figure 5.1 Viewing Shares of Individual Channels in Britain 2008[381]

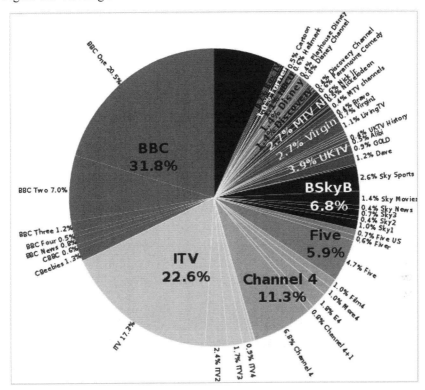

Source: from Wikipedia

Seaton attributes the survival of the BBC to three allies – the government, a network of impartial institutions, and the public[382] – for they finally relearned and reconfirmed the value of the public service broadcasting by and large. This perhaps belongs to the Britishness or can be understood as part of the British conventions: the power of tradition remains immense. Therefore, the dual broadcasting system in Britain would be able to have a perfect symbiosis of the public service broadcasting and commercial broadcasting, whereby the existence of the BBC helps raise standards of programming for the whole broadcasting market,

---

381 Television in the United Kindom. In Wikipedia. http://en.wikipedia.org/w/index.php?title=Television_in_the_United_Kingdom&action=historysubmit&diff=431507869&oldid=421063146#cite_note-barb-53. Last visited in June 2011.
382 James Curran and Jean Seaton. *Power without Reponsibility (7. edition).* London and New York: Routledge, 2010. p. 231.

and the existence of the commercial broadcasting endeavours to promote competitiveness in broadcasting sector.[383]

5.1.2.3. West Germany: the introduction of private broadcasting in 1984

Similar to Britain, the political powers were also very active during the post-war development of West German broadcasting system. Especially in the adversarial party politics, broadcasting policy was often used as a chessman in the political struggles between the two main political parties in the West German Parliament, the Christian Democratic Union (CDU) and the Social Democratic Party (SPD). Since the 1950s, the then governing party CDU had a long-standing dissatisfaction with the public law broadcasting institutions because it thought that the programmes of the public law broadcasting institutions were often critical of the federal government, while the journalists from the public law broadcasting institutions inclined to favour the social democrats. The (unsuccessful) attempt to establish a pro-state second television programme by the Adenauer Government (CDU) in 1960 aimed at breaking up the monopoly of the public law broadcasters as well as at achieving a balance of political sympathies in broadcasting from the perspective of the federal government. However, the first ruling on broadcasting made by the Federal Constitutional Court in 1961 reiterated the principle of distant from the state (Staatsfernheit) in broadcasting issues which was first set by the Allies. The first ruling on broadcasting also made it clear that the arrangement of broadcasting was the legislative competence of the Länder, and the competence of the Bund was exclusively for the transmission technology, not for the content. These decisions had led to the withdrawal of the Bund from the field of broadcasting policy and to the consequence of the consolidation of the public law broadcasting in the ensuing decades.

As a remedy for the failure of establishing pro-state broadcasting, some members in the CDU had gradually turned to support the ideas of introducing private broadcasting into the existed broadcasting system since the late 1960s, whilst the advancement of cable and satellite technologies worldwide – especially in the USA and Japan – in the late 1960s and the early 1970s also offered technological possibilities of increasing broadcasting channels. How to develop, organize and arrange the future communications sector, ranging from the service of the telecommunications to broadcasting, were fiercely discussed among the politicians in West Germany at the beginning of the 1970s. However, as Eifert and

---

383 Mark Oliver, "The UK Public Service Broadcasting Ecology", in *Can the Market Deliver?: Funding Public Service Television in the Digital Age*. UK: John Libbey Publishing, 2005. pp. 39-59.

5.1. Dual broadcasting system: the advent of the market logic and its impact

Hoffmann-Riem observed, these political discussions soon fell into a kind of "self-blockade"[384] on the grounds that the two main political parties in the Parliament, the CDU/CSU and the SPD, had very different standpoints on the future communications policy. The advocates for private broadcasting from the CDU/CSU and the interested groups like the publishing houses set their argument on the ideas of economic competition, which was equivalent to the principle of free organisation for a free communication system. In this theory, the recipients were equated with consumers, and the economic market was connected with the marketplace of ideas. At the constitutional level, they further equated the understanding of freedom of broadcasting with the freedom of the individual broadcasting entrepreneur, and accordingly claimed permission for private broadcasters since the special situation of insufficient spectrums did not exist any more.

The opponents of private broadcasting from the SPD and public law broadcasting institutions, on the contrary, emphasized the democratic and cultural mission of broadcasting in the social development, therefore the guarantee of the real diversity of opinion was the centre of concern. This could only be realized through a reformed public law broadcasting system. Foreign experiences also showed that private broadcasting tended to be oriented towards the taste of the masses, so the essential diversity of contents could not be provided. From the constitutional perspective, the functional understanding of the freedom of broadcast illustrated by the Federal Constitutional Court should be the criterion for the arrangement of broadcasting system, according to which the freedom of the formation of individual and public opinion was a significant point. A basic right to the arrangement of broadcasting should be therefore refused.[385]

These two main streams of opinions on private broadcasting were so irreconcilable that it became impossible to reach a consensus about the future media policy among the politicians from the two main parties. Some actions related to broadcasting issues throughout the 1970s, such as the appointment of the "commission for the development of technical communication system" (KtK) by the Brandt Government (SPD) in 1973 to give suggestions for the future development of communications system and the future technical development in broadcasting as well, the local cable pilot projects in four selected cities in search of the future model of media landscape planed in 1978 and conducted since 1984, the drafting of Land media law concerning the introduction of private broadcast-

---

384 Martin Eifert and Wolfgang Hoffmann-Riem, "Die Entstehung und Ausgestaltung des dualen Rundfunksystems", in Dietrich Schwarzkopf (ed.) *Rundfunkpolitik in Deutschland (Band 1): Wettbewerb und Öffentlichkeit*, pp. 50-116. München: Deutsche Taschenbuch Verlag GmbH & Co. KG, 1999. pp. 53 ff.
385 Ibid, p. 55.

ing in many Länder since 1980, were all attempts made by different political powers to enforce their own propositions of broadcasting policy. Furthermore, these actions had mostly only resulted in the sharpening of the contradiction between the two "camps".

Under such circumstances of political stalemate, the third and fourth rulings on broadcasting made by the Federal Constitutional Court, the Ruling of FRAG (FARG-Urteil) 1981 and the Ruling of Niedersachsen (Niedersachsen-Urteil) 1986, eventually dealt with the theme of freedom of broadcasting with regard to the problems of introducing private broadcasting from the constitutional perspective. These two rulings of the Federal Constitutional Court also formed the basis for the dual broadcasting system in West Germany.

In the Ruling of FRAG 1981, the Court consistently started its argument from the freedom of broadcasting guaranteed by Article 5 Section 1 Sentence 2 of the West German Basic Law, and expounded the interpretation on the freedom of broadcasting as a *"serving freedom" ("dienende Freiheit")* for the freedom of the formation of opinion. The legislature should establish a positive order through material, organisational and procedural regulations to "safeguard the diversity of the existing opinions could be expressed as wide and complete as possible"[386]. The necessity of regulation "still exists even after the special situation caused by insufficient spectrums and high start-up costs vanishes in the course of modern development"[387]. How the legislature would like to perform its task, according to the Court, was left to its own decision. This has made it in principle possible to introduce private broadcasting from the constitutional perspective, only if the private broadcasting would also perform the task of serving the freedom of the formation of opinion, but not for the interests of the individual entrepreneur. Moreover, the state responsibility of arrangement also covered a limited state supervision on the private broadcasting as well as a procedure of admission and rules of selection for the permission of the private broadcasters.[388]

The Court further differentiated two models of the arrangement of broadcasting for safeguarding the diversity of opinions: the so-called *"internal pluralistic" model (der binnenpluralistische Model)*, where a variety of opinions could be heard in the programmes of one broadcaster; and the so-called *"external pluralistic" model (der außenpluralistische Model)*, where the full range of opinions would be reflected by the totality of the programmes of all broadcasters together[389]. This differentiation indicated that the existed public law broadcasting institutions stood for the "internal pluralistic" model, while the "external pluralistic"

---

386   BVerfGE 57, 295. p. 320.
387   Ibid. p. 322.
388   Eifert and Hoffmann-Riem, p. 58.
389   Ibid. pp. 325 ff.

5.1. Dual broadcasting system: the advent of the market logic and its impact

model (possibly through various private broadcasters) was also an alternative for safeguarding the diversity of opinions so long as the totality of the prospective broadcasters could provide a full range of opinions in their programmes.

The private broadcasting has started to co-exist with the public broadcasting in West Germany since 1984. Under the guidelines of the Ruling of FRAG 1981, the Land media acts (Landesmediengesetze) have been successively enacted in the individual Länder since 1984 in order to regulate the development of the private broadcasting. The local cable pilot projects, with the active participation of private broadcasters, have also been conducted since this year. However, there was still a bitter controversy among the two "camps" for or against the private broadcasting by then. In the opinions of the Parliament members of the SPD, the essential provisions of the first Land media act in West Germany, namely the Land Broadcasting Act of Lower Saxony (Niedersächsische Landesrundfunkgesetz), was in violation of the Article 5 Section 1 of the West German Basic Law and therefore as a whole unconstitutional. A constitutional examination on the first group of Land media acts became imperative.

The Ruling of Niedersachsen 1986 made by the Federal Constitutional Court, consequently, examined the conformity of the Land Media Act of Lower Saxony with the West German Basic law. This ruling has exerted a far-reaching influence on shaping definition of the dual broadcasting system, with which the co-existence of the public law broadcasting and the private broadcasting sustained a framework. This framework was later arranged through the State Treaty of Broadcasting 1987 (Rundfunkstaatsvertrag 1987). The significance of the Ruling of Niedersachsen lies, moreover, in its clarification of the relationship between the private and the public law broadcasting in the statement of grounds of the Ruling with two important key phrases: *"basic provision" (Grundversorgung)*, and *"guarantee of existence and development (of the public law broadcasting)" (Bestands- und Entwicklungsgarantie)*. According to the Court, it was the task of the public law broadcasting institutions to guarantee the basic provision for the whole population with broadcasting programmes aiming to fulfil the essential functions of broadcasting for the democratic and cultural life in West Germany. With this end in view, the public law broadcasting institutions were given adequate technical, organisational, personnel and financial facilities as guarantees of their existence and development. So long as the public law broadcasting institutions could effectively assume these tasks, it seemed unnecessary to impose the same strict requirements in terms of the variety and diversity of the programmes on the private broadcasters like those on their public law counterparts.[390]

---

[390] BVerfGE 73, 118. p. 118.

Through the Ruling of Niedersachsen 1986, the private broadcasting was finally legitimised in West Germany, while the dual broadcasting system was eventually established with two unequal columns: the private broadcasting with reduced requirements on the variety and diversity of the programmes on the one hand, and the public law broadcasting as the primary supporting pillar to provide the whole population with broad and diverse programmes on the other hand. The detailed arrangements of the dual broadcasting system were stipulated in the State Treaty to the New System of Broadcasting 1987 (Rundfunkstaatsvertrag 1987).

The dual broadcasting system was hereafter erected in West Germany. The later rulings made by the Federal Constitutional Court[391] made further constitutional modifications to the dual broadcasting system and consequently consolidated it. The fifth and sixth rulings of broadcasting, the Ruling of Baden-Württemberg 1987 and the Ruling of WDR 1991, deliberated on the dynamic definitions of broadcasting and "basic provision". "Basic provision" did not mean "minimum provision", so that the scope of the programmes of the public law broadcasting should not be limited to the information and political niches, as the advocates for the private broadcasting often suggested. These two rulings also enhanced the capacity of the public law broadcasting for its existence and development with regard to: a) mixed financing, by which advertising financing was also allowed to public law broadcasting institutions, and b) new services similar to broadcasting such as "on-line services", or other new forms and contents open in the programmes of the public law broadcasting institutions which were to be stimulated by means of new technology and new transmission paths[392] (cable and satellite technologies by then).

Throughout a decade (from 1981 to 1991), the basic framework and fundamental principles of the West German dual broadcasting system were generally clarified through four rulings of broadcasting (the third, the fourth, the fifth and the sixth) at the constitutional level. These fundamental principles included:

- The basis of the order of broadcasting in the Federal Republic of Germany: Article 5 forms the basis for all regulations for the broadcasting freedom and the order of broadcasting. The broadcasting freedom functions as "a serving freedom" for the freedom of the formation of opinion. The legislature is obliged for the arrangements of the broadcasting freedom.
- The precondition for the introduction of private broadcasting: it is in principle possible to introduce private broadcasting from the constitutional per-

---

391 From 1987 to 2008, the Federal Constitutional Court have made other nine rulings of broadcasting under the framework of the dual broadcasting system, namely from the fifth (1987) to the latest thirteenth (2008).
392 BVerfGE 74, 297, and BVerfGE 83, 238.

5.1. Dual broadcasting system: the advent of the market logic and its impact

spective, only if the private broadcasting would also perform the task of serving the freedom of the formation of opinion, but not for the interests of the individual entrepreneur.
- The requirements for the arrangement of private broadcasting: the totality of the programmes of all private broadcasters together could be an alternative for safeguarding the diversity of opinions so long as the totality of the prospective broadcasters could provide a full range of opinions in their programmes (the "external pluralistic" model).
- The roles of the public law broadcasters in the dual broadcasting system: it is the task of the public law broadcasters to guarantee the basic provision for the whole population with broadcasting programmes which aim to fulfil the essential functions of broadcasting for the democratic and cultural life in West Germany. Moreover, "basic provision" does not mean "minimum provision", so that the scope of the programmes of the public law broadcasting should not be limited to the information and political niches. The public law broadcasters are given adequate technical, organisational, personnel and financial facilities as guarantees of their existence and development.
- The roles of the private broadcasters in the dual broadcasting system: the private broadcasting is complementary to the public law broadcasting in the whole provision of broadcasting programmes; therefore the private broadcasters are imposed with reduced requirements of the variety and diversity of the programmes. And there is no strict task sharing between the public broadcasting and the private broadcasting.
- The problem of financing: the public law broadcasting is financed by mixed revenues, by which advertising financing is also allowed so as to enhance the independence of public law broadcasting besides its main financial source of the license fee.

After these fundamental principles were settled, the establishment of the dual broadcasting system has been by and large completed in West Germany.

5.1.2.4. German broadcasting in the era of the dual broadcasting system

The ensuing development of the dual broadcasting system in (the reunited) Germany stayed largely consistent with the fundamental principles mentioned in last section. Throughout the 1990s and the 2000s, the Federal Constitutional Court has made more rulings of broadcasting to clarify other important problems of the dual broadcasting system. Among the latest seven rulings of broadcasting, three of them were related to the public law broadcasting sector and mainly involved the problem of financing. The seventh ruling of broadcasting, the Ruling of Hessen3 1992[393], concerned the fundamentals of the financing of the public law broadcasting, by which the guarantee of financing is part of the freedom of broadcasting, and a ban on advertising is permissible arrangement of the freedom of broadcasting. The eighth and twelfth rulings of broadcasting, the Ruling of License Fees 1994[394] and the Ruling of License Fees II 2007[395] concretised the requirements for financing the public law broadcasting. These two rulings emphasised that the process of determining the price level of licence fee should safeguard an adequately functional financing of the public law broadcasters and must follow the principle of distant from the state (Staatsfernheit). A three-stage-process was developed for the legislature as a model to follow.[396] And the organisation for the administration of financing of broadcasting, the Commission of Determining the Financing Requirement of the Broadcasters (die Kommission zur Ermittlung des Finanzbedarfs der Rundfunkanstalten, KEF), should be neutral and free from hidden political influences. Its suggestion served more than mere decision guidance for the legislature.

Two other rulings of broadcasting made by the Federal Constitutional Court were related to the private broadcasting sector. The eleventh ruling of broadcasting, the Ruling of "Extra Radio" 1998[397], dealt with the question of who are the entities of exercising the fundamental right of the freedom of broadcasting (Grundrechtträgerschaft): they can be all licensed broadcasters as well as the applicants for a broadcasting license regardless of legal status. Before then, only the public broadcasters and the Land media authorities, who supervise the private broadcasting, but not the private broadcasters themselves, were allowed to exercise the fundamental right of the freedom of broadcasting. This ruling of broadcasting has acknowledged the private broadcasters as the entities of exercising the fundamental right of the freedom of broadcasting. The thirteenth ruling of broadcasting, the Ruling of "Participation of Parties in Broadcasting Companies" 2008[398], dealt with the relationship between political parties and private broadcasting. An absolute prohibition for political parties on participating in arranging private broadcasting, from the viewpoint of the Federal Constitutional Court, was not a permissible legal arrangement of the freedom of broadcasting. Only those parties, which were closely connected with state, should be limited to

---

393 BVerfGE 87, 181.
394 BVerfGE 90, 60.
395 BVerfGE 119, 181.
396 The three stages of determining the price level of license fee are the application of requirement by the broadcasters, professional assessment through the KEF, and the determination of price level of the license fee through the Land-parliaments.
397 BVerfGE 97, 298.
398 BVerfGE 121, 30.

5.1. Dual broadcasting system: the advent of the market logic and its impact

the participation in arranging private broadcasting so as to prevent the exertion of political influence on broadcasting.

The rest two rulings of broadcasting made by the Federal Constitutional Court were related to other important general principles of the dual broadcasting system. The ninth ruling of broadcasting, the Ruling of the EU Guidelines on Television 1995[399], clarified that the federal government (the Bund) was the trustee for the Länder at the EU level. The tenth ruling of broadcasting, the Ruling of the Guidelines on Short News Report 1998[400], was related to the freedom of programme and football rights. The court acknowledged the free access to information in the public interest in terms of short news report on important cultural and sport events, and the boundaries of the commercial usability of information with general importance. A complete commercialisation of information through the organisers (of events) and (private) media would lead to a monopoly of information, and would consequently threaten the plurality of information sources which served the formation of free opinion.

Since the rulings of broadcasting made by the Federal Constitutional Court generally only worked on the principles and the newly emerged problems of the dual broadcasting system at the constitutional level, to which the regulators and decision-makers of German broadcasting and judges from other courts were obliged to adjust, the concrete arrangements of private broadcasting system were largely left to the legislature of individual Länder. The Land media authority (Landesmedienanstalt) in each individual Land[401] was established to take charge of licensing and controlling of the private broadcasting. These Land media authorities are public bodies financed by the license fee. They have similar organisational structures to the broadcasting councils of the public law broadcasters, which include an executive organ of Director and one pluralistic advisory council or commission appointed by the respective Land parliament. Besides their competence of licensing and controlling the private broadcasting, however, the Land media authorities have no active intervention to the arrangements of the private television and radio programmes. The control over the broadcast programmes can only be undertaken in a retrospective and therefore less effective way. The Land media authorities are also fairly powerless to deal with the problems in the private broadcasting sector, such as the increasing interweavements

---

399 BVerfGE 92, 203.
400 BVerfGE 97, 228.
401 Today, there are 14 Land media authorities in the Federal Republic of Germany, with exception of two joint Land media authorities of Berlin and Brandenburg, Hamburg and Schleswig-Holstein.

between the broadcasting companies, which could lead to the distortion of the process of opinion formation.[402]

As the complementary pillar in the German dual broadcasting system, German private broadcasting began to develop under the reduced requirements of public remit in terms of the variety and diversity of the individual programmes in a relatively deregulated broadcasting market, hence the private broadcasters made their full efforts to win popularity among the audience with overwhelming entertainment programmes of films, series and shows of various types. After 25 years of development and numerous fusion and acquisitions, today a relatively stable layout of market players has come into being in German private broadcasting. In the private television sector, two leading private broadcasting groups, RTL Group[403] and ProSiebenSat1. Media AG[404], have achieved a dominant position in the national television sector in terms of both market share and advertising revenue (see figure 5.2 and figure 5.3). However, this also indicates that it is very difficult for the majority of the private television companies to be commercially successful, for a large proportion of television advertising revenues goes to the two leading companies.

Figure 5.2 Market Shares of the German Television Market 2009[405]
Monday-Sunday, 3:00 am – 3:00 am

Source: AGF/DAP TV Scope

---

402 Konrad Dussel. *Deutsche Rundfunkgeschichte*. Germany: UVK Verlagsgesellschaft mbH, 2004. p. 274.
403 In Germany, RTL group owns the television channels of RTL, RTL II, Super RTL, VOX, n-tv, some pay-TV channels and reginional television channels. RTL group is the biggest television company in Germany and is distinctly stronger than other television companies. Arbeitsgemeinschaft der Landesmedienanstalten (ALM) (ed.). *ALM Jahrbuch 2009/2010: Landesmedienanstalten und privater Rundfunk in Deutschland*. p. 60.
404 ProSiebenSat1. Media AG owns the television channels of Sat.1, ProSieben, kabel eins, N24, some pay-TV channels and regional television channels in Germany. Ibid, p. 62.
405 Ibid. p. 86.

5.1. Dual broadcasting system: the advent of the market logic and its impact

Figure 5.3 Market Shares of the Gross Television Advertising Revenue in Germany 2009[406]

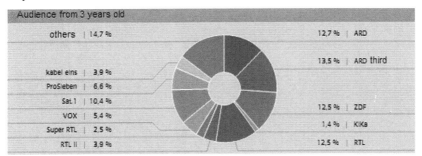

Source: Nielsen Media Research, February 2009

Unlike the private television market which is dominated by a few number of nation-wide full programme channels, the German private radio market has a stronger regional feature. The ownership and the market shares of private radio are also less concentrated in comparison with the private television market. Since the costs of radio programme producing are much lower than television programmes, some more private radios can have chance to survive and make profit in the market. The low producing costs of private radios are also reflected in the output of programmes. Music has become the most important (if not the only) content in the private radio programmes. Two types of format radio – adult contemporary music (AC) and contemporary hit radio (CHR) – currently dominate the private radio market[407], while other verbal contents of information, culture and education are largely left to their public law counterparts. The German private radio market with a larger number of players but uniform type of programmes is therefore by no means a good example of diversity.

After 25 years of competition as well as convergence, currently the public law broadcasting and the private broadcasting have well-balanced shares in the audience market, by which each pillar owns nearly half of the audience share. In the radio market, the public law radios had a slightly larger share than the private broadcasters in 2010[408]. However, as mentioned above, the public law radios

---

406 Ibid, p. 58.
407 Ibid, pp. 171-73.
408 In 2010, the market share of the entire private radio broadcasters (from Monday to Saturday) was 41.8%, and the market share of the radio services provided by the entire public law broadcasters (from Monday to Saturday) was 51.1%. Soure: *Media-Analyse 2011 Radio I, SWR Medienforschung/Programmstrategie*. See http://www.ard.de/intern/basisdaten/hoerfunknutzung/h_26_23246_3Brfunknutzung_20der_20privaten_20program/-/id=55142/15m44p5/index.html and http://www.ard.de/intern/basisdaten/hoerfunknutzung/h_26_23246_3Brfunknutzung_20der_20ard-programme_20_28m/-/id=55126/1ilrjo6/index.

provide the listeners with a richer diversity of programmes ranging from information, music, to culture and education, while the private radio programmes concentrated almost exclusively on music. The reason that public law radios can provide a full range of various programmes also lies in the fact that the public law radios are financially much stronger than the private radios. The license fee paid for the public law radios alone are already nearly five times more than the advertising revenues received by the private radios[409]. The good financial situation of the public law radios even enables them to become the main source of subvention for the public law television which suffers a long-term deficit.[410]

In the television market the audience share of private broadcasters was slightly larger than that of the public law broadcasters[411]. However, among the five broadcasters with the largest market shares (over 10 per cent) in 2009[412], the public law television had overall a larger market share than the private television. When the structure of programmes is examined more closely, Figure 5.4 indicates that the public law television broadcast considerably more programmes with distinct public remit character than the private television, such as the genres of information, sport, children's and youth's, while the private television broadcast more non-fictional entertainment (variety shows) than the public law television. In the genre of fiction (films and series), it has accounted for around one third of the total transmission time on both the public law and the private television. In the genre of advertisement, private television financed by advertising revenue naturally spent nearly one fifth of their transmission time on advertisement, while the public law television has only a very moderate part of 1.4 per cent.

html. Last visited in May 2011. See Marktanteile der AGF- und Lizenzsender im Tagesdurchschnitt 2010. *AGF/GfK Fernsehforschung*. http://www.agf.de/daten/zuschauermarkt/marktanteile. Last visited in May 2011.
409 In 2001, for example, the revenues of the public law radio were 5.179 million Mark (4.803 million Mark of license fee and 0.379 million Mark of advertising revenues), while the advertising revenues of private radios were only 0.950 million Mark. Dussel, p. 305.
410 Dussel, p. 304.
411 In 2010, the market share of the public law television broadcasters was 43.1%, and the private television broadcasters 56.9%. Source: AFG/GfK Fernsehforschung; TV Scope; Fernsehpanel D+EU. See Marktanteile der AGF- und Lizenzsender im Tagesdurchschnitt 2010. AGF/GfK Fernsehforschung. Cf. figure 5.2 on p. 180.
412 ARD Third (13.5 per cent), ARD (12.7 per cent), ZDF (12.5 per cent), RTL (12.5 per cent) and Sat. 1 (10.4 per cent). See figure 5.2 on p. 180.

5.1. Dual broadcasting system: the advent of the market logic and its impact

Figure 5.4 Genres of Programmes by ARD, ZDF, RTL, SAT. 1 and ProSieben 2008 (length of transmission in %)

	ARD	ZDF	RTL	SAT. 1	ProSieben
Information	42.7	48.2	33.3	17.6	23.5
Sport	7.8	7.0	1.5	0.6	0.2
Non-finctional Entertainment	4.1	8.8	11.4	28.7	15.3
Music	1.3	1.2	2.3	1.1	1.1
Children's and Youth's	5.0	4.2	1.3	0.1	3.5
Fiction	35.4	26.9	25.0	30.7	37.5
Other genres	2.4	2.3	4.7	6.3	5.2
Advertisment	1.4	1.4	20.6	15.0	13.7
Total	100.0	100.0	100.0	100.0	100.0

Period of the study: From 1. January to 31. December 2008, 3:00 am – 3.00 am.

Source: Udo Michael Krüger and Thomas Zapf-Schramm. "Politikthematisierung und Alltagskultivierung im Infoangebot. Programmanalyse 2008 von ARD/Das Erste, ZDF, RTL, SAT.1 und ProSieben". In: *Media Perspektiven* 4/2009.

Apart from others, the most direct media economic consequence of introducing the private broadcasting is the emergence and rapid development of television advertising market. As showed in Figure 5.5, television advertising market has grown from only accounting for 17 per cent market shares in the public law broadcasting era of 1984, to be the biggest and significant branch with 50 per cent of the market shares in the German gross advertising market in 2010. As Figure 5.4 shows, the vast majority of television advertising revenue goes to the private television companies. Although the advertising revenue remains financially inconsiderable for the public law broadcasters, the introduction of private broadcasting largely compensates the absence of market principle as well as competition in German broadcasting system, which helps the public law broadcasters to become increasingly cost-conscious and efficiency-conscious.

Figure 5.5 Media Shares in German Gross Advertising Market (from 1984 - 2010) (in %)[413]

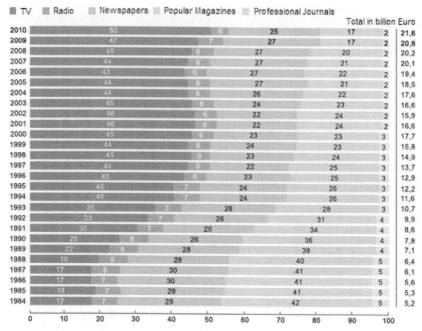

Source: Nielsen Media Research   Data in %

Although the dual broadcasting system appears fairly stable in Germany, it also faces various challenges resulting from the latest technological advancements and social changes, such as the development of Internet, the technology of digitalisation, the harmonisation of EU television market, and the process of globalisation. The public law broadcasting has been frequently criticised for the tendency of "content homogeneity" with the mass appeal programmes of the private broadcasting, and the increase of the license fee remains always controversial. The private broadcasting is also confronting criticisms of ownership concentration and the tendency of deteriorating tabloidisation of programmes. Nevertheless, these lately arising challenges and problems related to the dual broadcasting system will not be discussed here for lack of space. The further analysis will focus on the core of the dual broadcasting system: the dual understandings of broadcasting in a unified system, and the consequences of different decision-making models of broadcasting system.

413 AFG/GfK Fernsehforschung. TV data: Advertising market: Spendings on advertising. See http://www.agf.de/daten/werbemarkt/werbespendings/. Last visited in May 2011.

5.2. Co-existence, conflicts and coordination in the dual broadcasting system

In Chapter 4, the principles and the characteristics of the public service broadcasting system, and the understandings of broadcasting in the public service broadcasting system have been examined in depth[414]. As an expansion of the public service broadcasting system, the dual broadcasting system not only follows many of these principles, characteristics and understandings from the purely public service broadcasting system era, but also integrates some principles of the commercial broadcasting system into it. Nevertheless, the dual broadcasting system differentiates notably from the purely public service broadcasting system or the purely commercial broadcasting system. New ideas and revisions to the existed ideas, which kept emerging during the introduction of the commercial broadcasting and the ensuing development of the dual broadcasting system, make the result other than one-plus-one, i.e. the dual broadcasting system as a whole is more than public service broadcasting plus commercial broadcasting.

Another interesting feature of the dual broadcasting system lies in the fact that there exist two different sets of principles and understandings of broadcasting from the public service broadcasting and the commercial broadcasting respectively within one integrated broadcasting system. Many of the ideas of the two different sets of broadcasting are often incompatible with each other, or even adversarial. Reconciliation and harmonisation of these adversarial ideas become a paramount task for the arrangements of broadcasting system. Different decision-making models of broadcasting system also produce different consequences. Therefore, the focus of this sector is firstly to analyse the co-existing and sometimes adversarial understandings of broadcasting within the dual broadcasting system, and further to compare two different decision-making models of broadcasting system in Britain and Germany.

---

414 Cf. pp. 114 ff.

Figure 5.6 Two different sets of understandings of broadcasting within the dual broadcasting system

	Public service broadcasting[415]	**Commercial broadcasting**
Technological dimension	Public utility; universal infrastructure for all members in the country	Necessary platform for business; utility with user-pays principle
Economic dimension	Non-profit public service; financed by license fee, with (Germany) or without (Britain) very limited advertising revenues	For-profit business; solely financed by advertising revenues, sponsorships, subscriptions or other types of commercial revenues
Cultural dimension	Catering for national identity and community as well as for minorities (Britain); within the domain of culture on a federalist basis (Germany)	Audio-visual products being regarded as free trade goods; no strict requirement for cultural function
Social dimension	Catering for all interests and tastes (Britain); democratic function as the "serving freedom" for the freedom of the formation of opinion (Germany)	Entrepreneurial freedom
Audience	Citizens	Consumers
Programme	Full range programmes of diversity and pluralism; comprising information, education and entertainment	Entertainment with mass appeal
Regulation	Established under public law; under the supervision of national or regional legislature	Established under private law; advocating deregulation

Source: compiled by the author.

Figure 5.6 indicates the main differences of the understandings of broadcasting by the public service broadcasting and the commercial broadcasting respectively. These two sets of understandings co-exist within the dual broadcasting system, however, the co-existence was hardly peaceful as the experiences of Britain and Germany in the 1980s showed. To a large extent, it is left to the legal/political decision-makers to conciliate the conflicts between the two "camps", which can be roughly described as one "camp" who lay more emphasis on the socio-cultural dimensions of broadcasting (supporters of the public service broadcasting), and another "camp" with more emphasis on the techno-economic dimensions of

---

[415] Cf. figure 4.1 "characteristics of public service broadcasting", p. 116.

5.2. Co-existence, conflicts and coordination in the dual broadcasting system

broadcasting (supporters of the commercial broadcasting). If the legal/political decision-makers render more support or emphasis to the socio-cultural dimensions of broadcasting, the public service broadcasting will act as the basic pillar in the dual broadcasting system while the commercial broadcasting becomes the complementary pillar, which is the case of Germany. On the contrary, if the legal/political decision-makers lay more emphasis on the techno-economic dimensions of broadcasting, the dual broadcasting system will incline to be dominated by the principles of the market logic, which is the case of Britain, particularly during the 1980s and 1990s. (See Figure 5.7)

Figure 5.7 The scales of dimensions in the arrangements of broadcasting system

Source: illustrated by the author

As revealed in Figure 5.6, the dual broadcasting systems in both Britain and Germany share much in common in terms of the theoretical understandings of broadcasting, since most ideas – especially those of the public service broadcasting – of the German broadcasting system were adopted from the British broadcasting system in the post-war period. Therefore, the fact that currently the dual broadcasting systems in both countries display different landscapes is largely ascribable to the different decision-making models of broadcasting system in these two countries. In Britain, the Parliament is the final decision-maker for the arrangements of broadcasting system. In Germany, however, the Federal Constitutional Court can review the constitutionality of the statutes passed by the individual Land parliament upon request. To demonstrate this difference, typified (somehow also simplified) processes of decision-making in the two countries are illustrated in Figure 5.8 and Figure 5.9 respectively.

Figure 5.8 Process of decision-making in the British dual broadcasting system (an example)

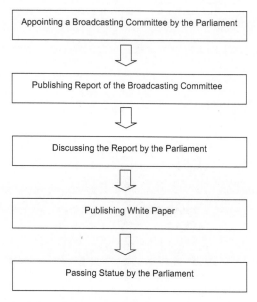

Source: illustrated by the author

Figure 5.9 Process of decision-making in the German dual broadcasting system (an example)

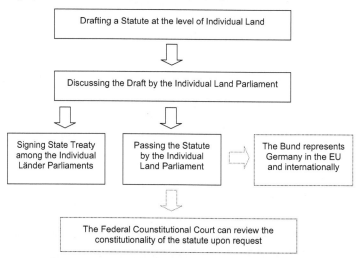

Source: illustrated by the author

5.2. Co-existence, conflicts and coordination in the dual broadcasting system

The rulings made by the German Federal Constitutional Court deal with the disputes at the constitutional level and are independent from political influences. Concerning the broadcasting issues, the most important criterion for the judicial review of the German Federal Constitutional Court comes from Article 5, Section 1, Sentence 2 of the German Basic Law, which guarantees freedom of reporting by broadcasting as well as freedom of opinion and freedom of press. So far the German Federal Constitutional Court has made thirteen rulings of broadcasting since 1961, among which eleven rulings of broadcasting were made during the time of dual broadcasting system except the first two rulings of broadcasting. Besides, four rulings of broadcasting are directly related to the establishment of the dual broadcasting system: Ruling of FRAG 1981, Ruling of Niedersachsen 1986, the Ruling of Baden-Wüttemberg 1987 and the Ruling of WDR 1991.[416] These rulings of broadcasting made by the German Federal Constitutional Court involve the clarification of the fundamental principles for the arrangements of the dual broadcasting system, such as the basis of the order of broadcasting, the functions of broadcasting, the preconditions and requirements for the introduction and arrangements of private broadcasting in Germany, the roles of public law broadcasting and private broadcasting in the dual broadcasting system respectively, and the problem of financing.[417] The significant functions of the rulings of broadcasting made by the German Constitutional Court for the arrangement of the dual broadcasting system lie in the following three aspects:

Firstly, the rulings of broadcasting made by the German Federal Constitutional Court only concern the fundamental basis of the order of broadcasting at the constitutional level, or, more precisely, the freedom of broadcasting is at the core concern. So the rulings of broadcasting made by the Federal Constitutional Court are to a large extent independent of political influence and above party lines. The common respect for the German Basic Law makes the rulings made by the Federal Constitutional Court acceptable by all political powers, although some of the opinions in the rulings of broadcasting remain controversial. The legislature is also legally bound by the rulings of broadcasting made by the Federal Constitutional Court. Hence, the fundamental principles clarified in the rulings of broadcasting made by the Federal Constitutional Court work as the "constitution" for the arrangements of the dual broadcasting system. This helps to reconcile the conflicts of ideas among various interest groups in practice, though arbitrating

---

416 For details cf. pp. 174 ff.
417 For details cf. pp. 176 ff.

political disputes dose not belong to the official task of the Federal Constitutional Court.[418]

Secondly, one specific property of the judicial review is that it has high consistency in all rulings made by the Federal Constitutional Court at various periods. The argumentation in the rulings of broadcasting made by the Federal Constitutional Court has to come down in one continuous line. Therefore, the understandings of the functions and roles of broadcasting in various rulings can not be changed in a drastic way. In addition, the judges of the Federal Constitutional Court are particularly cautious about the issues concerning the arrangements of broadcasting system. They hold the opinion that it is nearly irreversible once the broadcasting system moves towards an undesirable direction.[419]

Last but not least, though not explicitly stated, the rulings of broadcasting made by the Federal Constitutional Court function not only as an integration of viewpoints from the latest debates on broadcasting, but also as an integration of the discussions within the relatively small and less influential circle of media academia into the broader and highly influential socio-political arena. In the grounds (Begründung) of the rulings, opinions and viewpoints from the adversarial parties are comprehensively, systematically examined and consistently considered by the judges at the constitutional level. Nevertheless, the final decision is made by the judges independent from any external intervention. This function of integration of the rulings of broadcasting made by the Federal Constitutional Court ensures that all significant voices are to be heard in the decision-making of broadcasting system. Thus, it prevents any party or voice from being totally underrepresented in the decision-making of broadcasting system. More importantly, it also avoids the irreconcilable split between the strong political-economic forces and the small, often marginalized[420] left media academia. This helps to integrate the discourses on the role of media (in particular broadcasting) in a modern democracy into the mainstream of social and political discourses.

These three significant functions of the rulings of broadcasting made by the German Constitutional Court do not exist in the British decision-making model of broadcasting system, where the Parliament is the final decision-maker for the arrangements of broadcasting system as above mentioned. This could explain the quite different outcomes in these two countries when the supporters of the commercial broadcasting vigorously attempted to redefine broadcasting with the market logic in the 1980s. At that time, the conflicts between the supporters of

---

418 Wolfgang Hoffmann-Riem. *Regulating Media: the licensing and supervision of broadcasting in six countries*. New York: The Guilford Press, 1996. pp. 119 ff.
419 Cf. BVerfGE 57, 295 /323; BVerfGE 73, 118/160; BVerfGE 95, 163 /173.
420 James D. White. *Global Media: the television revolution in Asia*. New York and London: Routledge, 2005. p. 79.

5.2. Co-existence, conflicts and coordination in the dual broadcasting system

the public service broadcasting and the commercial broadcasting were so fierce that it was almost impossible for the two "camps" to reconcile with each other by political means. In Britain, where there is no written constitution and the values of public service broadcasting were largely regarded as part of the British conventions, it became particularly difficult for the conflicting groups to reach common views when the consensus collapsed. The forceful head of the British government, Mrs. Thatcher, who had a large majority in the Parliament, asserted her dominance in the reform of broadcasting. This has led to a direct consequence that the market logic prevailed over the public logic throughout the 1980s and the 1990s. The supporters for the public service broadcasting were politically powerless.

In West Germany, the conflicts between the two "camps" were as fierce as those in Britain while the political disputes also fell into a serious self-blockade. However, by resting on the German Basic Law, the rulings of broadcasting made by the Federal Constitutional Court not only defused tension between the two conflicting "camps", but also further clarified the fundamental principles of the arrangement of a dual broadcasting system. Unlike the British Parliament which became embroiled in power struggles in the extreme case during Mrs. Thatcher's governance, the German Federal Constitutional Court was a politically independent, neutral third party, whose rulings were eventually accepted by all conflicting parties. Unlike politicians who sometimes prone to make radical reform, what the judges of the Federal Constitutional Court most concern is the consistency of the interpretation of the freedom of broadcasting and to avoid undesirable development of broadcasting system.

The finding here that the German decision-making model of broadcasting system is to a larger extent immune from political interventions than the British model differs from some of the criticisms of German broadcasting system of being institutionally politicised[421] while the British broadcasting system enjoys a higher independence from political influences. These criticisms mainly refer to the politicisation of the regulatory bodies of German broadcasting. In Britain, the regulatory bodies of broadcasting conventionally follow the trusteeship model, which means that ideally the members of the regulatory bodies are no "experts" of broadcasting and no representatives of particular interests, but "persons of judgement and independence, who would inspire public confidence by having no interests to promote other than the public service"[422]. The appointments of the Board of Governors of the BBC (now Trustees of the BBC Trust), Board of ITA (later IBA, ITC, Ofcom), and the chairman and members of Broadcasting Committees all adopt this model of trusteeship. In Germany, on the contrary, the

---

421 Humphreys. pp. 152-53.
422 Briggs (1965), p. 393.

regulatory bodies usually follow the principle of proportionality (Proporz), borrowed from the organisational principle of parliament. The members of the broadcasting regulatory bodies come from various "socially significant groups" to reflect the principles of democracy and pluralism in broadcasting. The problem is that the parliamentarians are also included as members of the broadcasting regulatory bodies, along with other representatives from trade unions, churches, universities, etc. The various "social significant groups" also tend to have clear political allegiances. The links between the broadcasting system and the political influence have been in turn reflected in the political bias of the regional "third" channels.[423]

However, the extreme case in Britain in the 1980s reveals that the independence of the trusteeship model from political intervention could also be very fragile when conventions were no longer respected by radical politicians. In the era of the dual broadcasting system, the conflicts between the two (sometimes even more) adversarial ideas are often so fierce that it becomes very hard for the conflicting groups to reach a consensus within the parliament decision-making model. The decision-making of broadcasting system is therefore likely to fall into sharp power struggles, which could result in unstable and inconsistent decision-making.

The German decision-making model of broadcasting system, on the contrary, stays relatively neutral from political power struggles. The rulings made by the Federal Constitutional Court tackle problems solely within the boundaries of law. Problems beyond the boundaries of law, such as political or economic considerations, are not taken into account by the judges. This means that political considerations stay political. The legislature reserves its full competence for the arrangements of broadcasting system, when these arrangements do not violate the fundamental principles of the freedom of broadcasting. At the same time, thanks to the rulings of broadcasting made by the Federal Constitutional Court, a necessary consensus among the conflicting groups could be achieved, so that bitter controversies, brutal power struggles, severe inconsistencies of decision-making can be best possibly avoided.

In most countries of the world, decision-making of broadcasting system remains practically within the domain of politics. The experience of Germany offers an alternative perspective by which a politically independent third party, the German Federal Constitutional Court, can review the decision-making of broadcasting system within the boundaries of law for the sake of guaranteeing the fundamental values of the freedom of broadcasting, and further prevent the decision-

---

423 Humphreys, ibid.

making of broadcasting system from being a battlefield of sheer political power struggles.

5.3. Beyond the market myth: the criticism of the American purely commercial broadcasting by the dual broadcasting system

The USA has always been a pathfinder of modern broadcasting worldwide. The technological innovations, the broadcasting economy and the way of organising the American broadcasting system are widely regarded as a model to be imitated by many countries, just like what was happening with Chinese broadcasting in the past decade. However, countries of the dual broadcasting system such as Britain and Germany have been highly critical of the American broadcasting system, or, more precisely, of the American purely commercial broadcasting system. These countries also repudiate a fully commercialisation of broadcasting in principle.

In the British history of broadcasting, the American broadcasting system is also one of the most frequently referred broadcasting systems by British decision makers of broadcasting system. However, the British decision makers of broadcasting system twice refused (or partially refused) the American purely commercial broadcasting system. As early as at the founding stage of British broadcasting, the British decision makers were shocked at the "chaos of the ether" in the USA and decided to establish a commercial monopoly of the BBC instead.[424] Later Reith proposed the idea of public service broadcasting and transferred the BBC to a public corporation in 1927. Besides the practical considerations of technical, economic and political reasons, namely the scarcity of spectrum, the opposition from the press and the self-interested considerations of the Post Office, the most important argument for establishing the public service broadcasting was that it can better serve the public interest than the commercial broadcasting in terms of standards of programmes, efficiency of management and planned growth of broadcasting. Not only in Britain, there was a general tendency towards non-commercialism in Western Europe (except Luxemburg). This has been a feature of western European broadcasting where broadcasting was regarded more as a culture domain than as commodities in a free market like in the USA.

At the beginning of the 1950s, Britain decided to introduce commercial television into the existed public service broadcasting system in order to break up the monopoly of the public service broadcasting which was believed a damage of

---

[424] Cf. pp. 123 ff.

freedom by the post-war liberals, and to enhance competitiveness within the British broadcasting system.[425] Market mechanism was no longer completely rejected by the British broadcasting decision makers. Nevertheless, the decision makers of British broadcasting system were still very cautious about the issue of advertising. The American system of programme sponsorship, in which advertisers pay for individual programmes, was not allowed in British commercial television on the grounds that advertisers might have direct power over programme content.[426] Only spot advertising was permitted under very strict conditions. The prohibition of sponsorship[427] and the restrictions on spot advertising in British commercial television were regarded as a guarantee of the independence of programme-making from the influence of advertisers. Though financed commercially through advertising revenues, the British commercial television still differed enormously from its American counterpart in that it was highly constrained by the public service obligations.

However, in the broadcasting reform led by Mrs. Thatcher in the 1980s, the American purely commercial broadcasting system was regarded more as a successful model of market logic than an object of criticism for British politicians. In resonance with her American neo-liberal colleague Ronald Reagan, "deregulation" and "commercialisation" have been the buzzwords in Mrs. Thatcher's agenda of reforming broadcasting. Her successors of British government also followed this course of market logic concerning the issues of broadcasting policy. Distinct evidence was the fusion of five regulatory bodies of British commercial broadcasting and telecommunications in 2003 to establish a FCC-like umbrella regulatory body, the Office of Communications (Ofcom), which focuses more on the technological and economic aspects of broadcasting than on the journalistic perspective of broadcasting as a mass medium.

If the refusal and criticism of the American purely commercial broadcasting in Britain were, to a large extent, political decisions without written constitutional backing, the criticism of the American model of broadcasting system in Germany was mainly based on different understandings of the function of constitution. According to German contemporary theory of constitution, there are two dimensions of human rights. One dimension lies in their capacity as subjective rights of individuals which oblige the state to refrain from certain actions (the defence against state actions). The other dimension lies in their capacity as objective principles, by which the state is obliged to fulfil its protective duty (Schutzpflicht) to take action in order to secure or effectuate individual liberties

---

425 Cf. pp. 158 ff.
426 Curran and Seaton (2003), p. 185.
427 The prohibition of sponsorship of all programmes (except news and current events) was lifted in 1988. See Curran and Seaton (2003), ibid.

5.3. The criticism of the American purely commercial broadcasting system

against societal risks or dangers. Freedom of broadcasting, guaranteed by Article 5 Section 1 Sentence 2 of German Basic Law, also has these two capacities as both subjective rights and objective principles. Therefore, on the one hand, the freedom of broadcasting requires the principle of distance from the state (staatsfern) to defend against state interference in broadcasting. On the other hand, the freedom of broadcasting is understood as a "serving freedom" ("dienende Freiheit") which serves the purpose of free formation of individual as well as public opinions. Only free broadcasting organisations can provide unrestricted information about all relevant events and ideas which are essential for the free formation of opinions. The freedom of broadcasting requires that the broadcasting system as a whole is freely organised. Therefore, the state is obliged to take action in order to ensure the freedom of broadcasting from dominant social forces such as market forces (marktfern).[428] The public law broadcasting institutions, freely organised by the state to be independent from both state interference and market forces, are therefore a good example of the protection of basic rights by organisation (Grundrechtsschutz durch Organisation)[429]. In the dual broadcasting system, by which the public law broadcasting no longer has the status of monopoly, two most important preconditions for the introduction of private broadcasting are: 1) the freely organised public law broadcasting is responsible for the "basic provision" as well as "full provision" of broadcasting programmes for the general public, and, 2) the public law broadcasting is granted the "guarantee of existence and development" in terms of programme, technology and financing, which ensures the public law broadcasting to be competitive with the private broadcasting.

In the USA, on the contrary, although the Supreme Court also acknowledges that the freedom of broadcasting is guaranteed in the interest of viewers and listeners other than in the interest of the broadcasters, it is not prepared to require the government to take action to safeguard the ends of the freedom of broadcasting.[430] This means that the freedom of broadcasting has only the dimension of defence against state interference in the USA. The notion of a protective duty of the state elaborated by the German Federal Constitutional Court does not exist in the American understandings of human rights. Therefore, the broadcasting regulation in the American system is not about to require a "positive" safeguard of the broadcasting system, but only to produce the minimum requirements for a

---

428 Dieter Grimm. "Human rights and judicial review in Germany", in David M. Beatty (ed.) *Human rights and judicial review: a comparative perspective*. USA: Kluwer Academic Publishers, 1994. pp 267-95. pp. 276 ff. See also Dieter Grimm, *Anforderungen an künftige Medienordnungen*. In Arbeitspapiere des Instituts für Rundfunkökonomie Nr. 176. Germany: Institut für Rundfunkökonomie an der Universität zu Köln, 2003.
429 Grimm (1994), p. 281.
430 Grimm (1994), p. 282.

functional broadcasting order instead, in a similar manner of the "traffic regulations".[431] The regulatory body of broadcasting, the FCC, whose main task was to take charge of broadcast licensing, was established by the Communications Act 1934 largely with an intention to end the "chaos of the ether" of that time. Since the frequencies were scarce resources, the regulation in broadcasting had to take "public interest" into consideration in order to legitimise the criteria of allocation. Nevertheless, there are no further regulations for a positive arrangement of the structure of the broadcasting order and the programme performance of broadcaster in the Communications Act.

As Seaton points out, "in America, there are public service ideals in the media – but no institutions to put them into practice", especially after the newspaper industry is in severe collapse in recent years.[432] Many American intellectuals have for a long time realised the underperformance of American commercial broadcasters of educational, cultural and informational programmes. Started from a group of educational television stations of the universities, the highly dispersed American public television and radio stations, including the some larger national organisations like the Public Broadcasting Service (PBS) and the National Public Radio (NPR), were established in the late 1960s to remedy the deficiency of educational and cultural programmes of American broadcasting. However, the public broadcasting in the USA is largely marginalised as the so-called "cultural ghetto" for elites and minority groups by filling the programming void left by commercial television. And financially, the tight yet unstable budgets of public broadcasting stations from the vastly mixed sources of subscriptions, government funding and foundation grants etc. make them heavily rely on foreign producers (notably the BBC) and uncompetitive with American commercial networks (ABC, CBS, NBC, and many others).[433]

The criticism of American purely commercial system by the dual broadcasting system, either from the ideological perspective of the British decision makers before the 1980s, or from the constitutional perspective of the German Federal Constitutional Court, is of special importance for the two following reasons. Firstly, as Seaton points out, if the main threat to the existence of the public service broadcasting was political for the first sixty years (from the 1920s to the 1980s), today it is more economic as a result of the cut-throat competition launched by the huge, rapacious and rich international conglomerates. Market forces, along with their market logic, were once so pre-dominant in the world-

---

431 Hoffmann-Riem (1989). p. 41.
432 Curran and Seaton (2010), p. 226.
433 James Ledbetter. "Funding and Economics of American Public Television", in Eli M. Noam and Jens Waltermann (eds.) *Public Television in America*. Gütersloh: Bertelsmann Foundations Publishers, 1988. pp. 73-94.

5.3. The criticism of the American purely commercial broadcasting system

wide decision making of the future development of broadcasting since the 1980s. However, the dominance of any social group as a predominant power of opinion, particularly the dominance of economic power, is enormously disadvantageous for both consumers and democracy. The market forces and their business activities should therefore stay by no means unrestricted in the broadcasting sector.

Secondly, the American purely commercial broadcasting system has always been the most influential and the most imitated broadcasting system worldwide. This is largely attributed to the leading position of American audio-visual products in the global media economy and cultural industry[434], and the globally political, economic and cultural dominance of the USA as a whole. However, the leading position of the USA in the global export markets of audio-visual products is to a large extent a uniqueness of the American film and television industry, which can be hardly replicated by any other country because of the "cultural proximity" of the culture consumption – television audience generally prefer watching indigenous programmes to imported programmes with the sole exception of American audio-visual products. Moreover, when observing some countries and regions whose broadcasting systems have been highly commercialised since the late 1980s, it is highly likely to cause problems such as excessive competition in the broadcasting market and deterioration of the quality of programmes, like in Taiwan for example[435]; and the increasing loyalty of commercial broadcasters to government despite their earlier contribution during the process of anti-totalitarian broadcasting system in Russia[436]. The democratic and cultural functions of broadcasting are therefore seriously damaged. After all, as Seaton puts, "media are politically and socially very important and economically of the middling rank".[437] The democratic and cultural functions should always be the first considerations to be taken into account in the decision making of broadcasting. Criticism of the purely commercial broadcasting system is therefore both necessary and topical.

Either of the models of the dual broadcasting system, British or German, has shown us an alternative for constructing a broadcasting order in addition to state-controlled or market-dominated broadcasting. Most important of all, the dual broadcasting system functions fairly well both in fulfilling the democratic and cultural functions of broadcasting, and in maintaining a dynamic media economy at the same time. The dual broadcasting system, therefore, can provide the deci-

---

434 See European Audiovisual Observatory. *Focus 2009 – World Film Trends.* http://www.international- television.org/tv_market_data/focus_world_film_market_trends_statistics.html. Last visited in June 2011.
435 The author's observation.
436 Grotech Co., Ltd. (ed.). *Digital television in Russia.* http://www.international- television.org/tv_market_data/digital_tv_in_russia.html. Last visited in June 2011. p. 40.
437 Curran and Seaton (2010), p. 226.

sion makers of broadcasting system worldwide a rich source of ideas and initiatives as a better and feasible third way beyond the state control and the market myth.

5.4. Is the dual broadcasting system an anachronism in the era of Internet?

The establishment and development of the dual broadcasting system often appear to be an interaction of particular ideas and concrete social conditions, especially technologies, because the development of broadcasting is connected closely with the advancements of technologies. The examples concerning the advancements of technologies are – the scarcity of airwaves justified the monopoly of (public service) broadcasters in many countries for a long period; contrariwise, the emergence of cable and satellite broadcasting throughout the 1970s led to the disappearance of the scarcity of available channels, and then required the break-up of monopoly. Some particular ideas or ethos are undoubtedly highly essential for the decision making of broadcasting system. For example, there was a close correlation between the Reithian conception of "public service" and the reforming ideal of the Victorian middle class, spouted in the late 19th century and developed by the newly emerging professional classes with an aim to reform the lower class with culture – "the best that has been thought and written in the world".[438] And the wave of privatisation and deregulation of broadcasting in the 1980s was evidently promoted by the prevailing neo-liberalism of the time. This ideas-conditions interaction concerning broadcasting sector seems to follow such a rule: it is usually the latest technologies that trigger off the imperative of regulation or decision making, and then different ideas come to compete with each other in order to be the leading idea of decision making. Unlike what technological determinism claims, technology acts rather as a catalyst than a determinant for changes in broadcasting sector. It is the ideas that set the general orientation of the overall decision making process in view of the fact that different decision-makers may develop fundamentally different strategies to deal with the latest technological or other sorts of imperatives.[439]

After the technologies of cable and satellite broadcasting greatly impacted on the decision making and the landscape of broadcasting in the 1980s, the next wave of technological advancement was the digitalisation of broadcasting since the 1990s. To respond to Japan's ambition of setting global standards for high-definition television (HDTV) using analogue technology, the USA developed the ATSC (Advanced Television Systems Committee) set of technical standards for

---

438 Scannell. pp. 55-56.
439 Cf. McQuail's media policy change model. pp. 18-20.

5.4. Is the dual broadcasting system an anachronism in the era of Internet?

both standard and high-definition digital terrestrial television in the 1990s with the support of the FCC.[440] This proves to have evoked a new wave of technological revolution of broadcasting. By digitalising the contents of broadcasting (television, voice and data) into a single stream of digital bits and compressing them, not only the capacity of transmission and the quality of broadcast contents have been unprecedentedly improved, digital broadcasting further delivers a new range of applications (such as interactivity services) and a number of new platforms and distributive outlets (for example, online, mobile, interactive games in addition to the conventional television set and radio) which were unimaginable in the era of analogue broadcasting. To date, most countries in the world have set their agenda of switchover from analogue to digital transmission around 2010 to 2015, while a number of advanced economies have already completed the switch off of analogue transmission, such as Netherlands (in 2006), Finland and Sweden (in 2007).[441]

The impact of digitalisation on broadcasting is on all accounts profound. At the micro-level, digitalisation has affected the operational and corporate strategies of individual broadcasters (both public and commercial). For example, it becomes imperative for many broadcasters to embark on multi-platform distribution strategies so as to better cater to the needs of audience, although this must not be profitable economically. At the middle-level, as the distribution of media content has been tremendously extended from single or few platforms to multi-platform through digitalisation, this has also affected the upstream phases of commissioning and production of content. Along with the emergence of a large number of new "windows" in the era of digitalisation, the process of "windowing", where media content is arranged to be released at particular sequence in order to maximise profit in different "windows", becomes much more complex than ever before.[442]

The biggest challenge arisen by digitalisation is nevertheless at the macro-level, namely the decision making of broadcasting. As a result of the convergence of information and telecommunications technologies which has been greatly accelerated through the digital technologies, conventional broadcasting (via television set and radio) is no longer the only, though still a very important platform for the distribution of media contents among a number of other platforms of online, mobile, interactive games etc. This indicates a tendency that now the decision making of broadcasting has gone beyond the broadcasting domain. Actual-

---

440 María Trinidad García Leiva and Michael Starks. "Digital switchover across the globe: the emergence of complex regional patterns", in *Media Culture & Society* 2009 31: 787. p. 788.
441 Leiva and Starks, p. 787.
442 Gillian Doyle. "From Television to Multi-Platform: Less from More or More for Less?", in *Convergence* 2010 16: 431.

ly, a number of governments have already integrated the decision making of broadcasting with the sectors of information and telecommunications to forge an umbrella authority for a variety of earlier separated sectors, such as the Federal Communications Commission (FCC) in the USA, the Office of Communications (Ofcom)[443] and its parent department – Department for Culture, Media and Sport (DCMS) in the UK, and the Ministry of Internal Affairs and Communications (MIC) in Japan.

If the technologies of cable and satellite in the 1980s had eroded some of the essential underpinnings for decision making of broadcasting in the terrestrial broadcasting era, such as the scarcity of spectrum and the regulation of broadcasting within national territory, the advent of digital broadcasting may radically nullify these once essential preconditions for the decision making of broadcasting, at least from the technological perspective. Now the scarcity of spectrum in the analogue era has been replaced by the plenitude of capacity in the digital era. The market share, which was once of high importance for legitimating the existence of the public service broadcasting and for assessing the advertising value of certain commercial programme, might therefore be enormously diluted when the emergence of numerous channels and programmes (and eventually via other new platforms) continues to fragment the broadcasting market. The rise of the online video platform like YouTube and individual video blogs appears to largely enrich the "external plurality" of broadcasting – now everyone can broadcast online. Broadcasting seems no longer the privilege of a small group of elites or the game of the rich. The conventional broadcasting seems to fall into decline.

However, this is just one side of the digitalisation coin. The decline of conventional broadcasting must not necessarily mean a decline of the conventional broadcasters, in particular the public service broadcasters (somehow beyond all expectations). As James Curran observed that the international media conglomerates have already started to respond to market fragmentation with corporate concentration since the years of multi-channels in the 1990s. The merging of media companies happened everywhere – in the USA, Britain and Germany. And the business portfolios of these international media conglomerates cover almost all media-related sectors: film and television production, a bunch of television channels, press and publishing, cinemas, music labels, sport teams and even theme parks.[444] The corporate concentration of international media conglomerates would inevitably increase the risk of opinion concentration, which would in turn hurt the principle of plurality in a modern democracy. Moreover, the majority of the newly emerging providers of media content are market-oriented and of-

---

443 The Ofcom regulates the broadcasting and telecommunications industries in the UK except the BBC.
444 Curran (2002), pp. 228-29.

5.4. Is the dual broadcasting system an anachronism in the era of Internet?

ten focus on entertainment. This means that the huge number of newly emerging "broadcasters" does not automatically convert into the external plurality of broadcasting in a democratic sense. They are more interested in demanding a slice of the (commercial) broadcasting market cake than fulfilling the democratic functions of broadcasting. The provision of media content by various interest groups or individuals, which can eventually become the real "public" media some day, is so far still at the amateur level and remains largely unorganised, though the impact of these individual "broadcasters" can be enormous because of particular events, such as during the recent Arabian Revolution 2011.

The public service broadcasters, instead, become pretty successful with their online services, particularly the online catch-up service like the BBC iPlayer or the online streaming contents, which gives the audience a chance to see programmes missed or to watch their favourite programmes over Internet again whenever they want. The high quality of programming has endowed "ratings" with a new dimension in the age of multi-platform brought about by digitalisation – the aggregate viewing. This means that the high quality programming would have much higher aggregate viewing in the long run. Broadcasting programming of high quality is no longer a one-off for the prime time, whose relatively high costs often chill cost-sensitive commercial broadcasters. The new dimension of aggregating viewing in the age of multi-platform not only rewards the public service broadcasters for appreciating and persistently producing high quality programming over a long period of time and hence extends public value, but also encourages the commercial broadcasters to adapt a commissioning model of "high production, high quality and high costs", which enables the commercial broadcasters to yield additional revenues in a prolonged distribution period.[445]

Moreover, since the proliferation of broadcasters in the era of digitalisation would most likely bring about a proliferation of entertainment contents, the full range of programme provisions offered by the public service broadcasting is of particular significance so as to guarantee the internal plurality of programming[446], which might be more valuable than before for a modern democracy in a generally over-commercialised media environment. Another noticeable tendency in the era of digitalisation is an increasing demand for integration when the broadcasting market becomes more and more fragmented as a result of the proliferation of broadcasters and niche channels. As the viewing shares in Britain and Germany show[447], the big public service broadcasters and commercial broadcast-

---

445 Doyle, p. 438.
446 Grimm (2003), pp. 7-8.
447 See *"viewing shares of individual channesl in Britain 2008"* (figure 5.1) on p. 171, and *"market shares of the German television market 2009"* (figure 5.2) on p. 180.

ers remain stably dominant in the individual national broadcasting markets although numerous niche channels are emerging. The majority of the audience seems to prefer taking the traditional full-range programmes as their daily feed of broadcasting, while on and off using a handful of (often too specifically segmented) niche channels as complementary stuff. The integration of society by broadcasting is of high significance for public discourse on socially relevant subjects in a modern democracy, which has even been regarded as the good reason for the existence of the public service broadcasting in the era of digitalisation.[448]

As mentioned before, many governments worldwide responded to this technological convergence brought about by digitalisation by forging an umbrella authority for a variety of earlier separated sectors. This is also the case in Britain. Five regulatory bodies – the Independent Television Commission, the Broadcasting Standards Commission, the Office of Telecommunications, the Radio Authority, and the Radio Communications Agency – merged in 2003 to become a new media and communications regulator, the Office of Communications (Ofcom), which received its full authority from the Communications Act 2003. The merger assumed a need for further deregulation in the commercial broadcasting sector and telecommunications industries in the era of digitalisation[449], while the Communications Act 2003 accordingly lifted many restrictions on cross-media ownership. This proves to follow a continuous line of the techno-economic dimensions of broadcasting as well as the principles of the market logic since the 1980s,[450] and resonates with the generally market-oriented telecom and media policies of the supranational authority, the European Commission (EU), and the international organisation for trade, WTO.[451]

However, not all countries unreservedly follow the techno-economic dimensions for the decision making of broadcasting in the era of digitalisation. Germany, for example, still insists on the socio-cultural dimensions as the main consideration for the decision making of broadcasting. In the 12th Ruling of Broadcasting made by the German Federal Constitutional Court, the Ruling of License Fees II 2007, the Court reinforced the guarantee of existence and development for the public service broadcasting (die Bestands- und Entwicklungsgarantie für den öffentlichen Rundfunk) by not considering the public service broadcasting and its financing through license fees despite new media and convergence as obsolete, but see them as indispensable for the formation of opinion and democracy.[452] The financial capacity of German public law broadcasters has also been

---

448   Grimm (2003), p. 8.
449   Curran and Seaton (2003), p. 394.
450   Cf. figure 5.7 on p. 187.
451   Curran and Seaton (2003), pp. 394-95.
452   BVerfGE 119, 181.

5.4. Is the dual broadcasting system an anachronism in the era of Internet?

further enhanced in the age of Internet by requiring an extra payment of license fee for Internet link of broadcasting since 2007 if the household does not register the conventional radio or/and television license. PCs, notebooks, PDAs or mobile phones are categorised as *novel receiving sets of broadcasting (neuartige Rundfunkempfangsgeräte)*, which stand in contrast to the *conventional receiving sets of broadcasting (herkömmliche Rundfunkgeräte)* such as television sets or radios which receive broadcasting programmes through antenna, cable or satellite.[453] When other public service broadcasters like the BBC have to constrain their budget planning in order to spend extra investments on new platform services[454], German public law broadcasters have been given extra (financial) support for embarking on new platforms of Internet and mobile which enables them to extend public value for the users of novel receiving sets of broadcasting. This seems quite exceptional when the commercial broadcasters still suffer greatly from the latest economic recession.

The decision making of broadcasting at the EU level is also not always merely favourable to the techno-economic dimensions of broadcasting. On many occasions, European institutions such as the European Parliament and the Council have reaffirmed the relevance of PSB in the new era and the importance for PSB to develop online. In spite of a constant tendency towards commercialisation of European media and the increasingly market-oriented European policies on television, a general consensus has been revealed about the core values embodied within PSB in numerous Recommendations made by the Council of Europe.[455] The democratic, cultural and social functions of broadcasting in the era of Internet have been declared in the 2001 Communication on State Aid to PSB by the EU that:

> "... the public service remit might include certain services that are not 'programmes' in the traditional sense, such as online information services, to the extent that while taking into account the development and diversification of activities in the digital age they are addressing the same democratic, social and cultural need of the society in question."[456]

However, as Brevini observes, as with broadcasting, today the development of policies concerning the online expansion of PSBs is still evidently framed within each national context even during the process of European integration and glob-

---

453 See http://www.gez.de/gebuehren/internet_pcs/index_ger.html. Last visited in August 2011.
454 Doyle, p. 444.
455 Benedetta Brevini. "Towards PSB 2.0? Applying the PSB ethos to online media in Europe: A comparative study of PSBs' internet policies in Spain, Italy and Britain". In *European Journal of Communicartions* 2010 25: 348. See footnote 2 on p. 361.
456 Ibid. Cited by Brevini. p. 349. However, a more restrictive approach has been recently adopted by the new EC Communication on state aid to PSB since 2009. See Brevini, footnote 3 on p. 361, and p. 359.

alisation. In countries like Germany, where the affairs of broadcasting in terms of programmes are placed within the domain of culture on a federalist basis (Kulturhoheit der Länder)[457], the considerations of the socio-cultural dimensions remain furthermore prior for the decision making of broadcasting.

As discussed above, the public service broadcasters in Britain and Germany have not only survived in the era of Internet, but also gain some advantage on grounds of its fixed revenue of license fee (and extra payment in the case of Germany) compared with the commercial broadcasters suffering greatly from the latest economic recession. Nonetheless, the vitally changed environment under the impact of digitalisation, globalisation, convergence, fragmentation and commercialisation has facilitated the public service broadcasting to expand beyond conventional platforms of broadcasting to embark on novel platforms of Internet and mobile phone. As the importance of the novel platforms for broadcasting keeps increasing, some scholars argue that this has become a main impetus for the public service broadcasting to be transformed into public service media. In other words, the public service broadcasting ethos have been applied to online media and may eventually "(with other civil entities such as libraries, universities, museums, charities, parliaments and local government) collaboratively construct a public forum that would help to exploit the public interest potential of the web rather than simply allowing its gradual commoditisation."[458]

5.5. *The failure and success of imitating the dual broadcasting system: the cases of post-Communist Europe and Eastern Asia*

The latest massive imitation of the dual broadcasting system, or, more precisely, the imitation of the public service broadcasting, happened in the transformation of the post-Communist countries since 1989. Most Central and Eastern European countries have established their own public service broadcasters which were believed essential for the transformation of the totalitarian Communist media system to the democratic media system, as well as to respond to the requirements of EU integration as candidate countries.[459] Nevertheless, the introduction of PSB

---

457 Cf. the 9th Ruling of Broadcasting made by the German Federal Constitutional Court, the Ruling of the "EU Guidelines for Television" 1995, which cleared the competence of the EU in the economic, not the cultural, problems of broadcsting. BVerfGE 92, 203.
458 Brevini, p. 360.
459 The Central and Eastern European countries that have established public service broadcasting organisations include Czech Republic, Slovak Republic, Armenia, Slovenia, Bulgaria, Albania, Hungary, Romania, Poland, Macedonia, Lithuania, Estonia, Croatia, Latvia, Bosnia-Herzegovina. See Karol Jakubowitz, "Ideas in our heads: introduction of PSB as part of media system change in central and eastern Europe", in *European Journal of Communication* 2004 19:53. p. 64.

5.5. The failure and success of imitating the dual broadcasting system: the cases of post-Communist Europe and Eastern Asia

in the post-Communist countries proved to be a futile attempt more than a decade later. The newly established PSB organisations in the post-Communist countries are either described as in "a state of crisis"[460], or become "empty shells".[461] In a dual broadcasting system with the co-existence of both public and private broadcasting, most PSB organisations in the Central and Eastern European countries are not only too weak to fulfil the democratic functions of broadcasting media in the transforming societies, but also have to battle for survival under the immense political and market pressures. In some other post-Communist countries which even do not bother introducing any public service broadcasting system, the status of press freedom even regresses to the pre-transformation years. In Russia, for example, the main national television channels are currently tightly controlled by the government through extensive media holdings, while the country retains a relatively liberal and plural print media system at the same time.[462] Being perceived as the most important means of communication, television has been utilised by the government (especially under Putin since 2000) as a powerful instrument to expand its own influence and to beat the opposition parties at the same time.[463]

Many scholars attempt to analyse the possible causes for the failure of introducing the PSB in the Central and Eastern European countries as well as the regression of media freedom in the post-Communist countries. Some scholars, such as Smaele, ascribe the failure of consolidating the freedom of broadcasting in the post-Communist countries to the factor of "culture". By following the Huntingtonian paradigm of distinguishing the differences between the western culture (which allegedly emphasises individualism and respects for the law and has a long tradition of democracy) and the eastern culture (which is characterised by the collectivism and respect for authority and share no tradition of democracy), Smaele argues that the media change in Russia and many other post-Communist countries is indeed a process of "westification" (or in other variations of "Europeanisation", "Germanification"). Since the Russian culture can be seen as a product of cross (western and eastern) cultures but has more in common with the eastern perspective, the western model of broadcasting can therefore not be

---

460 Sandra Hrvatin, cited by Jakubowicz. p. 63.
461 Karol Jakubowicz, cited by Julia Rozanova. "Public Television in the Context of Established and Emerging Democracy: Quo Vadis?", in *The International Communication Gazette* 2007 Vol 69(2): 129-47. p. 140.
462 See Jonethan Becker. "Lessons from Russia: a neo-authoritarian media system", in *European Journal of Communication* 2004 Vol 19(2): 139-63. p. 150.
463 Rozanova. p. 136.

simply transplanted to Eastern Europe in general because of huge cultural and ideological differences.[464]

Another similar yet more sophisticated opinion about the failure of media system transformation in the post-Communist countries is the theory of neo-institutionalism. It focuses on the more "intangible" part of institutions beyond the "tangible" part of legal framework, the organization of the state and other administrative, political and economic institutions, and defines institutions as "rules of the game", or "behaviour patterns" that govern individual and collective actions as rules of collective life. This theory suggests that "lingering elements of old social consciousness, civilization and culture may result in proposals for legal and organizational frameworks that are not in accordance with the new system being created", while the new organizational frameworks are usually created first as part of the top-down social engineering element of transformation. This "path dependence" effect hinders the post-Communist transformation from being successfully achieved within a short period, because the economic, political and cultural conditions in these countries were "shaped by the last 500 years of that country's history" and would continue exerting their impact on the process of post-Communist transformation in the foreseeable future.[465]

Different from the two arguments above which mainly focus on the historical and cultural legacies of the old institutions or of a wider context of culture, Becker revisits the classical but often maligned "Four Theories of the Press" approach, and criticises the regression of media system in Putin's Russia as a rise of neo-authoritarian media system. In the neo-authoritarian media system, the state (particular the executive branch) still retains an overwhelming control over the media system, particularly over the most influential medium of television and issues that are of central importance to the regime, such as national security (in particular Chechnya) and elections. The autonomy and independence of television broadcasters are seriously eroded through means of: the appointments to key positions which are linked to political loyalty; financial control by which subsidies, targeted tax advantages, government advertising and other forms of assistance are used to promote support; attacks on the critical or oppositional media that economic pressures are selectively applied through legal and quasi-legal actions against owners, as well as attacks on critical journalists by prescribing criminal and civil penalties concerning such issues as libel, state interests, national security and the image of the head of state, and this further facilitates a chill of fear and self-censorship among the majority of journalists. What the neo-authoritarian media system differs from the traditional ones is the false toleration

---

464 Hedwig de Smaele. "The applicability of Western Media Models on the Russian Media System". In *European Journal of Communication* 1999 (14): 173-89.
465 Jakubowicz. pp. 55-56.

5.5. The failure and success of imitating the dual broadcasting system: the cases of post-Communist Europe and Eastern Asia

of pluralism (for example, in print media) and ostensible commitment to democracy. This "managed democracy" in Putin's Russia, in Becker's opinion, has put the real democratic media system in jeopardy in that "formal democratic institutions may appear to exist but they are rotten at their core".[466]

Contrary to the theory of neo-institutionalism and "path dependence" approach, Becker ascribes the failure of media system transformation in the post-Communist countries to the "institutional incapacity", by which the executive branch of state remains the most important threat to the emergence of democratic media systems and has not yet been effectively reined through a more sophisticated state institutions, such as a powerful legislative and judicial protection of journalists and media outlets, as well as press freedom in general. In other words, the process of democratisation has still a long way to go and is far from accomplishment.

Concerning the aforementioned three opinions that attempt to explain the failure of media system transformation in the post-Communist countries, the imitation of the dual broadcasting system in Eastern Asia (Japan and Korea) has offered a convincing counter-example against the versions of culture and "path dependence" approach. Japan and Korea, which are, without doubt, more typically "eastern" both geographically and culturally, have established an (at least formally) fairly stable dual broadcasting system respectively. In Japan, a dual broadcasting system has been adopted since the 1950s, by which the national public service broadcaster NHK (Nippon Hoso Kyokai, the Japan Broadcasting Corporation) co-exists with other five major commercial terrestrial broadcasters (regional services but with headquarters in Toyko) and other newly emerged yet relatively small commercial cable and satellite broadcasters. NHK, which operates two terrestrial television services (one general and one educational), two satellite television services and three radio networks, is dominant in Japanese broadcasting for its highly reliable public image, high quality programming, strong financial capacity, and advanced technological advantages. In a survey conducted by NHK, the majority of the interviewed viewers and listeners regarded NHK reliable (82 per cent), useful (84 per cent) and sophisticated (76 per cent). About 88 per cent of the interviewed viewers and listeners chose NHK as their first news source when an earthquake or tidal wave struck.[467] This is of special importance in a country always confronting natural disasters. Another survey showed that NHK has been for a long period trusted even more than the National Diet, the courts of Law, and the government.[468] NHK provides a wide variety of programming with high quality, including news and public affairs, drama, docu-

---

466 See Becker, pp. 147 ff.
467 Hilliard and Keith. p. 45.
468 White. p. 79.

mentaries, and educational programmes, while many of them won international major awards.[469] NHK has one of the largest public broadcast budgets in the world ($6.9 billion in 2009), mainly thanks to the large Japanese population (ca. 127 million in 2009) and the longstanding prosperous Japanese economy. It is financed almost solely (97 per cent) by the "receiving fee" system (Japanese version of license fee). Unlike what happens in other countries like in Britain and German, where a license fee is first paid to a third agency, then later passed on to the broadcaster after the government had collected its percentage, NHK collects the "receiving" fees by itself. Moreover, NHK plays a world leading role in the advanced technological innovation of broadcasting, particularly in the areas of satellite television and high-definition TV (HDTV) in the past decades.[470] Next to NHK, the five major terrestrial broadcasters, whose programming mainly focuses on entertainment and expands to news and current affaires since the 1980s, share jointly the second most affluent advertising market of the world.

Although NHK is such a sound and influential public service broadcaster in Japan, it plays by no means the role of public monitor to criticise government as its western counterparts do or claim to do so. For Western scholars, NHK is rather part of the Japanese "establishment", which not only has close linkage with the governmental ministries, foremost the broadcasting policy-making body Ministry of Posts and Telecommunications (now merged into Ministry of Internal Affairs and Communications), as well as other big business, but also carefully follows its journalistic convention of not broadcasting any news that would cause "chaos" or "confusion" (for the government and society).[471]

This is part of the oddness of the post-war Japanese politics. Established as a BBC model of public service broadcaster in 1925, NHK once served as the mouthpiece of the Japanese military government propaganda during the Second World War. Similar to the West German broadcasting institutions, it has also been reconstructed by the Supreme Commander Allied Powers (SCAP) after the war. A Broadcast Law was passed in 1950, which has given NHK a uniquely autonomous status as well as guaranteed freedom of expression. The Broadcast Law 1950 explicitly prohibited government or other outside interference in NHK's programming, and guaranteed the financial independence of NHK through the "receiving fee" system.[472] However, there lacked a thorough self-reflection in Japanese politics on the war as what happened in the post-war West Germany. Not only has a former Class A war criminal, Kishi Nobusuke, become

---

469 Roya Akhavan-Majid. "Public service broadcasting and the challenge of new technology: a case study of Japan's NHK". In *International Communication Gazette* 1992 50: 21-36. p. 24.
470 White, pp. 88 ff.
471 Ibid. pp. 102-04.
472 Ibid. pp. 84-87.

5.5. The failure and success of imitating the dual broadcasting system: the cases of post-Communist Europe and Eastern Asia

Prime Minister of Japan in the later 1950s, the structure and personnel of NHK as well as many other governmental authorities were little touched by the Allied occupations after the war.[473] This could partly explain the highly conservative and undemocratic side of the Japanese society till this day. While NHK remains a highly autonomous yet fairly conservative institution and part of the establishment, the commercial terrestrial broadcasters have achieved a great success with the often critical news shows, such as "News Station" anchored by Kume Hiroshi on TV Asahi and "Chikushi Tetsuya News 23" anchored by Chikushi Tetsuya on TBS, since the 1980s.

This situation of the public service broadcasting in Korea is similar to that in the Central and Eastern European countries, where the democratisation of media has been the main focus of attention for media scholars and intellectuals during the process of democratisation since 1987. Unlike in the CEECs where public service broadcasters are relatively weak, public service broadcasting system has very solidified its position in Korea. Among the five national terrestrial television networks, four of them are public service broadcasters (KBS1, KBS2, Munhwa, EBS[474]), while only one national terrestrial television network SBS (Seoul Broadcasting Station) and many cable programme providers and system operators are commercial. The two main national broadcasters, the KBS (Korean Broadcasting System, with two terrestrial television services KBS1 and KBS2) and MBC (Munhwa Broadcasting Corporation), which were transformed from state broadcasters to public service broadcaster in 1987, are leading national broadcasters in Korea. The KBS and MBC have mixed funding sources, in turn reflected by their programming output: the KBS1 is free from advertisement and financed by license fee, whilst its programming ranges from news and current affairs, educational programmes for children, documentaries, drama; the KBS2 is financed with advertising revenues and its programming is featured with entertainment and drama aimed at family and young audience; MBC is also financed with advertising revenues and is particularly popular for its drama programming.[475] Dramas produced by the KBS and MBC are so popular in the entire Eastern Asia that this even promoted a cultural phenomenon of "Korean Wave" in the neighbour countries (regions) of China, Japan, Hong Kong and Taiwan in

---

473 Ibid. p. 86.
474 EBS (Korean Educational Broadcasting System) is an educational public service broadcaster, financed manily by publishing revenue (41 per cent), advertising revue and governmental subsidy (20.7 per cent) and television license fee (3 per cent). EBS is relatively small compared with KBS and MBC. See Research, Development and Evaluation Commission, Executive Yuan (Taiwan) (ed.). *The Policy Positioning and Research for further Improvement in the Public Service Broadcasting System in Taiwan* (in Chinese《我國公共電視體制之政策定位與治理研究》). 2010. www.rdec.gov.tw/public/PlanAttach/201008031129105338800.pdf. Last visited in September 2011.pp. 24 ff.
475 Ibid.

recent years, and further make Korea a leading exporter of cultural products in Eastern Asia.

In spite of the huge success of public service broadcasters in drama production and export, Korean journalists are generally unsatisfied with the media environment in terms of press freedom, especially with the direct intervention in the management personnel by the state and the self-censorship within the organisation,[476] which seems to conform to some of the key features in the aforementioned new authoritarian model of media system in CEECs developed by Becker.

The cases of Japan and Korea, where the public service broadcasters are fairly consolidated yet less democratic than their Western European counterparts, indicate that the process of democratisation has not yet reached the more sophisticated stage in these two countries, particularly in term of the principle of "distance from the state" in media sector. This has been achieved in Britain largely with the help of its liberal conventions, and in Germany by the powerful legislative and judicial protection. The later is of particular importance for countries which have to imitate more advanced systems. It would be fruitless for the further course of democratisation when the focus is merely put on the burden of the former Communist regimes or "path dependence". One should not forget that Germany still regarded itself as part of the "Central Europe" – both geographically and culturally – until the 19th century, and also suffered from the control of the extreme totalitarian Nazi regime in the mid-20th century, by which broadcasting has been notoriously instrumentalised as the mouthpiece for Nazi propaganda. The post-war experience of West Germany shows that a thorough self-reflection, the adoption of democratic ideas and institutions, and the respect of an independent and well functional judicial system may effectively facilitate the transformation from a totalitarian to democratic system. The historical and cultural legacies of the old institutions or of a wider context of culture should rather be consciously treated as part of the obstacles to be overcome in the path to a more democratic system rather than being seen as static, unalterable facts.

What specifically causes the failure of the introduction of public service broadcasting in CEECs, which offers meaningful lessons for those who show interest in, seems to be the following four reasons. Firstly, the introduction of public service broadcasting has been highly politicised in the CEECs and the democratic function of the public service broadcasting system has been overstated by its advocates. It is true that a democratic media system is of essential importance for the democratisation process in a country; nevertheless, democratic function is not the only function of the public service broadcasting system. Besides the democratic function, public service broadcasting system still has many

---

476 Jae-kyoung Lee. "Press Freedom and Democratization: South Korea's Experience and Some Lessons". In *International Communication Gazette*1997 59: 135.

5.5. The failure and success of imitating the dual broadcasting system: the cases of post-Communist Europe and Eastern Asia

other dimensions of the cultural, educational, informative and entertainment functions, which are as essential for a modern society as the democratic one. The excessive emphasis on the democratic function of the public service broadcasting system has made it in a particularly vulnerable position when the indispensable protective mechanism has not yet been established. The direct impact of the excessive emphasis on the democratic function of the public service broadcasting system is, as the experience in the CEECs showed, either the marginalisation of the PSBs, or the recapture of national broadcasting institutions by the more powerful political forces. A democratic media system can not exist by itself and be separated from a generally undemocratic society. The degree of the democratisation of a society is also reflected in its media. The introduction of the PSB in CEECs proved to be a premature failure during the process of democratisation of the media system.

Secondly, as Jakubowicz also pointed out, the timing of introducing the PBS in CEECs was, unfortunately, not a good one at all.[477] Throughout the 1980s and the 1990s, it was exactly the most difficult time for most PSB institutions in the world, particularly in the heartlands of PSB in Western Europe.[478] Not only has the legitimacy of the PSB been constantly questioned in the Western European countries, the ideas of the PSB as a whole have been severely attacked by neo-liberals who were then politically and ideologically more powerful. The introduction of PSB in CEECs happened in such unfavourable circumstances. The attitudes toward the introduction of the PSB were, if not totally sceptic, generally not as persistent as other earlier imitators of the BBC in the 1950s when it was the heyday of the BBC as well as the PSB system. The prototypes of the PSB, the BBC and other PSB institutions in Western European countries, were still struggling for survival at a time of crisis. Therefore, their support, either spiritual or practical, was far from sufficient as their inexperienced colleagues in the CEECs expected and actually needed. Strong attacks and pressures from the outside, insecurity and hesitation within the inside, and lack of firm foreign aid in need – all these have predetermined the congenital deficiency of the introduction of the PSB in the CEECs.

Thirdly, along with the dominant neo-liberal ideology throughout the 1980s and the 1990s, the market myth also pervaded the process of democratisation in

---

[477] Jakubowicz, pp. 63 ff.
[478] NHK was an exception during this period. It never faced any serious ideological pressure in the politically stable Japanese society, or pressures from commercial interests in the dual broadcasting system, by which the five major commercial broadcasters and their newpaper parents have absorbed much of the advertising money available in Japan. NHK also pioneered in broadcasting technology, which made it more successful and active in new technologies than its defensive counterparts in Europe. See Akhavan-Majid. pp. 25-28.

the CEECs. Concerning media sector, the contribution of market forces to the process of democratisation has been widely acknowledged through the early experience of commercial media since the advent of *glasnost* in Russia and other CEECs. The fact that newspapers of the oppositional parties and dissent fiercely criticised the existed Communist regime, was seen as a symbol of the advancement of democratisation. However, this has consequently led to the reliance upon the commercial media, instead of the PSB institutions or other civil media, as the main facilitator of the process of democratisation without assessing the sustainability and reliability of commercial media in the long-term process of democratisation. After the first passion for democratisation, the later performance of commercial broadcasters in the CEECs, many of which were subsidiaries of Western media conglomerates, showed that they were more interested in profit-making than in criticising the current governing regimes. The governments, in turn, skilfully use economic means to buy off or crackdown commercial media so as to indirectly control them.[479] The democratic contribution of commercial media was just like a flash in the pan, which has not been effectively institutionalised as a sustainable capacity of the media. The overestimation of the democratic function of commercial media has also hindered the PSB from being believed as the main institution for public missions. Being set up as a weak organisation was nearly a false start for the PSB in CEECs. A dramatic improvement afterwards could only be hardly possible.

The fourth reason for the failure of the introduction of PSB in CEECs may lie in the insufficient study on the dual broadcasting system as a whole. In most CEECs, the reconstruction of media system has been split into two non-interrelated sectors of a highly politicised PSB system and a fairly deregulated commercial media sector, while the media outlets in each sector basically only defended their own interests. The interrelationships between these two different sectors, the role and function of each sector within the media system as an integrated entity have not been investigated more carefully. The decision makers of media system failed to clarify the essential rules of game for the players from different sectors, leaving them fighting in brutal market competition or drawing into complicated political power struggles. An overall consideration of the wide discrepancies between the public and commercial media sectors and their interrelationship is of essential significance for the stable and healthy "evolution" of media ecology, as the experience in Britain (in particular before the 1980s), Germany and Japan shows. This is actually a more sophisticated stage of institution building than a blind imitation of an alien system.

---

479 Jakubowicz, p. 149.

Chapter 6
Theoretical Analyses of the Dual Broadcasting System and the Inspirations for Chinese Broadcasting Reform

Based on the illustrative analysis of the dual broadcasting system in last chapter, some theoretical analyses of the dual broadcasting system, which involve the patterns of adoption in individual countries, the evolution or development of the PSB as well as the dual broadcasting system, will be conducted in this chapter. Lastly, for those countries like China, where the broadcasting system remains state-owned and the most decision makers have little knowledge about the dual broadcasting system, can the dual broadcasting system be an alternative for the on-going broadcasting reform?

6.1. Some theoretical analyses of the dual broadcasting system

From the largely historically illustrative analyses on the public service broadcasting and on the dual broadcasting system in the last two chapters, we can observe that there are different patterns of adopting broadcasting systems in individual countries, which can eventually affect the results of adoption.

With regard to the establishment of the public service broadcasting, this has been basically conducted by the state (mainly by the legislative branch) in many countries, which often concerns an intricate process of legislation and painstaking arrangements thereafter. The patterns of adopting the PSB can be categorised according to 1) timing and backdrop for the establishment, and 2) the range and scope of the imitation.

After the public service broadcasting was first established in Britain in the 1920s, there were three groups of countries that have successively imitated the public service broadcasting, mostly modelled on the BBC style, in three different historical periods. And the historical backdrops for imitating the PSB varied in different historical periods, while the motives for imitation by individual countries were nevertheless quite similar in each historical period.

- *Legacy of the British Commonwealth in the pre-war years*: The earliest public service broadcasting institutions of the BBC style before World War II were mostly the legacy of British Commonwealth, in that most of the first group of the public service organisations emerged in the members of the British Commonwealth, such as Canada, Australia, etc.

Chapter 6 Theoretical Analyses of the Dual Broadcasting System

- *Legacy of war soon after World War II*: The second wave of imitating the BBC was in the post-war period, as the legacy of war, in dozens of countries, including Germany and Japan[480] as part of the reconstruction of a democratic society soon after the end of World War II.
- *Legacy of transformation at the end of the 1980s*: The latest wave of imitating the PSB, as legacy of transformation, happened at the end of the 1980s and the beginning of the 1990s. This was represented by the Central and Eastern European countries after the collapse of Communism and by Korea during the process of democratisation in these former totalitarian or authoritarian countries.

Although many countries have adopted the PSB, the range and scope of the adoption vary tremendously. The character or qualities of the PSB can be classified into three dimensions, namely the *"culture and education"* character, the *"information and entertainment"* character, and the *"democratic monitor"* character. That the more of these qualities possessed by a PSB tends to imply that the PSB is at a more advanced stage of development. Accordingly, there are four types of results of adoption in the countries (regions) with a PSB sector, including in those countries (regions) with a modest part of PSB within the overwhelming commercial broadcasting system, such as the USA and Taiwan (see Figure 6.1).

As Figure 6.1 shows, not only do the quantities of the PSB character matter to the range and scope of adopting the PSB, the sequencing of the PSB character also plays an important role for the results of adoption. The Central and Eastern European countries, for example, attempted to leap over the "culture and education" character and the "information and entertainment" character of the PSB to reach the more advanced stage of "democratic dog" character, largely as a result of the overemphasis on the democratic function of the PSB during the transformation process.[481] Unfortunately yet unsurprisingly, the efforts were in vain.

Furthermore, it is noteworthy that the "information" character and the "democratic monitor" character have not been fully developed at the very start of the BBC. These more advanced PSB qualities rather emerged gradually under the general principle of "public service" when the connotations of the "public service" expanded along with the development of modern society and modern democracy. This is also affected by the development level of the individual society, such as the extent of democratisation, the general consensus in favour of

---

480 Although NHK (the public service broadcaster in Japan) was modeled on the BBC in 1926, it has been nationalised during World War II and acted as the propaganda mouthpiece of the Japanese military government. NHK has been reconstructed after the war as a public service broadcaster with the promulgation of the Broadcast Law in 1950.
481 For the comprehensive explanation for the futility of the introduction of the PSB in the CEECs, see pp. 210 ff.

6.1. Some theoretical analyses of the dual broadcasting system

Figure 6.1 The spectrum and evolution of the PSB character in a few sample countries

Evolution stages	primitive stage	moderate stage	advanced stage
USA, Taiwan	culture & education		
Japan, Korea	culture & education	Information & entertainment	
Britain, Germany	culture & education	Information & entertainment	democratic monitor
CEECs			democratic monitor
			futile "flying leap"

Source: illustrated by the author

PSB among decision makers, journalists and the wider public. Some further concrete conditions, such as independent and adequate financial sources, or/and independent and powerful legal protection for the autonomy of the PSB system, also contribute to the sophistication and soundness of the PSB sector in a society. The impact of these socio-political, economic and legal conditions on the whole broadcasting landscape is even greater in the dual broadcasting system than in the purely PSB system.[482]

The adoption of the dual broadcasting system should actually be a more complex process in that there are more variables to be taken into consideration in the coexistence of the PSB and the commercial broadcasting than in a single unitary broadcasting system of the PSB (or a state-controlled system), such as the interrelationship between the PSB sector and the commercial broadcasting sector, the status and role of each sector in the whole broadcasting system, and different approaches of regulation in each sector, etc. However, the practice was largely reduced to a contest between the "public logic" and the "market logic" and their respective supporters for dominance over the rivals during the process of decision making.

Historically, there were two waves of adopting the dual broadcasting system – in Britain and Japan at the beginning of the 1950s, and on a much larger scale in dozens of countries during the 1980s and 1990s, most notably in the heartlands of the PSB in Western Europe. In the first wave of adopting the dual broadcasting system in Britain and Japan, the "public logic" still retained a dominant pos-

---

[482] Cf. Figure 6.2 on p. 218.

ition in the process of broadcasting system decision making. The British commercial broadcasters were set up as an extension of the public service concept and were strictly regulated by the PSB standards.[483] There was no significant difference between the PSB and the commercial broadcasting sector in terms of missions and standards, therefore, the British commercial broadcasting from the 1950s through the early 1980s was stated by Sepstrup as "commercial public broadcasting". In Japan, the situation was slightly different from that in Britain. The Japanese commercial broadcasters were only encouraged to comply with the Broadcast Law 1950, whose high standards of "public logic" mainly apply to NHK.[484] Therefore, the Japanese commercial television stations carry principally entertainment, ranging from sitcoms, crime and adventure, to music and dramas. Although the Japanese commercial broadcasting was highly lucrative in economic sense, NHK maintained a high prestige in Japanese society for its full range provision of programming and high-quality content.

In the second wave of adopting the dual broadcasting system since the 1980s, however, the conflicts between the "public logic" and the "market logic" intensified. The general tendency was the rise of the "market logic", which led to a trend towards "deregulation" of the broadcasting market in many involved countries. The results of this trend of "deregulation" were nevertheless drastically diverse in the selected sample countries of this thesis: in the cradleland of the PSB, Britain, the BBC stepped into a state of crisis for a fairly long period, and the "commercial public broadcasting" (terrestrial commercial broadcasting sector) was "reformed" by the Thatcher government to abandon the public remit in a radically deregulated broadcasting market; the PSB institutions retained dominant in Germany and Japan while the commercial broadcasting was deemed the complementary pillar in the dual system, which was largely a result of the legal (in Germany) or bureaucratic (in Japan) protection; in Korea, the PSB remained dominant, however, most PSB institutions have been operated in a more commercialised manner (or self-commercialisation); in the CEECs, where the PSB appeared to have a bad start-up timing, it was no surprise that the PSB organisations there were generally weak in the both politically and economically unfavourable circumstances. On the whole, the majority of the PSB sector worldwide suffered from scathing attacks, mostly politically or ideologically, and had to take up a defensive position for survival.

Up to this point, the development of the dual broadcasting system remains largely the prolongation of the contest between the "public logic" and the "market logic" as before. The understandings of broadcasting have greatly deviated from the traditional ones – more and more decision makers in individual coun-

---

483 For details, see pp. 159 ff.
484 Hilliard and Keith, p. 172.

6.1. Some theoretical analyses of the dual broadcasting system

tries tend to categorise broadcasting as an industry rather than a public service when developing new regulations. In extreme cases, such as in Britain during the 1980s, the broadcasting audience were termed "consumers", which implied an ideological shift in the connotation of audience from a public service version of "citizen" to a commercialised version. Nevertheless, some countries have instead developed a balanced and comprehensive theory of the dual broadcasting system. In Germany, for example, the key problems on the dual broadcasting system have been consistently and systematically clarified in the rulings made by the German Federal Constitutional Court, such as the interrelationship between the PSB sector and the commercial broadcasting sector, the status and role of each sector in the whole broadcasting system, and different approaches of regulation in each sector, etc.

Therefore, the adoption patterns of the dual broadcasting system, if any, can be divided into two types of decision making mechanism for the system adoption. One type is, represented by Britain yet prevailing in many countries nowadays, the *politics-centric* decision making mechanism. In this type of decision making mechanism, the executive branch of the state, which actually has a large majority in the legislature, often acts as a leading force for decision making of broadcasting policy. The politics-centric decision making mechanism might be able to respond to the imminent challenges with high flexibility, however, this also contains the risks of arbitrary decision and inconsistency in decision making, or even a danger of split of consensus within the society in extreme case.

The second type is, represented by Germany, the *judiciary-centric* decision making mechanism. The judicial branch of the state offers an extra check at the constitutional level on the profound decisions made by the executive or legislative branches of the state. The high degree of independence of the judiciary guarantees the detachment of the rulings made by the courts from the manipulation of individual political or other socially powerful interests. It also ensures the consistency of the decision making in broadcasting sector by constantly revisiting the basic rights guaranteed by the constitution, according to which one of the core functions of broadcasting in modern democracy is to serve the fundamental purpose of free formation of private as well as public opinions. It also works as an integration or mediation between the fiercely conflicting ideas so as to help in avoiding a deep split of social consensus.[485] In consequence, the executive branch of the state cannot decide arbitrarily or react as flexibly as the governments with the politics-centric decision making mechanism.

---

485 Cf. p. 190.

Chapter 6 Theoretical Analyses of the Dual Broadcasting System

Figure 6.2 The results of different decision making mechanism in selected dual broadcasting systems

	Politics-centric mechanism				Judiciary-centric mechanism
	Britain	*Japan*	*Korea*	*CEECs*	*Germany*
PSB tradition	long	long	short	short	long
Financial independence of PSB	high	high	medium*	medium*	high
Deregulation of private sector	high	medium	medium	high	medium
Legal protection	low	medium	n.a.	n.a.	high
Extent of democratisation	mature	semi-mature**	modest	modest	mature

Results:
With politics-centric mechanism: an overwhelming tendency of commercialisation in broadcasting sector.
Britain:
the BBC survives from crisis thanks to the deep-rooted PSB tradition in British society, and remains fairly stable today. Nevertheless, it also arouses controversy that the BBC World Service has got more involved in business-style operations. Moreover, the media landscape as a whole has become far more commercialised.
Japan:
NHK remains largely stable, yet at the same time it is getting actively involved in cooperation with big business and commercial investments. The deregulation of broadcasting market is limited.
Korea:
the PSB sector is fairly self-commercialised. The drama output of the public service broadcasters has been strikingly popular, yet also arouses controversy about the tendency of vulgarity. The deregulation of broadcasting market is limited.
CEECs:
the PSB sector is generally weak (except in Poland, where the Polish public service broadcaster TVP holds a leading position in the market); commercial broadcasting sector has a dominant position.
With judiciary-centric mechanism: a fairly coordinated and less conflicting co-existence of the PSB and commercial broadcasting.
Germany:
the PSB sector has been endowed with the responsibility for the basic provision of programming for the whole population. The legitimacy of the PSB has been since then less questioned in Germany than in Britain. The commercial broadcasting is economically successful, yet less influential in media politics.

Source: illustrated by the author

Notes:
* The PSB in Korea and most CEECs have a mixed financing of licence fee, advertising revenue and state grants.
** Japan has well-established democratic insitutions. However, the Japanese society as a whole is highly conservative. Hence the operation within individual institutions retains largely undemocratic.

Figure 6.2 shows the latest developments of dual broadcasting system under these two different types of decision making mechanism. Overall, the "market logic" has gained the upper hand in broadcasting sector since the 1980s. The majority of the governments worldwide tended to incorporate broadcasting into a

6.1. Some theoretical analyses of the dual broadcasting system

broader market of tele-communications and information technology as a result of technology convergence. This was partly also the side effects of the laissez-faire ideology vigorously promoted by the neo-liberals since the 1980s. The technological/economic considerations prevailed over the social/democratic considerations in the process of decision-making. This profound shift of ideas of broadcasting has led to an overwhelming tendency of commercialisation in broadcasting sector worldwide. Although most public service broadcasters retain their positions as leading broadcasters of the country, the macro environment has become more commercialised than it used to be. This has consequently affected the overall development and operation strategies of the public service broadcasters themselves. As figure 6.2 shows, most public service broadcasters tended to operate more likely in business-style; this has nevertheless aroused controversies and even some hostile questioning on the legitimacy of the PSB. To go into business and compete with the aggressive commercial rivals, or to stay out of it for the sake of legitimacy – this has been the biggest dilemma that almost all public service broadcasters have to face today.

In German broadcasting sector, on the contrary, where the rulings of broadcasting made by the German Federal Constitutional Court have set out the most fundamental principles for the development of the dual broadcasting system from the very beginning, the atmosphere has been generally more peaceful. The commercial players make their efforts to compete in the affluent German advertising market, and seem less aggressive in challenging their public service counterparts (both politically and ideologically). The public law broadcasting institutions have been endowed with the responsibility for the basic provision of programming for the whole population. This has, in turn, given the public sector a "guarantee of existence and development" (Bestands- und Entwicklungsgarantie), including but not limited to adequate technical, organisational, personnel and financial facilities. It is noteworthy that German government did not react differently from other governments during the overwhelming trend of commercialisation and deregulation throughout the 1980s and 1990s. The extra check made by the judicial branch of the state has nevertheless produced different outcomes.

The most important achievement of the judiciary-centric decision making mechanism is therefore the capacity to resolve conflicts and to clarify confusion at the constitutional level, with which all uncompromising parties are also bothered during the process of decision making. To revisit the basic rights constantly such as freedom of broadcasting helps in reconstructing certain consensus in a highly pluralistic modern society. The core values in the constitution should be the base points for the decision makers to start off and to end in. The concrete arrangements of a broadcasting system – either PSB or commercial broadcasting, license fee or advertising revenue – are actually the adaptive means, which basically remain the domain of politics, to better serve the aims in an era of change. For example, it has been deemed legitimate for the German public law broadcasters to broadcast advertisements so long as this has been done for appropriate ends and under appropriate conditions. Commercial broadcasting is also an alternative means of safeguarding the diversity of opinions (the "external pluralistic" model) according to the German Federal Constitutional Court.[486] However, the democratic function of commercial broadcasting cannot be overrated because of the probable "market failures" – the underrepresentation of socially and economically weak groups, the narrow arc of opinions (which are mostly pro-right-wing), and the domination of entertainment in programming, among others.[487]

A well functioning judiciary-centric decision making mechanism requires some essential conditions, such as a strong and independent judicial branch in a given country, and the common respect for the constitution and rulings made by the judiciary among all socially important groups in the society. Nevertheless, this only implies the importance of the legal protection for maintaining a coordinated dual broadcasting system. As figure 6.2 shows, other socio-political and economic conditions are as indispensable as the legal conditions for the healthy development of the dual broadcasting system.

6.2. The theoretical significance of the dual broadcasting system

Most researches on public service broadcasting, especially in English literature, used to adopt inductive approaches to generalise the principles or characteristics of the PSB, since there lacks a universal and explicit definition of the PSB.[488] This has been part of the vagueness on the one hand, but also the flexibility on the other hand, of the researches on the PSB. However, for many people who are unfamiliar with the ideas and contexts of the public service broadcasting, it is sometimes quite confusing for them to understand the particularities of the PSB, in that the general principles of the European PSBs – *citizenship, universality, quality* and *trust*[489] summarised by Brevini – seem not the exclusive characteristics of the PSB. The state-owned Chinese broadcasting, for example, also emphasises the universality of broadcasting for the whole nation and demands quality for programming. The democratic role of media, according to traditional liberal theory, is to act as a public watchdog against the state. So long the media are

---

486 Cf. p. 174.
487 Curran (2002). pp. 227-31.
488 Cf. section 4.1., pp. 114 ff.
489 Brevini, p. 349.

6.2. The theoretical significance of the dual broadcasting system

free (in the free market), they would fulfil their democratic functions as a check on the state.[490] The theoretical significance of the PSB is therefore hardly to be completely understood with such kind of generalisations about the principles or characteristics of the PSB. Moreover, there also lacks sufficient researches on the dual broadcasting system as an interrelated integrity in English literature. Most academic works focus either on the PSB or on the media economy. The conflicts between the supporters of the PSB and the advocates of commercial broadcasting since the 1980s also deteriorate the conflicts of ideas among the "left" and "right" media academia.

Meanwhile, German scholars have offered different perspectives for a better understanding of the theoretical significance of the PSB and its later extension of the dual broadcasting system. Largely based on the constitutionally guaranteed freedom of broadcasting by Article 5 Section 1 Sentence 2 of the (West) German Basic Law, three main principles (among others) have been systematically developed and consolidated mainly through the Rulings of Broadcasting made by the German Federal Constitutional Court:

1) the principle of *distance from the state (staatsfern);*
2) the principle of *distance from the market (marktfern)*[491]; and
3) *the protection of basic rights by organisation (Grundrechtsschutz durch Organisation)*[492].

In historical retrospect, the state seemed a "natural" organizer or administrator of broadcasting at the start phase in that the allocation and use of airwaves needed to be regulated by the state. However, the decision makers in both Britain and the USA refused the direct control of broadcasting by the state largely under the influence of liberalism. In Britain, the principle of "arm's length" was preferred to tackle with the relationship between the state and other bodies, such as the legal system, the press, or the arts, and in particular the public service broadcaster in this case. The Americans preferred the market liberalism, by which the market system has been seen as morally preferable because it fosters freedom and self-reliance.[493] Although the Reithian ideas of public monopoly have rejected the market mechanism in British broadcasting, his arguments were less theoretical but rather for factual reasons: to avoid the "chaos of the ether" and vulgarity of programming that happened in the USA, to maintain efficiency of management and planned growth of broadcasting, and to guarantee a greater degree of freedom and independence of broadcaster. These factual reasons became later so arguably weak when the advocates of market system and commercial broadcasting

---

490 Curran (2002), pp. 217 ff.
491 Grimm (2003).
492 Grimm (1994), pp. 281-82.
493 Curran (2002), p. 198.

Chapter 6 Theoretical Analyses of the Dual Broadcasting System

attacked the undemocratic and inefficient side of the public monopoly and thus broke it up in the 1950s. The same scenarios repeated three decades later and finally led to the fall of the non-commercialism in British broadcasting in the 1980s.

Although German public law broadcasting system has imitated the British public service broadcasting system and adopted the organisation principles of the BBC after WWII, the arguments were apparently following another line of reasoning. The constitutionally guaranteed freedom of broadcasting by Article 5 Section 1 Sentence 2 of the (West) German Basic Law was the most important fundamental to revisit. In the first Ruling of Broadcasting made by the German Federal Constitutional Court in 1961, the principle of *distance from the state (staatsfern)* has been established at the constitutional level, according to which "a state-operated television, in which form also whatever, is inconsistent with the freedom of broadcasting"[494]. Similar to the reasoning of the public monopoly in Britain, the Court deemed the monopoly of public law broadcasters consistent with the freedom of broadcasting because of two factual situations: one was the prevalent scarcity of airwaves, and the other one was the extraordinarily high start-up costs for the organisation of broadcasting. Nevertheless, the Court did not deem that the arrangement of broadcasting programming could only be made by the public law broadcasters. The private persons with legal capacity could also be the organisers of broadcasting, only if they could offer what the public law broadcasters could achieve in guaranteeing the freedom of broadcasting. In the Court's opinion, on behalf of the freedom of broadcasting, media – being in fact a thing of the general public – must not be handed over either to the state or to *one*[495] individual social group. Comparatively, the organisation form of public law broadcasters could better guarantee the freedom of broadcasting than state-owned or market-dominated broadcasting on the grounds that the general public could be better represented in the boards of public law broadcasters through the so-called socially relevant forces, such as churches, trade unions, universities, entrepreneurs, sport associations, women's associations etc.[496] The freely organised public law broadcasters act as the protection of basic rights – in this case the freedom of broadcasting – by organisation (Grundrechtsschutz durch Organisation). In the era of the public law broadcasting system before the 1980s, the main focus of guaranteeing the freedom of broadcasting in Germany was how to protect the public service broadcasting from the state interference by setting various requirements on the organisation form and the internal organisation of the public

---

494 Grimm (2003), p. 1.
495 Italicised in the original text of the first Ruling of Broadcasting made by the German Federal Constitutional Court.
496 Grimm (2003), pp. 1-3. And BVerfGE 12, 205-264.

6.2. The theoretical significance of the dual broadcasting system

law broadcasters. For example, the state was responsible for the allocation of frequencies and fixing the license fee, nevertheless, the state could do these only with the principle of distance from the state. The state must follow the neutral standards to allocate frequencies in the media laws. The process of fixing the license fee for the public law broadcasters should preclude the exertion of influence on the content of programming by the state. Some necessary external control over the budget of the public law broadcasters would be conducted by the independent expert committees, whose recommendations could not be unreasonably withheld by the Parliament.

In the 1980s, when the scarcity of airwaves was gradually diminishing with the introduction of cable and satellite broadcasting, the public monopoly has also been put in question and the participation of the market forces in organising broadcasting appeared inevitable. In the third Ruling of Broadcasting made by the German Federal Constitutional Court in 1981, the principle of *distance from the market (marktfern)* has been further explicated, when the organisation of private broadcasting demanded legal regulation (by the state) so as to guarantee the freedom of broadcasting. The Court refined the freedom of broadcasting as a "serving freedom" ("dienende Freiheit"), a freedom which serves the self-development of individuals and the self-regulation of people. The freedom of broadcasting is not only an objective freedom, but also a subjective right. Therefore, the freedom of broadcasting as a "serving freedom" endows the state with a double role. On the one hand, the principle of distance from the state must be stuck to so that no influence with regard to contents could be exerted on broadcasting. On the other hand, the state is constitutionally obligated to guarantee the autonomy of broadcasting against any threat from third party, because the instrumentalisation of broadcasting either by the state or by the private operators is inconsistent with the freedom of broadcasting as a "serving freedom".[497] In the dual system, which the legislature (of German federal states) has chosen after the end of monopoly of the public law broadcasting, the principle of distance from the market (marktfern) has been established at the constitutional level to protect the journalistic autonomy of broadcasting from market pressures.

Among others, two arrangements of the private sector in the dual broadcasting system embody the principle of distance from the market (marktfern). One arrangement is to position the private broadcasting as the complementary role to the public law broadcasting in the dual broadcasting system. Since the private broadcasting is likely to run into difficulties with advertising financing if it has to completely fulfil the constitutionally required mission of broadcasting, the private broadcasters are imposed with reduced requirements of the variety and di-

---

[497] Grimm (2003), pp. 4-6. And BVerfGE 57, 295-335.

versity of the programmes. However, this could only be valid under the presupposition that the public law broadcasting can still undiminishedly fulfil its mission of programming, which is defined as the "basic provision". The "basic provision" through the public law broadcasting is full provision rather than minimal provision. The scope of the programmes of the public law broadcasting should not be limited to the information and political niches, whilst the private broadcasting can concentrate on the popular entertainment programmes. In other words, there is no division of work between the public law and the private broadcasting. In order to enhance the competitiveness of the public service broadcasting responsible for the basic provision in the dual broadcasting system, the public service broadcasting is endowed with the guarantee of existence and development (die Bestands- und Entwicklungsgarantie) in terms of programming, technology and financing. The strong public law broadcasting is also in the interest of the private broadcasting, since the performance capability of the public law broadcasting is the precondition for the introduction of private broadcasting.[498]

Another arrangement that embodies the principle of distance from the market (marktfern) in the dual broadcasting system is the organisation of the media authorities of the private broadcasting in individual Länder, the Landesmedienanstalten. The Landesmedienanstalten, which are in charge of licensing and controlling the private broadcasting in Germany, should have boards comprised of representatives of socially relevant forces following the model of the public law service broadcasters. This is essential for safeguarding the external plurality of private broadcasting, since the individual private broadcasters could not provide sufficient internal plurality as a result of their reduced requirements of the variety and diversity of the programmes.

As Grimm points out, the principle of distance from the market remains highly topical in the era of digitalisation. The number of broadcasters has proliferated in recent years as a result that the capacity of transmission has been enormously enhanced by digitalisation. However, the majority (if not all) of the newly emerging broadcasters are private, whilst many of them are affiliated to a handful of international media conglomerates through various investment connections. This has led to the tendencies of an over-commercialised media environment, the fragmentation of broadcasting, and the concentration of market forces, etc. In such circumstances, it is essential to retain the principle of distance from the market so as to reserve some non-commercialised islands in a further commercialised society, and to have integrated programming (provided by the public law broadcasting) which can reach the whole society and is for the interest of the general public.[499]

---

[498] Grimm (2003), pp. 4-6. And BVerfGE 57, 295-335.
[499] Grimm (2003), pp. 7-9.

6.2. The theoretical significance of the dual broadcasting system

Among these three principles in the dual broadcasting system, the principles of distance from the state and distance from the market act as threshold of guaranteeing the freedom of broadcasting. In other words, any broadcasting system should follow these two principles for the sake of guaranteeing the freedom of broadcasting. Public service broadcaster, consequently, is probably only one of the possible institutional forms that can better guarantee the freedom of broadcasting.

Therefore, it would come in vain to talk about public service broadcasting without recognising the significance of the principles of distance from the state and distance from the market. The failure of establishing well functioning public service broadcasting in the CEECs can largely be attributed to the neglect of the principle of distance from the state. The state, when there is no effective mechanism to prevent it from exerting influence on broadcasting, remains the major threat to the freedom of broadcasting. The market system, though it is supposed to function as a check on the state, also tends to make market failures, such as the concentration of opinions as a result of the concentration of media ownership, underrepresentation of minorities, invisible censorship by the market, the media's increasing orientation towards entertainment, etc.[500] This will, in turn, tremendously hinder the full fulfilment of the freedom of broadcasting and distort the democratic function of broadcasting in a modern society. The necessary distances of the state and of the market (or of any other single dominant social group) are indispensable for safeguarding the autonomy of broadcasting and then guaranteeing the freedom of broadcasting.

However, the necessary distances of the state and the market do not mean isolation from the state and the market. As discussed before, the state has actually a double role in the concept of the freedom of broadcasting according to modern German constitutional theory, namely from the formal perspective and the substantial perspective of freedom: defensive right (Abwehrrecht), and protective duty (Schutzpflicht)[501]. On the one hand, the state itself has to respect the freedom of broadcasting and to abstain from exertion of influence with regard to contents. Here freedom means the absence of state interference (Abwehrrecht). On the other hand, the state is obliged to fulfil its protective duty (Schutzpflicht) to actively defend the freedom of broadcasting from the threat of a third party.[502] In other words, the state has the constitutional obligation to establish a broadcasting order in which the individual and public opinion formation can be freely fulfilled within a representational plurality of a wide range of opinions and ideas,

---

500 Curran (2002), pp. 227-31.
501 Grimm (1994), p. 278.
502 Grimm (2003), p. 5.

but at the same time the state itself must not be a threat to the freedom of broadcasting during its active engagement of arranging the broadcasting order.

The market has also a similar double-sided role in the concept of the freedom of broadcasting. On the one hand, the overwhelming dominance of the market forces could be a hindrance to the full fulfilment of the freedom of broadcasting. On the other hand, the existence of broadcasting market and broadcasting economy is an inevitable and undeniable fact in the modern market economy. The market also facilitates competition among broadcasters and agiler consciousness of the needs of audience, which (when on an appropriate scale) could be very helpful in maintaining a healthy broadcasting system. Therefore, the market mechanism has not been completely excluded from German public law broadcasting. The German public law broadcasters keep a modest portion of advertising revenue (approximately 10% of the total avenue in 2010) as an essential measure to enhance some necessary consciousness of competition and sensitivity to the needs of audience and the market, as well as to avoid rigidity and arrogance – the commonest and frequently attacked illness among public bureaucracies.

If the principles of distance from the state and distance from the market can be understood as threshold of guaranteeing the freedom of broadcasting, the third principle of the dual broadcasting system, namely the protection of basic rights by organisation, could be understood as a feasible concept of fulfilling the freedom of broadcasting. This is the major contribution that Reith and the BBC have made to the world of broadcasting. The concrete arrangements of the public service institution, such as the organisation and structure, the autonomous status and self-regulation, the financing model with license fee, the ranges and standards of programming, and the performance of the BBC are all outstanding examples for institution planning and implementation. All these remain till today as an important source of inspiration for the design of broadcasting system. The conception and establishment of the BBC have proved once a successful story in the world broadcasting history, however, the later experience of the BBC throughout the 1980s and 1990s also revealed the apparent vulnerability of public service broadcasting institutions to the influence of the state and the market. A "perfect" public service institution alone is far from being a guarantee of the freedom of broadcasting. It needs to be included into wider and more comprehensive considerations of system design with regard to legal protection, active defensive regulations by the state, etc. How to safeguard the autonomy of the broadcasting institutions so as to effectively guarantee the freedom of broadcasting from the influence of the state and the market, or of any other single dominant social group, remains a paramount task for broadcasting decision makers in the past, at present, as well as in the future.

6.3. What can Chinese broadcasting learn from the dual broadcasting system?

After a painstakingly historical and theoretical review of the dual broadcasting system and its predecessor, the public service broadcasting system, in the previous analysis, now it comes to the finale of this thesis to answer the question posed at the beginning of this research: Is the dual broadcasting system an alternative for the ongoing Chinese television reform? Taking the conditions in China into consideration, what inspirations could be drawn from the dual broadcasting system for Chinese decision makers of television and media scholars?

Before answering the above posed questions, it is necessary to summarise the findings of this research in order to have a full view of the dual broadcasting system. In comparison with the British model, the German dual broadcasting system seems to provide a more feasible model for foreign imitations. By and large, what the British model provides is practical experience other than a comprehensive set of ideas on a broadcasting system, as what Briggs remarked on John Reith: "Reith's main achievement was to create a public corporation rather than to write about it"[503]. Moreover, the British experience has its peculiarities – it sometimes could only be well understood in the context of Britain, where social and political conventions function as part of the British common law. This can be a major obstacle to foreign imitators without common law tradition understanding and learning from Britain. The German model, on the contrary, has developed a comprehensive set of explicit and consistent ideas, principles and arrangements of the dual broadcasting system over the past decades. The refinement of theories and the abstractions of ideas enhance the universality of German model for foreign imitators to transcend the concrete conditions of a country and to pay more attention to the kernel of the dual broadcasting system.

Figure 6.3 and figure 6.4 illustrate the structure and further elaboration of the ideas, principles and arrangements of German dual broadcasting system. As figure 6.3 shows, the ideas, principles and arrangements of the German dual broadcasting system display a pyramidal structure with three levels. The top level is the ideas of the dual broadcasting system, the highest ends that the system is in pursuit of. In Germany, they are the freedom and the autonomy of broadcasting which are guaranteed by Article 5 Section 1 Sentence 2 of the German Basic Law. The second level is the principles of the dual broadcasting system, such as the three principles discussed in last section – distance from the state and from the market, and the protection of basic rights by organisation. These are the fundamentals of the system to achieve the highest ends. These two levels are ideological abstractions and universally recognisable. The third level of the structure

---

503 Briggs (Vol 2, 1995), p. 389.

Chapter 6 Theoretical Analyses of the Dual Broadcasting System

involves the concrete arrangements of the dual broadcasting system. This is the practical aspect of the system, which can be arranged by the decision makers according to the concrete conditions of a country. Therefore, there can be individual differences in the arrangements of the dual broadcasting system in various countries, but the general ideas and principles at the higher levels should remain overall unanimous.

Figure 6.4 elaborately displays some of the details of the ideas, principles, and arrangements of German dual broadcasting system. As figure 6.4 shows, the ideas and principles of the dual broadcasting system are the highest ends and the paramount fundamentals of the system, which are abstract, explicit, and universally recognisable. They are the guidelines for the concrete arrangements. The arrangements of the dual broadcasting system involve a great deal of concrete measures with the aim to realise the ideas by following the fundamental principles. In the case of Germany, where decision makers have chosen the coexistence of the public law and the private broadcasting, the arrangements of the broadcasting system have to deal with the arrangements of the public law broadcasting sector and the private broadcasting sector respectively, to which different approaches are adopted because of the discrepancies in broadcasting missions between these two sectors. Besides, the interrelationship between the two co-existing sectors is also an important concern of the arrangements of the dual broadcasting system. It is likely to cause conflicts if the decision makers cannot handle it well.

Figure 6.3 German dual broadcasting system I: the pyramidal structure

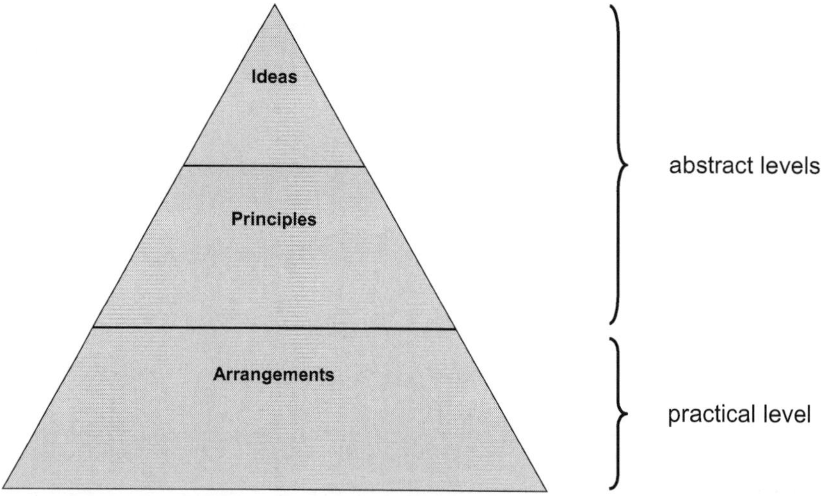

Source: illustrated by the author

6.3. What can Chinese broadcasting learn from the dual broadcasting system?

Figure 6.4 German dual broadcasting system II: ideas, principles and arrangements

	Further elaboration
Ideas	– guarantee of the freedom of broadcasting; – guarantee of the autonomy of broadcasting.
Principles	– broadcasting belongs to the domain of culture; – serving the interest of the general public; – distance from the state and from the market; – the protection of basic rights by organisation; etc.
Arrangements	
Public law broadcasting	– being set up by public law; – universal and free access to broadcasting services for the general public; – representation of the voices of the socially relevant forces; – independent financial source of license fee; – self-regulation and professionalism; – wide-ranging programming of culture, education, information and entertainment; – land-based broadcasting institutions; – high standards of programming in terms of quality and plurality; etc.
Private broadcasting	– being set up by Land media acts; – reduced requirements of the variety and diversity of private programming; – media authorities of the private broadcasting follow the public model; – regulation of ownership concentration; – external plurality; etc.
Interrelationship between public law and private broadcasting	– public law broadcasting is responsible for the basic provision of programming for the whole population; – the commercial broadcasting plays a complementary role; – cooperation between the public and the private broadcasting institutions; etc.

Source: illustrated by the author

Chapter 6 Theoretical Analyses of the Dual Broadcasting System

The ideas and principles, therefore, are the kernel of the foreign imitation of the dual broadcasting system, whilst the concrete arrangements can vary according to the concrete situations in an individual country. In the case of China, when comparing current Chinese television system with the dual broadcasting system, there are clearly wide discrepancies in ideas and principles as a result of the distinctly different cultural, social and political attitudes to broadcasting, especially the influence of political ideology and political system upon broadcasting system. Nevertheless, it is still possible to find some common ground despite the existing discrepancies. For example, broadcasting used to be perceived as a cultural good in China throughout a long period in the history, and the universal access to broadcasting for the whole population has always been one important goal to which the government has made concerted efforts. Therefore, the inspirations or the successful experiences of the dual broadcasting system that Chinese decision makers may use for reference can be set about from two aspects. One is the instantly doable aspect of the inspirations to correct the immediate negative effects of the commercialisation of television. Another aspect is rather from a long-term perspective. As the model of gradual transition in chapter 1 shows, if China continues it transition both economically and socially, it is reasonable to assume that China will go further in the process of democratisation. Actually, the Chinese government never gives up claiming its determination of political reform, but only keeps emphasising that this must be implemented with "Chinese characteristics". In other words, it has to be a self-determined process instead of being determined by others (among others, the West). Consequently, the democratisation of media also belongs to the agenda of political reform. The reference from the dual broadcasting system can be badly needed for system conception. A reservoir of ideas and some preparatory work can be started from now on among decision makers and scholars.

Therefore, the suggestions for the reform of Chinese television based on the research on the dual broadcasting system will be twofold. At present, what Chinese television can learn from the dual broadcasting system can mainly be drawn from the following three points. Firstly, it is essential to gain a full knowledge on the market failures caused by over-commercialisation of television and to come to a sober understanding about the negative consequences of the market logic for television. The market failures of Chinese television include, among others, the overuse and misuse of the market logic in assessing various genres of programmes and in the overall programming, the underrepresentation of peasants and other economically weak groups and the overrepresentation of the well-off, better-educated young urban "consumers", the high homogeneity and the tendency towards vulgarisation of television programmes, especially the entertainment programmes. Some Chinese scholars and journalists have been cognisant of

6.3. What can Chinese broadcasting learn from the dual broadcasting system?

these problems caused by the over-commercialisation of Chinese broadcasting and tried to correct these ill ends of over-commercialisation with the concept of "public television".[504] However, the lack of systematic argument and comprehensive knowledge about public service broadcasting made their criticism of market failures less convincing. The principle of distance from the market in the dual broadcasting system can therefore provide a valuable perspective for reflecting the ill effects of over-commercialisation, especially the criticism of the American purely commercial system made by the European scholars throughout the history of both public service broadcasting system and the dual broadcasting system can be a vital counterweight to the American-style of understandings on broadcasting which are now dominating in China.

Secondly, after a deep rethinking of the ill ends of over-commercialisation of Chinese television, the next thing is to facilitate a comeback of the cultural and social characters of television besides the economic and entertaining characters, in that the public characters of television in terms of information, culture and education used to be part of the mission of Chinese television. As Kops suggests, from the media economy perspective, television programmes as economic goods have both marketable and non-marketable properties.[505] Some essential functions of television, such as cultural, social and political ones, are most unlikely to be successful economic goods in the free market, and are therefore non-marketable in such circumstances. The more sophisticated understanding on the marketable and non-marketable properties of broadcasting helps decision makers of Chinese television to deal with each case on its merits. Programmes with the non-marketable property, such as news and current affairs, documentaries, programmes about science, nature and other part of the world, educational programmes, high quality programmes on the Arts, should be therefore largely exempt from the domain of market logic. The assessment of the programmes with non-marketable property should be quality-oriented instead of being ratings-oriented or profitability-oriented. Preferential support, especially financially and administratively, is necessary for programmes with non-marketable property in order to maintain the functional capacity and competitive capacity of these programmes. Only a full range of programmes with both marketable and non-marketable properties can better cater for the needs of general public for public communication.

Thirdly, it is also imminent to correct the misconception about the "public interest" broadcasting and the misunderstanding of other public service broadcasters like the BBC of Britain, the NHK of Japan, or the PBS of the USA. It is

---

504 See p. 85.
505 Manfred Kops. *The German Broadcasting Order. A Model for China?* Working Papers of the Institute for Broadcasting Economics Cologne University No. 215e. Germany: Institute for Broadcasting Economics, University of Cologne, 2006.

seriously misleading to equate "public interest" broadcasting with state-controlled broadcasting, which happened in China. Actually, what the founders and the advocates of the public service broadcasting strive for is the independence of broadcasting from political and commercial powers, and to keep broadcasting within the domain of the public since broadcasting is regarded as a "public utility". In the public sphere, the public are the citizens who "gather as public bodies to discuss issues of the day, specifically those of political concern"[506]. There are fundamental distinctions between the state, the public sphere, and the private economy in the modern political philosophy. The public sphere, in Habermasian conception, refers to the "realm of social life where the exchange of information and views on questions of common concern can take place so that public opinion can be formed"[507]. Assembly and association of the citizens were the common forms of the public sphere in the eighteen century in Western Europe. In the modern society, the mass media have become the chief institutions of the public sphere in that the public opinion is often generated in the mass media rather than in the assembly of relatively small numbers of citizens.[508] Therefore, public broadcasting is by no means state broadcasting. On the contrary, the state has always been regarded as a threat to the autonomy of broadcasting. The principle of distance from the state has been first established in Britain with the establishment of the BBC as a public service broadcaster, and later explicated by the German Federal Constitutional Court as a fundamental principle of the public law broadcasting system. The administrative, editorial, financial autonomy of broadcasting, and self-regulation of journalists, have been regarded as the distinguishing features of the public service broadcasting. What the state, or more precisely, the legislature, does with broadcasting is to set the legal framework for broadcasting, whilst the government is responsible for short-term and long-term policy making at the macro-level. The daily administration and the editorial issues remain foremost within the domain of the public service broadcasters. The public service broadcasters – the BBC, the NHK, or the PBS – are no equivalents to Chongqing Satellite TV, by which the Department of Propaganda of Chongqing municipal Party committee still holds the control over editorial guidelines and the high-ranking personnels. It is of essential importance to clear the misconception and misunderstanding of the public service broadcasting in China, otherwise it will be a giant obstacle to introduce the ideas of the PSB to China.

In the long run, the dual broadcasting system can be a rich source of inspiration for the future reform of Chinese television system once the democratisation

---

506 Peter Dahlgren. *Television and the Public Sphere: citizenship, democracy and the media.* London and Thousand Oaks: Sage Publications, 1995. p. 7.
507 Ibid.
508 Ibid.

6.3. What can Chinese broadcasting learn from the dual broadcasting system?

of Chinese media system takes place. At the theoretical levels, as Figure 6.3 and Figure 6.4 show, the ideas and principles of the dual broadcasting system present comprehensive perspectives on understanding the functions of broadcasting in a democratic society. The starting point is the idea that the freedom of broadcasting functions as "a serving freedom" for the freedom of formation of both individual and public opinions. All further principles and frameworks are developed to serve this end. Some most important principles include, as Figure 6.4 shows, the distance from the state and from the market, the protection of basic rights by organisation, etc. This in turn requires the establishment of a set of basic frameworks – such as the legislative and judicial protection of journalists and broadcasting institutions, independent and adequate financial sources for public broadcasters, the wide scale and scope of programming of public broadcasters, etc. – to ensure the broadcasting system can reach its wide-ranging ends in a democratic society. The establishment of the frameworks which are essential for the guarantee of the freedom of broadcasting cannot be realised through the reform of media system alone. It can only be achieved in a broader process of political democratisation.

At the practical level, the realities of China also confirm that the future reform of Chinese television has to be paralleled by the process of political democratisation. And the experiences of successful imitations and vice versa in other countries also provide useful reference on the transformation from a state-controlled media system to a democratic one. Doubtless the most serious problem of Chinese television currently is that media have no genuine autonomy and are still controlled primarily by the CCP, whilst the economic forces act as a secondary yet mighty outside interference. As the experience in CEECs shows, media often act as a pioneer in stimulating public discourses at the start stage of political democratisation. However, the media itself is especially vulnerable to political pressures, by which economic means are often used to exert pressures. Without sufficient legal and judicial protection of the autonomy of media, and without necessary resources (financial, organisational, personnel, and technical ones), the media can be severely debilitated with its democratic function. Therefore, once China sets about the process of political democratisation and the democratisation of media, it is highly essential to develop awareness of how political and economic forces will jeopardise the autonomy of media. On the one hand, it is necessary to dispel the market myth, which is believed by a number of Chinese scholars that the free market can facilitate the democratisation of media. On the other hand, the principle of distance from the state is of paramount importance during the democratisation of media, especially for the countries with an authoritarian history. As the discussions on media reform often happen within a relatively small and less influential circle of media academia, they are simply too

Chapter 6 Theoretical Analyses of the Dual Broadcasting System

feeble to incorporate this important theme into the broader and highly influential socio-political arena. This becomes the main challenge for the decision makers and scholars in media sector to arouse a strong consciousness of the threat to the freedom of media by the state in the mainstream of social and political discourses. In fact, the principle of distance from the state and the democratic function of media belong to the characteristics at the most advanced stage in the evolution spectrum of broadcasting. There is a high correlation between the political autonomy of media and the extent of democratisation in a country. Only a few countries hitherto have successfully come close to this ideal, such as in Britain and Germany. Some other countries have not soundly achieved it so far (Japan, Korea), whilst some countries just failed in keeping distance from the state in the media sector (Russia).

Since the practice of introducing the dual broadcasting system is a highly intricate project, all the details of arrangements need painstaking argumentation, and various possible schemes should be developed and compared on the basis of the situations in China. This has gone beyond the scope of this thesis and has to be left for the future researches. Anyhow, several focal points will be stated at the end of this thesis to stimulate further discussions on the feasible schemes of arranging the dual broadcasting system in China.

- The public service broadcaster, as the important institution to put the public service ideals into practice, remains a paramount part of the imitation of the public service broadcasting. Without the establishment of one or a group of independent and well-functioning public service broadcaster(s), the adoption of the ideas and principles of the dual broadcasting system can hardly be successful. The advantage of establishing public service broadcaster in China in the future is that the existing state-owned broadcasters are well-established and have some characters of the public service ideals as above discussed. They could be transformed into public service broadcasters. In fact, this has happened in many newly industrialised or newly democraticised countries (regions), such as in Korea, Taiwan and CEECs. The main point is how to ensure a successful transformation from the state-owned broadcaster to public service broadcaster. Again, the principles of distance from the state and from the market remain the most important principles to follow. The concrete arrangements can be made by following these two principles. This involves not only the organisation of the public service broadcaster self, but also the external conditions as a framework for the well functioning public service broadcaster. As Figure 6.4 shows, there is a great deal of criteria for what an independent and well functioning public service broadcaster should be (self-regulation, independent funding, wide-ranging programming, etc). Nevertheless, the external framework, foremost the legal protection by the legislative

6.3. What can Chinese broadcasting learn from the dual broadcasting system?

and judicial branches, is of vital importance in defending the public service broadcaster against political and economic pressures. Without effective external protection, the public service broadcaster itself is particularly vulnerable to both political and economic pressures.
- Besides the efforts from the decision makers in the conversion of ideas and establishing framework in favour of the dual broadcasting system, a much serious challenge might come from the audience side. As a country with vast territory and wide regional disparities in economic prosperity, Chinese government always strives for bridging the gap between rich and poor regions. The access to broadcasting has been seen as one effective means to narrow the regional disparities in culture. The "four-level system" policy in the 1980s which enabled the fast expansion of television across whole China, including rural areas and the western mountainous and desert areas[509], and projects like "television access in every village" ("村村通" or "cun cun tong") or "Project of (full television coverage in) Tibet and Xinjiang" (西新工程 or xi xin gongcheng) in the 1990s[510], all indicate the public function of television in China. Regrettably, today the 31 provincial satellite TV channels have become battlefields of cut-throat competition for ratings – and for the enormous advertising profit the ratings can bring – with all sorts of popular entertainment programmes. Can the public service broadcasters maintain their influence among the audience, especially those poorly educated or living in backward areas, who interest themselves less in "dry" political issues than entertainment stuff for fun? A possible solution is that the public service broadcasters have to find a balance between the public remit of television and its entertaining function. On the one hand the public service broadcasters must maintain their public remit for all citizens in fields of information, culture and education, which is similar to the open access to public libraries for all citizens; while on the other hand, they should maintain their popularity. This has always been a hard nut for all public service broadcasters all over the world. Nevertheless, the public service broadcasters have a good reason to persevere in providing "dry" yet essential stuff such as political and current issues, while (or simply because) their private counterparts do not have to.
- It is noteworthy that the public service broadcasters should also take on their responsibility when competing with the private broadcasters for popularity. Today many public service broadcasters are frequently criticised for content convergence of entertainment programmes with the private broadcasters. In my opinion, it is not "guilty" for the public service broadcasters to have con-

---

509 See pp. 41-45.
510 See p. 71.

tent convergence with private broadcasters in order to maintain their popularity among audience. Entertainment is also one of the important functions of public service broadcasting. Therefore, public service broadcasters should produce entertainment programmes with high popularity, so long they also conscientiously cater to other public functions of broadcasting, such as information, culture and education. Nevertheless, public service broadcasters should be ready to bear more risk of innovation, including developing new programming formats, contents for minority groups, and technological advancements, etc. The problem of content convergence can only be transcended through innovation.

- How to finance the public service broadcaster, which used to be the most controversial topic in many dual broadcasting system countries, can also be a key issue for related discussions in China. Chinese audience are used to the free access to broadcasting content, hence a levy of license fees is very likely to cause resentment or boycott by the audience. The current funding of advertising revenue or state subsidies like the case of Chongqing Satellite TV will also be problematic in that this may jeopardise the independence of the broadcaster. However, these questions are not going to be discussed at length here and left for the future research. After all, the financial model of individual broadcasters depends on the overall design of a broadcasting system, which not only involves the public service sector, but also involves the arrangements of a separate private broadcasting sector (which dose not exist in China at present) and the interrelationship between the public and the private sectors in the future.

Bibliography

A. Cited English and German literature

Abercrombie, Nicholas. *Television and Society*. UK: Polity Press, 1996.

Akhavan-Majid, Roya. "Public service broadcasting and the challenge of new technology: a case study of Japan's NHK". In *International Communication Gazette* 1992 50: 21-36.

Asa Briggs. *The BBC: the first fifty years*. Oxford and New York: Oxford University Press, 1985.

_____. *The History of Broadcasting (Vol. 1): the birth of broadcasting*. Oxford and New York: Oxford University Press, 1961 and 1995 (reprint).

_____. *The History of Broadcasting (Vol. 2): the golden age of wireless*. Oxford and New York: Oxford University Press, 1965 and 1995 (reprint).

_____. *The History of Broadcasting in the United Kingdom (Vol. 3): the war of words*. London and New York: Oxford University Press, 1970 and 1995 (reprint).

_____. *The History of Broadcasting in the United Kingdom (Vol. 4): sound and vision*. Oxford and New York: Oxford University Press, 1995 (reprint).

_____. *The History of Broadcasting in the United Kingdom (Vol. 5): competition*. Oxford and New York: Oxford University Press, 1995.

Bausch, Hans. *Rundfunkpolitik nach 1945: Erster Teil 1945-1962*. München: dtv, 1980.

_____. *Rundfunkpolitik nach 1945: Zweiter Teil 1963-1980*. München: dtv, 1980.

Becker, Jonethan. "Lessons from Russia: a neo-authoritarian media system". In *European Journal of Communication* 2004 Vol 19(2): 139-63.

Brevini, Benedetta. "Towards PSB 2.0? Applying the PSB ethos to online media in Europe: A comparative study of PSBs' internet policies in Spain, Italy and Britain". In *European Journal of Communicartions* 2010 25: 348.

Camilleri, Joseph. *State, Markets and Civil Society*. Asia Pacific: the political economy of the Asia-Pacific region, Volume I. USA: Edward Elgar, 2000.

Chan, Joseph Man. "Administrative Boundaries and Media Administration: a comparative analysis of the newspaper, TV and Internet markets in China". In Chin-Chuan Lee (ed.) *Chinese Media, Global Contexts*. London and New York: RoutledgeCurzon, 2003. pp. 159-76.

Chen, Pu. *Economic Reform and the Transition from Plan to Market: a model for the gradual approach of transition in China*. Münster (Germany): LIT Verlag, 1996.

Cho, Young Nam. "Political Reform without Substantial Change". *Asian Perspective*, Vol. 28, No. 3, 2004, pp. 61-86.

Collins, Richard. "'Ises' and 'Oughts': public service broadcasting in Europe". In Robert C. Allen and Annette Hill (eds.) *The Television Studies Reader*. London and New York: Routledge, 2004. pp. 33-51.

Crisell, Andrew. *An Introduction History of British Broadcasting*. London: Routledge, 1997 (1st Edition) and 2002 (2nd Edition).

Bibliography

Curran, Charles. *A Seamless Robe*. London: William Collins Sons & Co Ltd, 1979.

Curran, James. *Media and Power*. London and New York: Routledge, 2002.

_____ and Seaton, Jean. *Power without Responsibilities*. London and New York: Routledge, 1997 (5th Edition), 2003 (6th Edition) and 2010 (7th Edition).

Dahlgren, Peter. *Television and the Public Sphere: citizenship, democracy and the media*. London and Thousand Oaks: Sage Publications, 1995.

de Smaele, Hedwig. "The applicability of Western Media Models on the Russian Media System". In *European Journal of Communication* 1999 (14): 173-89.

Doyle, Gillian. *Media Ownership*. London: Sage Publications, 2002.

_____. "From Television to Multi-Platform: Less from More or More for Less?", in *Convergence* 2010 16: 431.

Dussel, Konrad. *Deutsche Rundfunkgeschichte*. Germany: UVK Verlagsgesellschaft mbH, 2004.

Eifert, Martin and Hoffmann-Riem, Wolfgang. "Die Entstehung und Ausgestaltung des dualen Rundfunksystems". In Dietrich Schwarzkopf (ed.) *Rundfunkpolitik in Deutschland (Band 1): Wettbewerb und Öffentlichkeit*. München: Deutsche Taschenbuch Verlag GmbH & Co. KG, 1999. pp. 50-116.

Feng, Chien-San. "Is it Legitimate to Imagine China's Media as Socialist? The state, the media and 'market socialism' in China". In *Javnost* (2003), Vol X (4). pp. 37-52.

Fewsmith, Joseph. "China's New Leadership: a one-year assessment". *Orbis: a Journal of World Affairs*, 2004, 48, 2, Spring, 205-15.

Friedman, Lester (ed.). *Fires Were Started: British cinema and Thatcherism*, USA: University of Minnesota Press, 1993.

Frith, Simon. "Entertainment". In James Curran and Michael Gurevitch (eds.): *Mass Media and Society (2nd edition)*. London (a. o.): Arnold, 1996. pp. 160-78.

Frolic, B. Michael. "State-Led Civil Society". In Timothy Brook and B. Michael Frolic (eds.) *Civil Society in China*. New York and London: M. E. Sharpe, 1997. pp. 46-67.

Goodwin, Peter. *Television under the Tories: broadcasting policy 1979-1997*. London: bfi publishing, 1998.

_____. "The Role of the State". In Jane Strokes and Anna Reading (eds.) *The Media in Britain: currant debates and developments*. London: Macmillan Press Ltd, 1999. pp. 130-42.

Grimm, Dieter. "Human rights and judicial review in Germany", in David M. Beatty (ed.) *Human rights and judicial review: a comparative perspective*. USA: Kluwer Academic Publishers, 1994. pp. 267-95.

_____. *Anforderungen an künftige Medienordnungen*. In Arbeitspapiere des Instituts für Rundfunkökonomie Nr. 176. Germany: Institut für Rundfunkökonomie an der Universität zu Köln, 2003.

Grotech Co., Ltd. (ed.). *Digital television in Russia*. http://www.international-television.or g/tv_market_data/digital_tv_in_russia.html. Last visited in June 2011.

Guo Zhenzhi. *WTO, "Chanye Hua" of the Media and Chinese Television (also in Chinese, WTO, 媒介"产业化"与中国电视 or WTO, Meijie Chanyehua yu Zhongguo Dianshi)*. Working Papers of the Institute for Broadcasting Economics, University of Cologne, No. 189 (Chinese version: No. 189c). Germany: Institute for Broadcasting Economics, University of Cologne, 2004.

A. Cited English and German literature

He, Zhou. "How do the Chinese media reduce organisational incongruence? Bureaucratic capitalism in the name of Communism". In Chin-Chuan Lee (ed.) *Chinese Media, Global Contexts*. London and New York: RoutledgeCurzon, 2003. pp. 198-214.

Head, Sydney W. *World Broadcasting Systems: a comparative analysis.* USA: Wadsworth Publishing Company, 1985.

Hesse, Albrecht. *Rundfunkrecht: die Organisation des Rundfunks in der Bundesrepublik Deutschland (3. Aufl.).* München: Verlag Franz Vahlen München, 2003.

Hill, John. *British Cinema in the 1980s*. Oxford and New York: Oxford University Press, 1999.

Hilliard, Robert L. and Keith, Michael C. *Global Broadcasting System*. USA: Focal Press. 1996.

Hoffmann-Riem, Wolfgang. *Rundfunkaufsicht im Ausland: Großbritannien, USA und Frankreich.* Düsseldorf: Presse- u. Informationsamt d. Landesregierung Nordrhein-Westfalen, 1989.

_____. *Regulating Media: the licensing and supervision of broadcasting in six countries*. New York: The Guilford Press, 1996.

Hong, Junhao. *The Internationalization of Television in China.* Westport in the USA: Praeger Publishers, 1998.

Hu, Zhengrong. "The Post-WTO Restructuring of the Chinese Media Industries and the Consequences of Capitalisation". In *Javnost*, 2003 Vol. X 4: p. 19-36.

Huang, Yu and Green, Andrew. "From Mao to the Millennium: 40 years of television in China (1958-98). In David French and Michael Richards (eds.) *Television in Contemporary Asia.* New Delhi: Sage, 2000. pp. 267-91.

Humphreys, Peter. *Mass Media and Media Policy in Western Europe.* Manchester and New York: Manchester University Press, 1996.

Hutchings, Graham. *Modern China.* London: Penguin Books, 2001.

Jakubowitz, Karol. "Ideas In Our Heads: introduction of PSB as part of media system change in central and eastern Europe". In *European Journal of Communication* 2004 19:53.

Jones, Janet. "PSB 2.0 – UK Broadcasting Policy after Peacock". In O'Malley and Jones (eds.) *The Peacock Committee and UK Broadcasting Policy*. UK: Palgrave Macmillian, 2009. pp. 187-206.

Keane, Michael. "Civil society, regulatory space and cultural authority in China's television industry". Philip Kitley (ed.) *Television, Regulation and Civil Society in Asia.* London and New York: RoutledgeCurzon, 2003. pp. 169-87.

Kitley, Philip. "Introduction: First principles – television, regulation and transversal civil society in Asia". In Philip Kitley (ed.) *Television, Regulation and Civil Society in Asia.* London and New York: RoutledgeCurzon, 2003. pp. 3-34.

Kops, Manfred. *What Is Public Service Broadcasting And How Should It Be Financed? (Summary)* In Working Paper of the Institute for Broadcasting Economics, University of Cologne, No. 145. Germany: Institute for Broadcasting Economics, University of Cologne, 2001.

_____. *The German Broadcasting Order. A Model for China?* In Working Papers of the Institute for Broadcasting Economics Cologne University, No. 215e. Germany: Institute for Broadcasting Economics, University of Cologne, 2006.

Bibliography

Krüger, Udo Michael and Zapf-Schramm, Thomas. "Politikthematisierung und Alltagskultivierung im Infoangebot. Programmanalyse 2008 von ARD/Das Erste, ZDF, RTL, SAT.1 und ProSieben". In: *Media Perspektiven* 4/200.

Kumar, Keval J. "Cable and Satellite Television in Asia: The role of advertising". In David French and Michael Richards (eds.) *Television in Contemporary Asia*. New Delhi: Sage, 2000. pp. 111-29.

Ledbetter, James. "Funding and Economics of American Public Television". In Eli M. Noam and Jens Waltermann (eds.) *Public Television in America*. Gütersloh: Bertelsmann Foundations Publishers, 1988. pp. 73-94.

Lee, Chin-Chuan. "Chinese Communication: prisms, trajectories, and modes of understanding". In Chin-Chuan Lee (ed.). *Power, Money, and Media: Communication Patterns and Bureaucratic Control in Cultural China*. Evanston, Illinios: Northwestern University Press, 2000. pp. 3-44.

Lee, Jae-kyoung. "Press Freedom and Democratization: South Korea's Experience and SomeLessons". In *International Communication Gazette* 1997 59: 135.

Leiva, María Trinidad García and Starks, Michael. "Digital switchover across the globe: the emergence of complex regional patterns". In *Media Culture & Society* 2009 31: 787.

Lin, Yifu. *Lessons of China's Transition from a Planned Economy to a Market Economy*. Working Paper Series of China Centre for Economic Research (2004-2), Peking University. http://ccer.pku.edu.cn/download/2963-1.pdf, last visited in March 2005.

Lynch, Daniel C. *After the Propaganda State: media, politics, and "thought work" in reformed China*. California (USA): Stanford University Press, 1999.

Livingstone, Sonia. "On the challenges of cross-national comparative media research", in *European Journal of Communication*, Vol. 18(4) 477-500. London: Sage Publications, 2003.

McChesney, Robert W. "Public Broadcasting: past, presemt and future". In Michael P. McCauley et al. (eds.) *Public Broadcasting and the Public Interest*. Armonk an New York: M.E. Sharpe, 2003. pp. 10-24.

McCormick, Barrett L. and Liu, Qing. "Globalisation and the Chinese media". In Chin-Chuan Lee (ed.) *Chinese Media, Global Contexts*. London and New York: RoutledgeCurzon, 2003. pp. 139-58.

McQuail, Denis (et. al). "A framework for analysis for media change in Europe in the 1980s". In Karen Siune and Wolfgang Truetzschler (eds.), *Dynamics of Media Politics: broadcast and electronic media in Western Europe*. London: Sage Publications, 1992. pp. 8-25.

————. "Mass Media in the Public Interest: towards a framework of norms for media performance". In James Curran and Michael Gurevitch (eds.) *Mass Media and Society (2nd ed.)*. London: Arnold, 1996. pp. 66-80.

————. "Commercialization and Beyond". In Denis McQuail and Karen Siune (eds.) *Media Policy: convergence, concentration and commerce*. London: Sage, 1998. pp. 107-27.

Murdock, Graham. "Citizens, Consumers and Public Culture". In Michael Skovmand and Kim Christian Schroder (eds.) *Media Cultures: Reappraising Transnational Media*. London: Routledge, 1992. pp. 17-41.

Negrine, Ralph. *Politics and the Mass Media in Britain (2nd ed.)*. London and New York: Routledge, 1994.

A. Cited English and German literature

Oliver, Mark. "The UK Public Service Broadcasting Ecology", in *Can the Market Deliver?: Funding Public Service Television in the Digital Age*. UK: John Libbey Publishing, 2005.

O'Malley, Tom. *Closedown? The BBC and government broadcasting policy 1972-92*. London: Pluto Press, 1994.

Ostroff, David. "United States of America". In Leen d'Haenens and Frieda Saeys (eds.) *Western Broadcasting at the Dawn of the 21st Centry*. Berlin and New York: Mouton de Gruyter, 2001. pp. 409-33.

Pan, Zhongdang and Chan, Joseph Man. "Building a Market-based Party Organ: television and national integration in China". In David French and Michael Richards (eds.) *Television in Contemporary Asia*. New Delhi: Sage, 2000. pp. 233-63.

Paulu, Burton. *British Broadcasting: radio and television in the United Kingdom*. USA: University of Minnesota Press, 1956.

Peacock, (Sir) Alan. "The 'Politics' of Investigating Broadcasting Finance". In Tom O'Malley and Janet Jones (eds.) *The Peacock Committee and UK Broadcasting Policy*. UK: Palgrave Macmillian, 2009. pp. 84-100.

Pei, Minxin. "The Growth of Civil Society in China". In James A. Dorn (ed.) *China in the New Millennium*. Washington D.C.: Cato Institute, 1998. pp. 245-66.

Peng, Bo. "The Policy Process in Contemporary China: mechanism of politics and government". In Catherine Jones Finer (ed.) *Social Policy Reform in China*. England: Ashgate, 2003. pp. 37-50.

Ros, Guido. "The Federal Republic of Germany". In Leen d'Haenens and Frieda Saeys (eds.) *Western Broadcasting at the Dawn of the 21st Centry*. Berlin and New York: Mouton de Gruyter, 2001. pp. 275-306.

Rozanova, Julia. "Public Television in the Context of Established and Emerging Democracy: Quo Vadis?". In *The International Communication Gazette* 2007 Vol 69(2): 129-47.

Scannell, Paddy. "Public Service Broadcasting: the history of a concept". In Edward Buscombe (ed.) *British Television: A Reader*. Oxford: Oxford University Press, 2000. pp. 45-62.

_____ and David Cardiff. *A Social History of British Broadcasting (Vol. 1 1922-1939): serving the nation*. UK and USA: Basil Blackwell, 1991.

Sepstrup, Preben. "Implications of Current Developments in West European Broadcasting". *Media, Culture & Society*, 1989 Vol. 11: 29-54.

Seymour-Ure, Colin. *The British Press and Broadcasting since 1945 (2nd edition)*. UK: Blackwell Publishers Ltd, 1996.

Siune, Karen and Hultén, Olof. "Dose Public Broadcasting Have a Future?". In Denis McQuail and Karen Siune (eds.) *Media Policy: convergence, concentration and commerce*. London: Sage Publications, 1998. pp. 23-37.

Smith, Anthony. *British Broadcasting*. UK: David & Charles, 1974.

Streeter, Thomas. *Selling the Air: a critique of the policy of commercial broadcasting in the United States*. Chicago & London: The University of Chicago Press, 1996.

Stuiber, Heinz-Werner. *Medien in Deutschland (Band 2): Rundfunk (1. Teil)*. Konstanz: UVK Medien Verlagsgesellschaft mbH, 1998.

_____. *Medien in Deutschland (Band 2): Rundfunk (2. Teil)*. Konstanz: UVK Medien Verlagsgesellschaft mbH, 1998.

Tracey, Michael. *The Decline and Fall of Public Service Broadcasting*. UK: Oxford University Press, 1998.

UNESCO. *Convention on the Protection and Promotion of the Diversity of Cultural Expressions*. 2005. http://unesdoc.unesco.org/images/0014/001429/142919e.pdf

van Zoonen, Liesbet. "Imagining the Fan Democracy". In *European Journal of Communication*, 2004, Vol 19(1): 39–52.

White, James D. *Global Media: the television revolution in Asia*. New York and London: Routledge, 2005.

Yu, Jinlu. "The Structure and Function of Chinese Television, 1978-1989". In Chin-Chuan LEE (ed.) *Voices of China: The Interplay of Politics and Journalism*. New York: The Guilford Press, 1990. pp. 69-87.

Zhao, Bin. "Mouth Piece or Money Spinner?: the double life of Chinese television in the late 1990s". *International Journal of Cultural Studies*, 1999 Vol. 2(3): 291-305.

Zhao, Yuezhi. *Media, Market and Democracy in China: between the party line and the bottom line*. Urbana and Chicago: University of Illinois Press, 1998.

_____. "Media and Elusive Democracy in China". *Javnost*, 2001 Vol. 2: 21-44.

(N.N.). "Leading Publication Shut Down In China" in Washington Post, http://www.washingtonpost.com (accessed in January 2006)

B. Cited Chinese literature

Cui, Baoguo (ed.). *A Report on the Development of Chinese Media Industry (2004-2005) (in Chinese,《中国传媒产业发展报告（2004-2005）》or Zhongguo Chuanmei Chanye Fazhan Baogao (2004-2005))*. 2005. http://www.china.com.cn/chinese/zhuanti/chuanmei/903305.htm. Last visited in February 2012.

Dai, Yuanguang. *Chinese Journalism and Communications in the Twentieth Century: Band of Communications (in Chinese,《二十世纪中国新闻学与传播学：传播学卷》or Ershi Shiji Zhongguo Xinwenxue yu Chuanboxue: Chuanboxue Juan)*. Shanghai: Fudan University Press, 2001.

Feng, Chien-San. *The Political Economics of Broadcasting Capital Movement: an anlysis to the traditions of Taiwanese broadcasting media in the 1990s (in Chinese.《广电资本运动的政治经济学》or Guangdian Ziben Yundong de Zhengzhi Jingjixue)*. In a research series of Taiwan (Taipeh): A Radical Quarterly in Social Studies (in Chinese,《台湾社会研究》丛刊 or Taiwan Shehui Yanjiu) 05, 1995.

Guo, Zhenzhi. *History of Chinese Television (in Chinese,《中国电视史》or Zhongguo Dianshi Shi)*. Beijing: Renmin University of China Press, 1991.

_____. "*My View on Political Economics of Communications*" (in Chinese, "传播政治经济学之我见" or "*Chuanbo Zhengzhi Jingjixue zhi Wojian*"). http://academic.mediachina.net/article.php?id=2963. Last visited in Febuary 2012.

Huang, Shengmin. *Analysis to Chinese Advertising Behaviour with Positivist Approach (in Chinese,《中国广告活动实证分析》or Zhongguo Guanggao Huodong Shizheng Fenxi)*. Beijing: Beijing Broadcasting Institute Press, 1992.

B. Cited Chinese literature

Li, Liangrong. "Retrospections and Expectations of the Press Reform in the Past 15 Years" (in Chinese, "十五年来新闻改革的回顾与展望"or "shiwunian lai Xinwen Gaige de Huigu yu Zhanwang"). In *Journalistic University (in Chinese, 新闻大学 or Xinwen Daxue)*, 1995 Spring: 3-8.

Li, Zhijian. *A Forecast on Foreign Investment in Chinese Television in 2005 (in Chinese. 2005 外商投资中国电视业展望 or 2005 Waishang Touzi Zhongguo Dianshiye Zhanwang)*. http://media.people.com.cn/GB/40724/40727/3121990.html. Last visited in Febuary 2012.

Lu, Di. *A Research on the Development Strategy of Chinese Television Industry (in Chinese, 《中国电视产业发展战略研究》or Zhongguo Dianshi Chanye Fazhan Zhanlue Yanjiu)*. Beijing: Xinhua Press, 1999.

―――. "2004 Report on Chinese Television Industry" ("2004年中国电视产业报告"or "2004nian Zhongguo Dianshi Chanye Baogo"). In Cui, Baoguo (ed.) *A Report on the Development of Chinese Media Industry (2004-2005) (in Chinese, 《中国传媒产业发展报告（2004-2005）》 or Zhongguo Chuanmei Chanye Fazhan Baogao (2004-2005))*. 2005. http://www.china.com.cn/chinese/zhuanti/chuanmei/903496.htm. Last visited in February 2012.

Lü, Yu-Nü. *Satellite Era: development and challenge of Continental China's television industry (in Chinese, 《卫星时代中国大陆电视产业的发展与挑战》or Weixing ShidaiZhongguo Dalu Dianshi Chanye de Fazhan yu Tiaozhan)*. Taipei: Shi-Ying Publishing House, 1999.

Mao, Zhongyuan. *CCTV conducts a full-scale reform: ratings and revenue become hard indexes (in Chinese. 央视全面改革：收视收益成硬指标 or Yangshi Quanmina Gaige: Shoushi Shouyi cheng Yingzhibiao)*. http://news.xinhuanet.com/ent/2005-10/10/content_3600531.htm, accessed in February 2012.

Research, Development and Evaluation Commission, Executive Yuan (Taiwan) (ed.). *The Policy Positioning and Research for further Improvement in the Public Service Broadcasting System in Taiwan (in Chinese 《我國公共電視體制之政策定位與治理研究》 or Woguo Gonggongdianshi zhi Zhengce Dingwei yu Zhili Yanjiu)*. 2010. www.rdec.gov.tw/public/PlanAttach/201008031129105338800.pdf. *Last visited in September 2011.*

Wang, Jifang and Li, Xing. *An Interview to the President of Guangxian Television WANG Changtian: To develop film and television should not merely depend on television stations. (光线电视总裁王长田：发展影视不能只管电视台 or guangxian dianshi zongcai wang changtian: fazhan yingshi buneng zhiguan dianshitai)*. http://news.xinhuanet.com/newmedia/2004-10/10/content_2071640.htm. Last visited in February 2012.

Wang, Jiong. *The regions "close the door", and the landing of satellite channels confronts a conundrum of "non-market"(地方"闭门"卫视落地遭遇"非市场"难题 or difang "bimen" weishi luodi zaoyu "fei shichang" nanti)*. http://news.xinhuanet.com/newmedia/2006-03/29/content_4360287.htm. Last visted in February 2012.

Wang, Xuewen. *An Analysis of the Structure and Market Share of Chinese Media (in Chinese, 中国传媒结构与市场份额分析 or zhongguo chuanmei jiegou yu shichang fen'e fenxi)*, 2004. http://www.china.com.cn/chinese/zhuanti/2004whbg/504166.htm. Last visited in February 2012.

Bibliography

Wu, Dong and Cao, Heng. *2003: Analysis of the Viewer Behaviour of Chinese Television Audience and the Competition of Viewer Market* (in Chinese, 2003 年中国电视观众收视行为与收视市场竞争分析 or *2003nian zhongguo dianshi guanzhong shoushi xingwei yu shoushi shichang jingzheng fenxi*). http://wenku.baidu.com/view/b81f41b765ce050876321363.html. Last visited in February 2012.

Wu, Jin. *An analysis of the developing opportunities of civilian-run television* (in Chinese. 解析民营电视的发展机遇 or *jiexi minying dianshi de fazhan jiyu*). http://qnjz.dzwww.com/gdst/t20060224_1365785.htm. Last visited in February 2012.

Wu, Xinxun. *The Imbalance of Media Economy between eastern and western China and Countermeasures* (in Chinese, 中国东西部传媒经济的失衡与对策 or *zhongguo dongxibu chuanmei jingji de shiheng yu duice*), 2005. http://media.people.com.cn/GB/22100/51194/51195/3572501.html. Last visited in February 2012.

Xia, Yu. *"CCTV showes red and yellow cards: ten programmes are eliminated"* (in Chinese. "央视亮出红黄牌：10 个节目被罚下" or *Yangshi Liangchu hong huang Pai: shige jiemu bei faxia*). In 南方周末 or *Nanfang Zhoumo*, June 27, 2003. http://news.sohu.com/50/96/news210509650.shtml, last visited in February 2012.

Xie, Yungeng and Wang, Caiping. *A Report on Chinese Entertainment Programmes* (in Chinese. 中国电视娱乐节目报告 or *Zhongguo Dianshi Yule Jiemu Baogao*). In 《新闻界》 or *Xinwenjie*, Vol. 4, 2005.

Xu, Guangchun (ed.). *A Brief History of Broadcasting in the People's Republic of China: 1949 – 2000* (in Chinese. 《中华人民共和国广播电视简史：1949-2000》 or *Zhonghua Renmin Gongheguo Guangbo Dianshi Jianshi: 1949-2000*). Beijing: Chinese Broadcasting Press, 2003.

Yu, Guoming, "Six key Points of the Development of Chinese Media Industry" (in Chinese, "中国传媒业发展的六个关键词", or *"Zhongguo Chuanmeiye Fazhan de liuge Guanjianci*), a speech given on 30. May 2003. http://media.sohu.com/14/34/news209663414.shtml. Last visited in February 2012.

Zhang, Liwei. *Five genres of radio and television contents should not be commercialised* (广播电视不能商业化的五种内容 or *Guangbo Dianshi buneng Shangyehua de wuzhong Neirong*). In 《新闻战线》 *Xinwen Zhanxian* 2005:9.

Zhang, Ning. *A Ratings Analysis to the Bidding of Advertising Spots on CCTV* (in Chinese, 中央电视台广告招标段位收视分析 or *Zhongyangdianshitai Guanggao Zhaobiao Duanwei Shoushi Fenxi*). http://www.a.com.cn/cn/mtyj/mtalfx/2001/hyzl-ssfx.htm. Last visited in February 2012.

Zhang, Ying. *Super Girl: four million audience, over one million revenues from three sources* (in Chinese. 超级女声节目观众四亿 三大项收入数以亿计 or *Chaojinüsheng Jiemu Guanzhong siyi, sandaxiang Shouru shuyi yiji*). In *People Net* (on August 19, 2005). http://finance.people.com.cn/GB/42775/3628404.html. Last visited in January 2012.

Zhu, Hong. *The Status Quo and Development Strategy of the Chinese Radio, Film and Television Group* (in Chinese, 中国广播电影电视集团的现状和发展战略 or *Zhongguo Guangbo Dianying Dianshi Jituan de Xianzhuang he Fazhan Zhanlue*). http://www.people.com.cn/GB/14677/22114/26417/26443/1752509.html, last visited in February 2012.

Modern Adervertising Magazin. *Chinese Advertising Industry over the Past Two Decades: a compilation of statistic data.* (中国广告业二十年：统计资料汇编 or *Zhongguo Guanggao Ershinian: tongji ziliao huibian*). Beijing: China Statistic Press, 2000.

B. Cited Chinese literature

(N.N.). *CCTV Yearbook 1998, 1999 (in Chinese,)*. Beijing: Chinese Radio & TV Press, 1998, 1999.

(N.N.).*Yearbook of Chinese Radio & TV 1997, 1999 (in Chinese)*. Beijing: Yearbook Press of Chinese Radio & TV, 1997, 1999.

(N.N.). Chongqing Satellite TV. Press release on January 1st, 2011. http://tv.cbg.cn/content/2011-01/01/content_5603367.htm. Last visited in September 2011.

(N.N.). Press release of the Chongqing Satellite TV on March 2nd, 2011. http://v.cqnews.net/first/2011-03/02/content_5807633.htm. Last visited in September 2011.

(N.N.). *The Rankings of All-China TV Programmes (in Chinese, 全国电视栏目收视率排名 or quanguo dianshi lanmu shoushilü paiming)*, 2004. http://data.icxo.com/htmlnews/2004/11/26/480455.htm. Last visited in February 2012.

(N.N.). *The CCP further controls television (in Chinese. 中共进一步统管电视 or zhonggong jinyibu tongguan dianshi)*. www.kanzhongguo.com, accessed in October 2005. This web page was found to have been removed by the author's final check in February 2012.

(N.N.). An interview with HE Shizhong, the Head of the Department of Propaganda of Chongqing municipal Party committee, on *Chongqing Daily* on March 3rd, 2011. http://fl.cqnews.net/html/2011-03/03/content_5811831.htm. Last visited in September 2011.

Index

advertising revenue *51, 55, 58, 62-63, 65, 70, 95, 100, 105, 119*
- advertising industry *164-65*
- ban on advertising *123-24, 130, 134, 157-58, 194*
- by type of medium *47, 60, 184*
- of British commercial television *135, 159, 167*
- of Chinese television *45-48, 59-62, 77-78, 101-02*
- of German private broadcasting *180-84*
- of German public law broadcasting *123, 144, 157, 176*
- revenue structure *90-91*
- soft advertising *48*
- USA *122, 134, 141*
aggregating viewing *201*
Allies *139, 141, 142-43, 146, 150, 172*
American commercial networks *196*
American purely commercial broadcasting system *193-98, 231*
ARD *152, 154, 181-83*
"arm's length" *137, 138, 221*
ATSC *198*
audience
- as citizens *33, 129-31, 170, 186, 217, 232, 235*
- as consumers *53, 71, 73, 130, 134, 158, 166, 173, 186, 197, 217, 230*
- research *60, 92-94, 129*
audio-video exemption *57, 81, 121*

"basic provision" *175-77, 218, 219, 224*
BBC *87, 114, 115, 117-31, 131-35, 142, 155, 157-61, 163-68, 169-71, 193, 196, 200, 201, 203, 216, 218, 226, 231-32*
- Board of Governors *191*
- BBC iPlayer *201*
- BBC model *135-39, 143, 146-48, 208, 211, 213-14*
- BBC Trust *191*
bidding system *60, 61, 70, 94*
British broadcasting acts
- Broadcasting Act 1990 *167-68*
- Television Act 1954 *135, 159*
- Sound Broadcasting Act 1972 *167*
British broadcasting committees *118, 188, 122, 125*
- Annan Committee *121*
- Beveridge Committee *158*
- Crawford Committee *120, 122*
- Peacock Committee *166*
- Pilkington Committee *160*
- Sykes Committee *118, 122, 124-25*
British Commonwealth *136, 213*
British Empire *113, 132, 136*
Broadcasting Research Unit *131*

cable broadcasting *43, 53, 57-58, 61, 65, 79, 155, 161, 165, 167-68, 170, 172, 173, 175, 176, 198, 203, 207, 209, 223*
CCP *33-39, 41-42, 49-50, 53, 56, 67, 72, 73, 86, 87, 89, 223*

247

Index

CCTV *13, 43, 46, 55-56, 58, 59-62, 65, 68, 70, 71, 77-80, 82, 85, 93, 101*
CDU *172-73*
civil society *48-51, 68, 71, 100, 129*
civilian-run television *79-81*
commercial broadcasting *25-27, 48, 54, 56, 59-63, 66-67, 81, 87, 92-94, 99-108, 133-35, 157-61, 164-68, 168-72, 186, 191, 193-97, 200-02, 207, 209, 212, 214-20, 221, 229*
commercialisation *19, 48, 53, 63-64, 67, 94, 106, 167-68, 179, 193, 194, 203, 218-19, 230-31*
– self-commercialisation *16, 31, 34, 35, 52, 71, 81, 88, 91, 93-94, 95-98, 99-103, 216*
common law *227*
Communications Act 1934 *122, 196*
Communications Act 2003 *202*
competition *133, 155, 157-61, 167, 169, 173, 181, 196, 212, 226, 235*
– competitive mechanism *92*
– excessive competition *101, 106, 197*
concentration *156, 169, 200, 225, 229*
conglomeration *57, 73-74, 81, 91*
Conservative Party *133, 163*
consumer society *48, 160, 166*

decision making mechanism *217-20*
– judiciary-centric *217-18*
– politics-centric *217-18*
democratisation *16, 19, 52, 85, 98, 105, 129, 137, 140, 156, 207-12, 214-15, 230-34*
Department of Propaganda *38-39, 69, 87, 102, 232*
deregulation *29, 186, 198, 202, 216, 218, 219*

Deutsche Welle *140*
Deutschlandfunk *140*
digitalization *198-204, 224*
discourse theory *170*
distance from the market *19, 221, 223-26, 229, 231*
distance from the state *195, 221-27, 229-34*
domain of culture *121, 186, 204, 229*
dual broadcasting system *16-20, 108, 113-14, 135, 152, 155-56, 162, 168,, 179-80, 184, 185, 186, 187-92, 193, 195, 197, 198, 204, 207, 212, 215-20, 221-26, 227-36*
– framework and principles *174-77*

entrepreneurial freedom *186*
European Broadcasting Union *139*
"external pluralistic" model *174-77, 220*
extrinsic transition *22-25, 30, 89-92, 94, 96*

FCC *196, 199, 200*
four-level policy *41-45, 47, 86, 235*
"Fourth Estate" *126*
freedom of broadcasting *140-43, 151-52, 153, 173-74, 176, 178, 189, 191-92, 195, 219, 221-22, 225-29, 233-34*
functions of broadcasting *33, 49, 69-72, 128, 151, 153, 155*
– democratic function *95, 137, 170, 186, 210-12, 214, 220, 225, 234*
– propagandist function *33, 43*

GATT Uruguay Round *121*
German Basic Law *140, 145, 151, 153, 191*
– Article 5 *150-51, 152, 174-75, 189, 195, 222*

German Federal Constitutional Court *140, 141, 144, 151-56, 172-77, 177-79, 188-92, 195-96, 202, 217, 219, 221-23, 232*
German media act *175*
gradual transition *21, 228*
– of Chinese economy from plan to market *21-25*
"guarantee of existence and development" *175, 195, 202, 219, 224*

HDTV *198, 208*
homogeneity *184, 230*
human rights *194-95*
– defensive right *225*
– objective principles *195*
– protective duty *194-95, 225*
– subjective rights of individuals *195, 223*

industrialisation *56-57, 72-74, 98*
Internet *76, 169, 184, 198-204*
intrinsic transition *23-25*
IPTV *72, 77, 82-83, 170*
ITA *133-35, 159, 161, 167*
ITC *167*
ITV *167*
"internal pluralistic" model *174*

juridification *140, 150-54*

Labour Party *133, 135, 159, 167*
Land media authority *179*
license fee *26, 40, 116, 119, 123, 149, 152, 154, 169, 177, 178, 179, 182, 184, 186, 202, 204, 208-09, 220, 223, 226, 229, 236*

market economy *14, 22, 33-34, 45-46, 52, 54-63, 64, 72, 96, 98, 226*
market logic *64, 67, 157, 159-62, 163-68, 169, 187, 190-94, 196, 202, 215-16, 230-31*
mass logic *35-36, 38, 41, 50, 101*
military government *139, 142, 147-50, 208, 214*
monopoly *16, 30, 76, 78, 83, 101-02, 106, 115, 119, 154, 157-61, 179, 195*
– breakup of monopoly *133, 172*
– public monopoly of the BBC *122-32, 221-23*
multi-channel era *58, 80, 163, 220*
multinational media conglomerates *13, 35, 57, 67, 81-82, 88, 98-99, 164, 196, 200, 212, 224*
multi-platform *199, 201*

NAZI *121, 131, 138, 141-42, 150, 210*
neo-authoritarian media system *205-06*
news reform *68*
NHK *87, 136, 207-09, 211, 214, 216, 218, 231-32*
non-commercialism *116, 123-24, 193, 222*
NPR *196*

Ofcom *169, 191, 194, 200*

party logic *35, 38, 49, 52, 95*
PBS *87, 136, 196, 231-32*
post-Communist countries *204-07*
press freedom *14, 17, 52, 102, 109, 126, 153, 189, 205, 207, 210*

Index

private broadcasting *114, 155, 162, 172-77, 178-84, 189, 195, 205, 223-24, 228, 229, 236*
privatisation *198*
– of the BBC *163, 166-67*
producer mechanism *55, 67*
propaganda *33, 35-36, 38, 42, 48-49, 72, 89, 119, 131, 138, 146, 208, 210, 214*
ProSiebenSat1. Media AG *180, 183*
protection of basic rights by organisation *195, 221-22, 226-27, 229, 233*
provincial satellite channels *62, 77-79, 83, 101, 235*
public channel *86*
public discourse *49, 76, 202, 233*
public law broadcasting *119, 121, 123, 148, 151-54, 157, 172-77, 184, 189, 195, 219, 222-24, 228-29*
public logic *41, 48, 49-51, 71, 191, 225-26*
public property *118-19, 122*
public service broadcasting *14, 16, 19, 26-27, 107-08, 113, 136, 146-47, 155-57, 160-61, 185-87, 191, 193, 200-04, 210-11, 213, 220, 222, 227, 231-32, 234, 236*
– –CEEC countries *204-07*
– international imitation *136-39*
– Japan and Korea *208-09*
– misapprehension in China *50, 99*
– –principles and characteristics *114-16*
– reform in Britain *164-72*
– –understanding of broadcasting *117-31*
public sphere *66, 68, 85, 95, 98, 101, 103, 107, 138, 170, 232*

ratings *13, 60-62, 71, 77-78, 84-85, 93-94, 101, 201, 231, 235*
"red channel" *87*
Reith, Sir John *114-15, 120, 123, 126-30, 157, 193, 198, 221, 226-27*
Royal Charter *119, 125, 127, 131*
RTL Group *180*
rulings of the German federal constitutional court *20, 140, 151-53, 174, 176, 177-79, 189-92, 217, 219-21*
– (~ chronologically ~)
– Ruling of Television (1961) *121, 145, 152, 153, 172, 222*
– Ruling of Value Added Tax (1971) *152, 153*
– Ruling of FRAG (1981) *174-75, 189*
– Ruling of Niedersachsen (1986) *174, 175-76*
– Ruling of Baden-Württemberg (1987) *176, 189*
– Ruling of WDR (1991) *176, 189*
– Ruling of Hessen3 (1992) *178*
– Ruling of License Fees (1994) *178, 202*
– Ruling of the EU Guidelines on Television (1995) *179, 204*
– Ruling of "Extra Radio" (1998) *178*
– Ruling of the Guidelines on Short News Report (1998) *179*
– Ruling of License Fees II (2007) *178*
– Ruling of "Participation of Parties in Broadcasting Companies" (2008) *178*

SARFT *39, 57, 64-66, 74, 77, 81-83, 86, 91*
satellite broadcasting 43, *162, 165, 168, 170, 198, 223*

separation between broadcasters and producers *80*
"serving freedom" ("dienende Freiheit") *174, 195, 223, 233*
shiye danwei (事业单位) *34, 40-41, 53-56, 59, 64, 73-75, 81, 82, 89*
"social market" *64-65, 99*
SPD *172-73, 175*
spillover effects *92-93*
State Treaty to the New System of Broadcasting 1987 (Rundfunkstaatsvertrag 1987) *175, 176*
Super Girl *84-85*
supervision by public opinion *68-71, 100, 105*

television market share *71, 77, 78, 84, 101, 102, 122, 180-83, 200*
"Ten Commandments" *142, 149*

Thatcher, Mrs. Margret *162-68, 191, 194, 216*
thought work *33, 35, 74*
Tian'anmen crackdown *34, 52, 64, 66, 96, 103*

UNESCO Convention on Cultural Diversity *121*

Weimar Republic *121, 141, 143-44, 148*
WTO *13, 35, 53, 57-58, 64, 67, 79, 81, 91, 105, 202*

ZDF *84, 152, 154, 182, 183*